We've Got to Start Meeting Like This

A Guide to Successful Meeting Management

Revised

Roger K. Mosvick & Robert B. Nelson

Park Avenue

We've Got to Start Meeting Like This!
A Guide to Successful Meeting Management

Revised Edition

© 1996 by Roger K. Mosvick and Robert B. Nelson

Published by: Park Avenue Productions
An imprint of JIST Works, Inc.
720 North Park Avenue
Indianapolis, IN 46202-3431
Phone: 317-264-3720 Fax: 317-264-3709
E-mail: JISTWorks@aol.com

Cover Design: Listenberger Design
Interior Design: Debbie Berman
Interior Illustrations: Doug Hall

Library of Congress Cataloging-in-Publication Data

Mosvick, Roger K.
  We've got to start meeting like this : a guide to successful meeting
management / Roger K. Mosvick & Robert B. Nelson. -- Rev.
    p.   cm.
  Includes index.
  ISBN 1-57112-069-6
  1. Business meetings.   2. Communication in management.
I. Nelson, Robert B.   II. Title.
  HF5734.5.M673 1996
  658.4'563--dc20   95-26612
                                                                      CIP

Printed in the United States of America

99 98 97 96 5 4 3 2 1

Library of Congress Cataloging-in-Publication Data Applied For

We have been careful to provide accurate information throughout this book,
but it is possible that errors and omissions have been introduced.

To Nona and Jennifer

P·R·E·F·A·C·E

There is a revolution going on in business today. It's a revolution about how work gets done, who decides what work gets done, and how it will be accomplished. It's a revolution about what goals an organization will strive for and who will be responsible for achieving them. It's a revolution that touches everyone in an organization — from the very top to the very bottom. What is this revolution? It's a revolution called *teams*; highly collaborative work groups that are often entirely self-directed, and self-managed.

Why teams? In the late 1980s and early 1990s global competition put intense economic pressure on the U.S. economy, forcing companies to seek ways of cutting unnecessary expenses. Teams offer an easy way to tap the knowledge and resources of *all* employees in an organization to solve problems. A well-structured team draws together employees from different levels of the organization who can help find the best way to approach an issue. Companies have learned that, to remain competitive, they can no longer rely on management to guide the development of work processes and the accomplishment of organizational goals — they need to involve those employees who are closer to the problems and to the organization's customers as well.

Perhaps management expert Peter Drucker best answered the question "why teams?" when he considered the preeminence of knowledge over status in the modern organization. According to Drucker, "No knowledge ranks higher than another; each is judged by its contribution to the common task rather than by inherent superiority or inferiority. Therefore, the modern organization cannot be an organization of boss and subordinate. It must be organized as a team" (Drucker 1992).

Until recently, large companies such as IBM, General Motors, Sears, and Xerox were not that different from the rigid, traditional, hierarchy of the Leader-Follower model. Employing hundreds of thousands of workers, these companies depended — and, to some extent, still depend — upon legions of supervisors and managers to control the work that workers did and when and how they did it. The fundamental flaw with the Leader-Follower model was that many supervisors and managers made little or no direct contribution to the production of a company's products or services. At its worst, many of these supervisors and managers actually impeded the ability of their organizations to get things done — dramatically adding to their costs of doing business.

Fortunately this revolutionary turn to team management was accompanied by a fortuitous explosion of computer technology, which greatly increased the speed and accuracy of information distribution. Bypassing the traditional information hierarchy of supervisors and middle managers, computers have given workers access to information in unprecedented amounts of detail. In the words of Frederick Kovac, vice president of planning for the Goodyear Tire and Rubber Company, "It used to be, if you wanted information, you had to go up, over, and down through the organization. Now you just tap in. Everybody can know as much about the company as the chairman of the board" (Stewart 1992). This newfound freedom of information eroded the traditional hierarchy in many firms, by removing supervisors and middle managers from their positions as brokers of information.

Today information technology facilitates and supports the use of widespread team-based work groups. To compress time and gain benefits, a company has to work in, and manage through, relatively small, self-managing teams made up of people from different parts of the organization. As Bower indicates, the teams must be small because large groups create communication problems. The teams must be self-managing and empowered to act because referring decisions back up the line wastes time and often leads to poorer decisions. The teams must be multifunctional because that's the best — if not the only — way to keep the actual product and its essential delivery system clearly visible and foremost in everyone's minds (Bower 1988).

One of the most important things to come out of this transformation of businesses from vertical to horizontal orgnanizations was the movement of authority and power from the very top of the organization down to the front-line workers who interact with customers on a day-to-day basis. With fewer middle managers involved, front-line employees were naturally granted more authority — and many accept it with real zeal.

More than ever before in American businesses, employees are being rewarded for *cooperating* with each other, instead of competing *against* one another. According to David Ehlen, chief executive officer with Wilson Learning, a leading management-training firm, advancement in the new business world of teams "is measured not only by your individual contributions but by how effective you are as a collaborative team member" (Schellhardt 1994). To cite one representative example, the management of Motorola considers employee teams to be a crucial part of its strategy for quality improvement. Self-directed teams at its Arlington Heights, Illinois, cellular equipment manufacturing plant not only decide on their own training programs and schedule their own work, but they also are involved in the hiring and firing of co-workers (Lee 1994).

The single most important forum where the potential of the team revolution is being realized is in the thousands upon thousands of organizational meetings which take place day after day. All of these other forces provide the context that surrounds this vital organizational activity. Despite the powerful electronic extensions of information processing, we cannot automate major decisions. Face-to-face meetings, whether real or televised, remain an inescapable fact of modern organizational life. When there is a problem, a meeting is called. When the status of a project is reviewed, it is often done in a meeting. When a new idea is needed or an old one re-evaluated, a meeting helps ensure that the most current and relevant perspectives are brought to bear.

The primary purpose of meetings has long been to share information and to make decisions. Many of these same forces that have come to characterize modern organizational life have simply exacerbated the typical and persistent problems of meeting management by adding a major dose of information overload.

But today, forces of accelerating change are severely restricting the effectiveness of organizational meetings. Few organizations are free from the pressure of constant meetings and the fragmented decision making which results from such pressures. More than ever before, managers are reporting an increase in time spent in meetings and a decrease in the effectiveness of those meetings.

Decisions are delayed as additional meetings are scheduled. Decisions are made with incomplete information as frustrated managers seek to avoid meetings altogether. Decisions are made by default as groups run out of time. Ineffective, wasteful meeting management is fast becoming a pervasive characteristic of American business and professional life, contributing significantly to our nation's diminished productivity and the growing void in effective leadership.

This book is a response to the growing problem of ineffective meetings. It seeks to answer two basic questions: (1) How have meeting management practices and attitudes changed in recent years? and (2) What are the most effective techniques for obtaining high-quality decisions in a timely manner from a group? Our answers to these questions come directly from the empirical evidence of a series of extensive surveys conducted over a fourteen-year period (1981–1995). The research reflects the experiences of over 1,600 managers and professionals, in several technology-oriented companies in the United States, Europe, South America, and Australia. Included are representatives from divisions or subsidiaries of 3M, Honeywell, General Dynamics, IBM, Control Data, Unisys, Digital, Unilever, Microsoft, Ford Motor Company, General Motors, and Volkswagen, as well as several United States Federal Agencies such as the Defense Communications Agency, the Federal Reserve Bank, and U.S. Treasury.

Our research focused on meetings, as they are most commonly defined in business environments; namely, small groups working together to solve problems. Other data came from follow-up interviews with this same group of managers and technical professionals, as well as from observations and interaction with numerous other business professionals in the course of the authors' combined sixty years of consulting experience.

The research process has been a potent reminder of the persistence of meeting problems in all organizations as well as a fairly startling vision of how much the world has changed in the nine years since the first edition of this book. On the one hand small group meetings continue to be plagued by the same old problems of chaotic information processing and suspect decision making. On the other hand business meetings increasingly mirror the trends of globalization, decentralization, and flexible self-managing teamwork, all driven by the powerful tools of computer-mediated communication. It is perhaps fitting that the final drafts have been edited not from our "home" offices but from Dusseldorf, Germany, where one author is completing a monthlong consulting and research stint, and from points along the way of the other author who is conducting a 30-city book tour of Canada and the U.S.

This book is divided into two major parts. Part One examines meetings as they occur today in most organizations. This in-depth analysis of current meeting practices will help the reader to more easily implement needed changes and techniques. Although the average reader probably realizes how poorly current business meetings are conducted, Chapter 1 gives some indication as to why business meetings have recently become so ineffective. Chapter 2 introduces a new way of understanding business meetings through analyzing the kind of information processing which occurs in the typical business meeting. Chapters 3 and 4 examine what is known about how groups work together — and what factors have a primary influence on the functioning of work groups.

Part Two focuses specifically on what the reader can do to have more effective meetings which take less time. Fundamentals of meeting planning are presented in Chapter 5. Chapter 6 discusses leadership in business meetings and explains how effective leadership can and should be a shared activity, a theme which is continued in Chapter 7, "The Participant's Role in Business Meetings." Chapter 8 looks at the meeting environments of the future, including high-technology influences on modern business meetings such as electronic and video conferences.

Special meeting formats and leadership styles are discussed in the appendices. A Meeting Planners' Packet is also included for ready reference in helping the readers incorporate ideas from the book into their own meeting practices.

Roger K. Mosvick
Robert B. Nelson

C·R·E·D·I·T·S

This book is the product of extensive work with key executives, managers, and technical professionals in many high-technology corporations, including organizations that have been assessed as some of the best-managed and most highly regarded firms in the United States. We are grateful for the extensive support we have received from these corporations over an extended time period for this research effort. We sincerely appreciate the time and commitment we received and the many interpretive insights that came from follow-up interviews with individuals within these corporations, allowing us to develop an extensive data base for this book.

To a great extent, this book represents the daily experience and frustrations of managers and executives with meetings in these organizations, which are representative of all companies throughout American industry. Although the individual contributions of organizational members are not specifically cited throughout this book, individuals may recognize many of their suggestions. We thank those people and their organizations for the consistent and extensive support and encouragement we received for this research project: 3M Company, General Dynamics/Electronics Division, Honeywell Inc., Systems Development Corporation/Burroughs (now UNISYS), Digital Equipment Corporation, IBM, Control Data Corporation, Unilever, Economics Laboratory, General Motors, National Computer Systems and Government Agencies of the U.S. Treasury, and the U.S. Defense Communications Agency.

We would also like to thank our many colleagues in business, government, and academia who contributed over the years to our thinking about this book in discussions and correspondence. We would particularly like to acknowledge the counsel and invaluable assistance of Dr. Suzanne Hagen and Dr. James W. Pratt, both of the University of Wisconsin-River Falls, who assisted us in this project from start to finish. Reviewers of the original manuscript provided many helpful suggestions to us for which we are most grateful. We would especially like to thank Marcus Alexis, Dean of the Business School of the University of Illinois-Chicago; Dr. Don Shields of the University of Missouri; Dr. Gordon Zimmerman of the University of Nevada-Reno; and Dr. Leonard Hawes of the University of Utah.

We would like to thank Macalester College for encouragement and support of this project and for seeing the value of a fruitful collaboration between the academic and business world.

We would like to thank Peter Economy, Reid McLean, Mrs. Jeanne Arntzen, Ms. Alison Humble, Amy Jensen, and Toby Heytens for their assistance in survey analysis, data processing, and manuscript preparation of the revised edition. The editorial and marketing staff of JIST Works, Inc., particularly Jim Irizarry, Thelma Silvola, and Sara Hall, receive our special appreciation for their encouragement and direction.

Finally, we deeply appreciate the general assistance, patience, and encouragement we received from our wives, Nona M. Mosvick and Jennifer W. Nelson, while sustaining both of us on this project.

—February 1996

A·G·E·N·D·A

Part One
Meetings: How We're Doing Today

4 Beneath the Surface

Hidden Variables Which Influence

Business Meetings 73

Part Two
Meetings: Doing Them Better Tomorrow

5 Preparing for Success and Avoiding Meeting Problems

Planning and Conducting Meetings That Work 105

6 Real Leadership

The Leadership Role in Business Meetings 135

7 Everyone Plays a Part
The Participant's Role in Business Meetings 167

8 Changing the Rules of the Game
The Changing Meeting Environment 189

Appendix A
Special Meetings for Special Purposes 221

Appendix B
Meeting Planners' Packet 253

PART 1

Meetings: How We're Doing Today

We've Got a Problem
Meeting Management in America

Today in countless rooms across America, thousands of managers, technical professionals, and executives are sitting down at tables to conduct our nation's business. The rooms differ in decor; some are comfortable and richly appointed, while others are crowded, plain, and windowless. But the goal is the same — the solution of business problems. Whether the meetings have been called for the purpose of long-range planning, coordinating complex operations, or cracking an emergency problem, they are a microcosm of American business at work, in which dedicated, well-educated, energetic experts carry out the most critical work of American business, processing information. How are they doing? We're glad you asked, because . . . we've got a problem. A big problem of ineffective meeting management.

Accelerating costs, wasted human resources, and a structural resistance to change are making this a problem of staggering proportions. The problem has seemingly been around forever and it is getting worse. The most depressing issue is that few organizations recognize the problem and even fewer groups are attempting to do something about it. It is part of our collective organizational amnesia.

The dimensions of this problem can be sketched in broad strokes by looking at some startling current facts of business life in America.

> *Most of the business of America gets done in meetings.* The largest segment of the American workforce, information processors, is estimated to be from 60 to 80 percent of all workers. Increasingly, meetings are becoming an indispensable feature of their organizational life. Because of broader corporate accountability, increased complexity of goods and

services, and greater need to coordinate specialized tasks, the business meeting is rapidly becoming the place where America's business gets done.

■ *The average manager and technical professional spend nearly one-fourth of their total work week in meetings.* Upper/middle managers spend nearly two days a week in meetings, and some senior executives spend as much as four days a week in meetings. The feeling which many of us have — that we spend most of our life in meetings — is no illusion. Studies show that on average we spend more time in meetings of three or more people than in any other communication activity except one-to-one meetings.

■ *The frequency of meetings is growing.* For a variety of reasons there is a slow, steady growth in the number of meetings attended each year. This is especially true of high-technology organizations. If present trends continue, high-tech government and business organizations can expect to see a 5 to 9 percent growth in the frequency of meetings in the next five years.

■ *Over 50 percent of the productivity of the billions of meeting hours is wasted.* Countless surveys and studies have revealed that there are too many meetings, lasting too long, and woefully mismanaged. Poor meeting preparation, ad hoc scheduling, and lack of participant training in meeting management are causing many companies to lose the *equivalent of 30 man-days and 240 man-hours a year for every person who participates in business conferences.*

■ *The compounded loss of man-hours represents a significant drain on American productivity.* One carefully costed-out analysis of a mid-size Fortune 500 company yielded a conservative esti-mate that this business lost *143 million dollars* a year because of ineffective meeting management! This analysis is of a company routinely judged to be one of the best-run corpora-tions in America. A Hofstra University survey noted that:

> Based on statistics in the October 1988 issue of *Monthly Labor Review* and other sources, unproductive time spent in poorly run meeting translates to a loss of nearly $37 billion annually. (Hosansky 1989)

In 1996 that figure is probably closer to $60 billion, constituting a serious threat to American productivity at the very moment we are striving to maintain our competitive edge in international markets. One can see a serious threat to American productivity at the very moment we are striving to maintain our competitive edge in international markets.

It is clear from this perspective that we've got a problem, a large and growing problem, directly affecting the efficiency and effectiveness of every major decision-making group in this country. Increasingly, the work of our postindustrial society is done in groups: committee work, business conferences, and meetings. And almost in inverse proportion to this growth in the frequency and length of those group activities, our capacity to manage this problem diminishes.

Ineffective meeting management is fast becoming a national disgrace. Poorly planned and poorly run meetings are the worst-kept secret of America's vaunted business skills. In competitive challenges at home and abroad they are our Achilles' heel. Contemporary business is a hotly contested race which requires that every component of our competitive position be examined. Yet, few companies have even begun to take a serious look at the largest remaining item of containable costs in most organizations.

It is doubtful that any econometrician, business leader, or think tank has the total cost picture in focus. The macro costs to our nation can only be hinted at. Although accurate dollar estimates for each business organization can be given, the psychological costs involved are truly incalculable. The personal psychological costs, well known to anyone who has weathered a disorganized, muddled, three-hour meeting, are apathy, resentment, and lack of commitment to the decision and to the group. In the modern business world, the times that try men's and women's souls seem to occur with increasing frequency right in the middle of one of those endless meetings.

That's the bad news. The good news is that we can do something about the problem. This is a management problem at heart, one requiring special management attention. We have the techniques and the learning designs to bring about a major change toward productive meeting management. What is needed is a broad raising of organizational consciousness about the problem and exposure to the analytical methods necessary to bring about change.

No one can promise to reclaim every hour of that wasted meeting time. We do claim, however, that any organization or department can significantly increase their productive time through relatively simple, inexpensive efforts. Our experience with scores of companies supports this claim. Any company can save 25 to 35 percent of their meeting productivity costs through an understanding of the basic techniques in this book and through proper training — the cost of which will be quickly recovered. Take a moment to determine the cost of quality for meetings in your own organization. We think you will be pleasantly surprised by the potential savings available and properly motivated to exploit the principles this book presents.[1]

Those are the broad charges of the problem we all seem to share. Now it is time to support those claims with hard data. To begin, let's consider the increasing use of meetings from the standpoint of "average" managers and technical professional groups, which constitute some of the fastest growing segments in the information revolution.

The Increasing Use of Meetings in Today's Organizations

Meetings are the critical nerve centers of the complex flow of organizational communication. They are the common ground where administrators, managers, executives, and technical professionals are brought together to translate their own perspectives and coordinate their varied goals and objectives. To many business professionals, however, meetings are the bane of their existence. They can't get along without them and they can't manage them well. This is a burden to professional managers who take pride in their ability to plan, organize, coordinate, and implement other management activities. Few areas are so frustrating as the endless, daily routines of a business meeting that seems to defy all attempts of rational management. Many managers have given up doing much about them by accepting that, in most organizations, meetings have a life of their own. Meetings seem to resist all attempts to reform more stoutly than any other single facet of organizational life.

---

[1] The calculation procedure to determine productivity costs is straightforward. First, compute (or estimate) the number of business professionals in your organization who are regularly involved in meetings. Second, multiply this figure by the average number of hours each management group spends in meetings (compute your own or use our standard figures: 9, 11 and 12 hours for lower management, middle management, and senior management, respectively). Third, multiply each of these figures by burden rate figures for your organization and region. These figures, which include salary, benefits, and all costs required to support workers at their jobs, are usually available in your organization or from a local university. Finally, multiply by 48, the typical annual work week figure. Divide this figure by 50 percent, the estimate of wasted productivity which has turned up in several studies including our own. You now have a rough estimate of the group productivity losses you are experiencing and the potential savings available to your organization.

If the preceding description rings a bell, join the crowd. All of us have felt a sense of hopelessness from time to time in the face of countless unplanned, poorly coordinated, and inconclusive meetings. But we can rest assured that this problem is not going to go away. Organizational prognosticators predict that our future is going to be filled with more and more meetings.

Meeting Management Surveys

In the last twenty-five years, there has been a steady increase in the use of meetings by business managers. Let's look at a few studies during this period that detail this growth at different levels, particularly among the new breed of technology managers. A benchmark study on meeting practices and attitudes about committee work found that while executives spend three and one-half hours in planned meetings each week (more in informal meetings) they displayed quite positive attitudes about committee work. Depending on their management level, 55 to 85 percent felt committees promoted coordination, creativity, and informed decision making. Only 8 percent would abolish committees if given a chance (Tillman 1960, 162–172).

Surveys in the 1970s, 1980s, and 1990s indicated an alarming growth in both the use of business meetings and mounting dissatisfaction with their effectiveness. For example, a survey of 600 chief executives representing all types and sizes of businesses in the Chicago area revealed the average top executive participated in six to seven meetings per week, almost twice as many as in the decade earlier. Equally alarming was the fact that 73 percent questioned the effectiveness of these meetings (Rice 1973).

Similar findings in meeting studies were seen throughout the 1980s. Sigband (1985) reported a study of 471 management leaders who said they attended more meetings than ever before, but liked them less, with few companies having guidelines or training on how to conduct meetings. In 1989 a study done by the Annenberg School of Communications at the University of Southern California discovered why meetings are so costly:

> *The typical meeting occurs with only two hours notice and has no written agenda or, if it has an agenda, the meeting often fails to cover it. . . . Furthermore, participants often believe their role in these meetings is limited. Of 903 managers at 36 companies who were asked about their last meeting, one-third said they had no impact on ultimate decision making. One-third felt pressure to back opinions they privately disagreed with (Hsu 1990).*

In another 1989 study of over 1,000 business leaders conducted by Hofstra University and Harrison Conference Services, 72 percent responding indicated they were spending more time in meetings than they had five years ago and that in only slightly more than half of the meetings "do participants understand the intended outcomes and do meetings achieve the intended outcomes" (Hosansky 1989).

During this booming period of organizational growth, it became evident that changes in technology were rapidly creating new managerial and administrative positions whose chief duties were to coordinate technical details through meetings. A great number of people in middle management coordinator positions (project leaders, coordinators, and committee chairpersons of key business committees, for example) reported spending as much as three to four days a week in various types of meetings. Some reported spending eight straight hours in one type of meeting alone. One study showed that program managers spent as much as 80 percent of their time in meetings (Van de Ven 1973).

Not all studies were directly comparable, but the general trend seemed evident. Business professionals at all levels, in different occupational roles, and in companies large and small, seemed to be spending more and more time in meetings while feeling increasingly negative about the value of this process.

Research in High-Technology Industries

Beginning in the 1980s, researchers were particularly interested in assessing communication practices in those organizations on the leading edge of the postindustrial revolution: large-scale, technology-intensive industries. These organizations are often described as complex, highly specialized, interdependent, and decentralized information environments driven by a computer-based technology. Their workforce is characterized by highly educated scientists and engineers and technical, financial, and business professionals who make up a diverse source of managerial and technical leadership.

In a real sense these organizations are windows on the future. It is within these types of organizations and populations that we are likely to uncover major changes in organizational communication patterns and practices. The electronic, data processing, aerospace, and military products industries have often been the trend setters in communication practices.

To assess this trend, three related surveys (Mosvick 1982, 1986, 1995) were conducted, encompassing nearly 1,600 managerial and technical

MEETING NOTES

Mosvick Study Description
(1981–1995)

Sample: Nearly 1,600 managers and technical professionals from three ranks: junior management, middle management, and senior management.

Surveys: Three surveys were conducted during a 14-year period. Detailed data were collected from 230 individuals during the first two-year period (1981–1982), from 720 individuals in the second four-year period (1983–1986), and from 626 individuals in the third nine-year period (1987–1995).

Firms: Ten firms in the United States, Europe, and South America. Eighty percent of the data were drawn from personnel at five Fortune 500 high-technology corporations in the United States: General Dynamics, Honeywell, Control Data Corporation, 3M Company, and Unisys.

Occupational Areas: Managerial and technical professionals, distributed over eleven general occupational areas, were sampled: research and development, financial/accounting, manufacturing data processing, quality assurance, marketing, sales, human resources and development, engineering, legal, administrative staff, and other.

Representativeness: No significant differences were found in any major demographic or background factors in groups from any of the major firms or government agencies. All major firms at the period surveyed were highly successful and well-managed firms. The populations surveyed seemed broadly representative of business professionals in large-scale, multinational, high-technology corporations or government agencies.

professionals, representing ten firms and government agencies in the United States and abroad (see *Meeting Notes,* page 9).

The major finding among the first, second, and third surveys was that there was a *sizable shift toward an increase in the number and length of meetings, with increasingly higher levels of dissatisfaction with meetings in general.*

Three Major Shifts in Meetings

More and Longer Meetings. In all surveys, meetings proved to be a constant and growing feature of the manager's and technical professional's life. To appreciate this dramatic upsurge, let us compare the results of the three surveys completed from 1981 to 1995.

In the first survey, business professionals indicated they attended meetings of three or more individuals seven times a week. They averaged about six meetings each week at work, plus one after-hours meeting. In total, meetings accounted for approximately six hours of their work time per week (Mosvick 1982).

In the second survey, four years later, these business professionals reported that they averaged *8.5 meetings a week* on the job, or a *gain of 2.5 meetings a week* over this short period of time. When one additional after-hours meeting was added, the average manager or technical professional in the second survey attended *9.5 meetings a week, which consumed nearly ten hours, or approximately 25 percent of the work week* (Mosvick 1986). In the third survey covering 1987–1995, the average number of meetings a week increased to 10, requiring 10.5 hours on the job plus 2 additional hours for the 1.5 work-related after-hours meetings, business luncheons, and the increasingly popular "power breakfast."

Although only a slight change was found between surveys in the length of meetings, that change did demonstrate *that more time was spent on each of the four main types of meetings.* This evidence indicated that meetings were becoming more frequent and steadily consuming more and more time each year. (Such conclusions lead one to sympathize with the two unhappy managers who reported the total percentage of their work week spent in meetings at 150 percent!)

More Interdepartmental and Problem-Solving Meetings. Although there was a slight increase between the first two surveys in staff meetings and policy meetings used routinely for administrative functions, the major gains were in problem-solving and interdepartmental meetings.

The 50 percent gain in the frequency of problem-solving meetings was reported between the first two surveys. Since the main function of business meetings is related to problem solving, some gain is expected, but not one of this size. This change is clearly related to the overall upsurge in all types of meetings experienced in every company surveyed (Mosvick 1982, 1986).

A similar gain, 40 percent, in the frequency of interdepartmental meetings underscores the growing importance of liaison interaction in today's organizations. These managers and technical professionals reported spending more time coordinating program activities with colleagues in other departments, work groups, and scientific disciplines than they did meeting with the staff within their own departments.

More Involvement of All Ranks and Occupational Specialties in Meetings. The time appears long past when one can opt out of meetings by specializing in a solitary profession or by remaining in a lower rank. Today, meetings involve virtually everyone in the organization.

No matter what a person's occupational specialty is, from research scientist to marketing representative, the average business professional can expect to participate *in at least six, or as many as eleven, meetings each week*. This can only be seen as a further indication of the growing interrelatedness of modern industry. No job provides a haven from meeting overload.

Rank holds many privileges, but when it comes to meetings the opposite appears to be the case. In general, being promoted automatically involves the manager or technical professional in both more and longer meetings. The data indicate that there is a general progression in rank, from junior management through middle management to senior management, toward more meetings of virtually all kinds. Follow-up interviews also revealed that a greater degree of their job effectiveness became increasingly dependent upon how effective they were in both participating in and leading meetings.

When analyzing these data, one is struck not so much by the differences between ranks but by their general similarity. While each higher rank generally attends slightly more meetings for a somewhat longer period, *the differences between attending nine or eleven meetings a week are not truly significant*. A great number of business meetings were expected of everyone from the most recent management recruit to the seasoned veteran. Knowledge of, and skill in, effective meeting management is requisite no matter what position or rank an individual holds in the corporation.

TABLE 1-1   Frequent Reasons Why Managers Call Meetings

1. Sharing Information and Monitoring Staff
"Telling and Selling"
(Primarily one-way interaction)
30–40% of total meeting time.

1. To brief my group on new information or organizational decisions.
2. To share relevant information with my own and other groups.
3. To "sell" my group on official organizational programs or decisions.
4. To instruct my group on new procedures or policies for doing things.

2. Decision Making and Problem Solving
(The true meeting with dynamic interaction)
40–50% of total meeting time.

5. To "troubleshoot" specific problems.
6. To identify a problem and solve it.
7. To make a decision on a main or sub task.
8. To solicit solutions and recommendations from a group.
9. To assign, clarify, coordinate, and monitor departmental or interdepartmental project tasks.
10. To reconcile conflicting views of a group.
11. To consider a range of solutions and choose the best solutions.
12. To assign action steps and specific responsibility in implementing a decision.

TABLE 1-1   Frequent Reasons Why Managers Call Meetings *(Continued)*

3. Creative Ideation
5–8% of total meeting time.

13. To "brainstorm" for new ideas.
14. To demonstrate new ideas or concepts.

4. Social/Ceremonial
Group identification
Cohesion and
  Commitment
8–10% of total meeting time.

15. To simply listen to my group's concerns; to let my group "ventilate."
16. To recognize and celebrate individual or group achievements.
17. To build group morale and solidarity; encourage group identification, participation, and group involvement.

5. Self-Aggrandizement

18. "To hear himself (herself) talk!"
19. To show that he (she) is the boss!
20. To blame others for his (her) poor decision.

It is important to appreciate the way rising meeting trends eat up time and energies. However, it is equally important to recognize meeting skills as an emerging new prerequisite to gaining a leg up the corporate ladder. Walter A. Green, founder of Harrison Conference Services Inc., is adamant on this point:

◆

"It is impossible to be regarded as a highly effective manager unless you run an effective meeting....According to research done by his company and Hofstra University, Green found that four out of five managers evaluated each other based on how they partici-pate in a meeting, and 87% judge leadership based on how a person runs a meeting" (Hsu 1990).

Meetings — What to Call Them?

One of the curious features of research on business meetings is that there is a good deal of confusion among survey makers and respondents over what to call various meetings in their organizations. Virtually all organizations identify the staff meeting, but there is little agreement on the many other planning, problem solving, and creative meetings that organizations sponsor. During our last survey completed in 1995, the categories of meetings were combined into four broad but clearer functional categories of meetings based on most frequently reported reasons why managers call meetings. They are listed in Table 1-1. As one can see, there is plenty of room for potential errors in managers misunderstanding the quite different purposes and dynamics of these four main types of meetings. Although the last category lacks interviewee estimates, several managers from several different companies have noted that it is often the real reason for a number of wasted meetings.

Now that we have a clearer picture of contemporary business, one is inclined to ask what can be done about it. Let's not, however, make the mistake of attempting to solve the problem before it is diagnosed properly. Instead, let's turn from these alarming statistics and ask what is *behind* the growing need for more meetings. Why are meetings taking on growing importance in our business and governmental organizations?

Part of the answer is that the historical reasons for meetings have not diminished. The "meeting" has been around a long time because it has served an important function for which no other activity could be substituted. There is a continuing need for staff meetings, for informational and persuasive meetings, and for problem-solving and decisionmaking meetings in virtually all business, professional, and government organizations. There are other important trends developing, however, which make meetings more important in their own right. These emerging trends include the accelerating changes in the business environment and character of organizational work, the emphasis upon participative management, and the increased expansion of new group media: computer-mediated communication.

Accelerating Changes in the Business Environment

We are in the midst of a technological revolution that is radically reordering how managers obtain and process information. The ongoing digital revolution, centered on the microprocessor, the computer, satellite communication links, and increasingly powerful internal and external networks, is significantly altering the very concept of managerial work. E-mail, faxes, the Internet, and electronic and video conferencing radically affect how organizations restructure and distribute work of all kinds. There is some evidence, however, that indicates that as machines take over more routine functions and allow faster access to better data, managers tend to graduate to higher priority job functions, which typically rely heavily on oral communication and small group skills (Josephs 1985). Few futurists were as prescient as Alvin Toffler who predicted the managerial work style of this age with dead-on accuracy (Toffler 1970).

Characteristics of Modern Organizations

- Recurring Reorganization
- Reliance on Task Force Management
- Collapse of Hierarchy
- Growth of Flat Organizations
- Changing Roles and Increase in Transient Relationships

Since then, these predictions have become reality, particularly among managers of large, multinational companies. They reflect the underlying thesis of most futurists — that change will occur ever more rapidly. As political and economic forces intensify, the external environment becomes highly volatile. As major firms compete aggressively for markets and scarce resources, a premium is placed upon organizational adaptation and fast, accurate information.

Experience has shown that both reliance upon task-force management and recurring reorganization are successful strategies against this volatile external environment. Recurring reorganization has now become virtually constant reorganization in many of the leading computer and electronic industries. Five years ago, when managers in various programs were asked the question, "When did your department or division last reorganize?" the typical answer was, "Two years ago." Today, the answer is more likely to be "Six months ago," "Last month," or "We're right in the middle of one." Managers have come to accept that rapid change in organizations is a way of life, knowing that it is simply part of the process of organizational survival.

The diminished power of the organizational hierarchy is also a present trend. A business cannot survive today if incoming orders are slowly processed up and down several management levels. The trend toward more efficient, flatter organizations with fewer communication barriers has been going on for many years. The fact that virtually all company information is widely and instantly available to technical professionals and managers at nearly all levels severely compromises a manager's ability to control through withholding information.

The changing roles and increase in transient relationships are also inevitable consequences of accelerating change. The organizations of today are increasingly adhocracies, i.e., rapidly changing, adaptive temporary systems, organized around problems to be solved by groups of relative strangers with diverse professional skills.

In a review of these characteristics of modern organizations, it is clear that the manager who is to survive this continual "future shock" must be a highly adaptable person skilled in all types of communication. The successful manager must be able to size up each new management work group rapidly and then to communicate in an appropriate style in ways which are fast, accurate, and effective. *If there is one absolutely vital skill the successful manager must possess, it is the skill to effectively plan and manage meetings of all kinds.*

A related emerging trend is the fast changing character of business organizations. Key issues are global competition, decentralization, interdependency, and redundancy. These forces are most evident in the United States with the emphasis upon automation, corporate downsizing, and shifts to temporary workers, in an attempt to remain globally competitive.

Fierce global competition has driven efforts to automate, downsize, and re-engineer all jobs toward the goal of greater efficiency and profitability. The steady erosion of dependable lifelong jobs, and the trend to outplace former organizational departments as independent contractors, has created great stress and a quite different working environment. As futures analyst Peter Leyden points out:

◆

> *Corporations began to farm out much of their nonessential work to smaller firms or individuals ... the tempting practices has become so widespread that Manpower Temporary Services in 1993 'employed' far more people, about 560,000, than General Motors with 365,000 or IBM, with 330,000.*
>
> *The work rhythms will be driven more by a never-ending succession of projects. Teams of individuals with specialized talents will form around these projects only to disband when projects are complete....It's not all that different from the way the movie industry works right now. A movie producer orchestrates the 'project' of producing a movie and then brings together a unique constellation of creative talent. Everyone from the lead actors to the makeup person goes into the project knowing they soon will have to find another project (Leyden 1995).*

As we sit around the meeting table, how will this new climate influence our commitment and effort? Will it make a difference that I am now interdependent upon my ever-changing nightshift in Djakarta or Bombay, individuals I will likely never meet except on the information superhighway? We are just beginning to explore the answers to these questions.

With the attempts of business to decentralize, downsize, and re-engineer to meet competition from abroad, there are accompanying tendencies toward interdependency as organizations become more international and work becomes more specialized.

There is a natural and unavoidable need for more meetings in order to coordinate and control organizational tasks. Many business and governmental projects are monumental in their conception and scope. They require tremendous coordination in planning, endless consultation among various occupational professionals, and elaborate machinery programmed to track the project toward completion. Modern organizations require greater numbers of project teams, or task forces, to handle not only the constant change but the complexity of large systems. The success of any large organization rests upon the success of its numerous subunits. The major rub in the contemporary business environment is that *individual success is often dependent upon the efficiency, degree of cooperation, and expertise of scores of other working groups both inside and outside a company*. Increasingly, individual work units do not control their own destiny. They must be constantly consulting and checking with other work units.

Increasing Emphasis upon Participative Management – The Team Revolution

The second trend that has influenced the increased importance of the meeting in contemporary business is the recent emphasis in organizations upon participative management and self-managing teams. Today the fastest growing trend in American and European business is decentralized, highly autonomous, self-directing teams of multifunctional professionals who are empowered to manage entire projects from start to finish. Although this trend is often associated with Japanese management practices, participative management, historically, has strong American roots. Some of the earliest experiments and innovations in participative management, such as the Scanlan plan, came from American industry. The move to involve subordinates in the decision making that affected them or their jobs was based on the twin concern for productivity and people: (1) that improved quality of decisions would result when subordinate expertise is tapped in deciding key organizational problems, and (2) that improved morale would result from meeting the subordinate's needs for recognition, autonomy, and achievement through these decision-making activities.

It has proven to be difficult to establish all of these assumptions, but there is sufficient research evidence to show that a participatory decision is superior to a nonparticipatory, or individual, decision in one vital area: it allows a wider range of information and expertise to be brought into the decision-making process, thereby improving the probability of a better, wiser decision. Participative management takes many forms in the United States and Europe, ranging from shop floor decision-making teams to worker representatives on boards of directors. Of course, participation and power sharing do have limits, which are brought about by the competitive realities of power and politics in any organization.

However limited, there has been very rapid growth in various types of participative and self-management designs each year. Unquestionably the stage for acceptance of the "team" approach was set by the steady adoption of the total quality movement during the 1970s and 1980s. The logic of requiring worker participation in all phases of product development as part of a powerful new management philosophy and method was undeniable. By 1982 a New York Stock Exchange study showed that 44 percent of all companies with more than 500 employees had quality programs. The study also estimated that 90 percent of the Fortune "500" companies had a total quality program in place (Lawler and Morhman 1985, 66).

This movement dramatically accelerated the trend toward more participative management overnight by adding hundreds of meetings in companies where there were none ten years ago. This additional layer of meetings, including for the first time shop floor-level workers, doubled the total meeting activity in many companies. This trend continues unabated in the late 1990s, reinforced by quality standards programs like the ISO9000 from Europe and the Malcomb Baldridge Quality Awards in the United States.

A recent analysis in a *Fortune* magazine article places a high-involvement workplace with self-managing teams and other devices for empowering employees first as one of the three most dominant forces shaping 21st century organizations (Stewart 1992). Several advantages of teams are claimed by those who use them.

■ Team decisions made at the lowest level result in better, faster decision making and a higher degree of involvement. Those closest to a job tend to know best the work and problems associated with the task at hand as well as the work styles and preferences of their co-workers. Consequently, decisions are faster without lag time lost going through channels. Decisions are potentially more realistic, and implementation is accepted since they are owned by the group that made them.

■ Teams are more flexible in adapting to the fast changing business environment. Customers have developed new expectations for delivery of the latest products and services: "today," not "three months from now." Large, bureaucratic organizations with clogged hierarchies have a hard time competing in the marketplace against smaller, more nimble competitors. Team size and flexibility provide real competitive advantages in time to market and in rapid response in error correction and customizing goods and services.

■ Teams can also lead to increased innovation. It is no wonder why the use of self-managing teams is so pervasive in innovative companies like 3M, Xerox, Microsoft, and General Electric.

Teams can also lead to increased innovation. According to then-Harvard economist Robert Reich, "As individual skills are integrated into a group, the collective capacity to innovate becomes something greater than the sum of its parts. Over time, as group members work through various problems and approaches, they learn about one another's abilities. They learn how they can help one another perform better, what each can contribute to a particular project, how they can best take advantage of one another's experience. Each participant is constantly on the lookout for small adjustments that will speed and smooth the evolution of the whole. The net result of many such small-scale adaptations, effected throughout the organization, is to propel the enterprise forward" (Reich 1987).

Teams are clearly an irresistible idea whose time has come. Given the trends of corporate downsizing, the adoption of teams may be less of a choice than an organizational survival move. A few years ago, Chrysler employed 1 salaried employee for every 25 hourly employees.

This ratio is now 1 salaried employee for every 48 hourly employees. Chrysler expects the ratio to be 1 salaried employee for every 100 hourly employees by the year 2000 (Boone and Kurtz 1993).

From a human resource management standpoint, the decision to turn to self-managing teams is a wise choice that is finding bottom line justification. In the last decade, while other Fortune 500 companies with dwindling earnings were slashing their workforces, General Electric was busy finding new ways to grow. In the decade from 1984 to 1993, General Electric's revenues and earnings more than doubled from 28 billion to 60.5 billion dollars and 2.3 billion to 5.2 billion dollars, respectively (*Hoover's Handbook* 1995). Much of this was due to GE's extensive development of teams in all phases of their operation.

Finally, the personal value of team involvement is incalculable. Although team decisions are but one part of the movement of worker empowerment, they are a critical element. Making job decisions that affect one's immediate working environment, taking pride in high quality self-corrected work, participating in the broader learning of cross-disciplinary teams are all widely recognized ways of developing work satisfaction and fulfilling managerial discretion and autonomy needs. It is not surprising that the national consulting firm, the Hay Group, in a recent survey of 248 large American firms found that 87 percent of the respondents were pleased with teams (Schellhardt 1994).

Expansion of New Group Media — Computer-Mediated Communication

There is a third trend moving inexorably into all organizations that must be recognized. It is intimately related to the other two trends since it serves as the main facilitator for accelerating changes in the business environment and the reinvention of the hierarchy into self-managing teams. We refer to the explosive growth of new group media, computer-mediated communication (CMC). These interactive communication technologies, sometimes called "virtual meeting," will transform our meeting practice in ways that are largely unforeseen. Recently *Time* magazine devoted a special issue to analyzing the impact of this revolutionary technological synergy. From this analysis it is evident that this family of related technologies — cable networks, satellite broadcast media, commercial on-line information services, interactive video conferences and e-mail, with internet linking 46,000 interconnected computer networks — has reached a critical mass all about to take off to reshape patterns of information processing and meeting interaction.

Computer-mediated communication is truly a new media, a hybrid, retaining some of the important features of human communication but different from conventional organizational interaction because it displaces time and space at little cost. A widely respected international communication expert, Everitt Rogers, with Marcel Albritton, recently examined the impact of this new media:

 It is exponentially *faster* than telephone or postal service. A user can send a message across the world in seconds, or in real time.

 It is a more *flexible* and *convenient* media. Some forms (e-mail, electronic conferences) permit individuals to send or receive messages when they wish to rather than use the same system simultaneously.

It brings powerful *tools to group work*, through major advances in information searches, and group decision support systems.

It is *conserving* of *human energies* and *organizational efficiency* by displacing costly travel, and by decentralizing control with a wider sharing of power and decision making.

It affords *unique properties* of organization and coordination of massive scientific projects by facilitating cooperation between professionals who are relative strangers (Rogers and Albritton 1995).

We will elaborate on many of these impressive new tools of meeting management at greater length in Chapter 9.

These three basic forces are generating a multiplier effect on managerial meetings. Prognosticators see no immediate letup in these patterns of accelerating changes in business environments, increased emphasis upon participative management and upon newly developed technology of computer-mediated communication. Although we are in the midst of changes having many-faceted potential for improvement of meetings, most of these trends point to more, not fewer, meetings. Like computers, which failed to generate the "paperless office," technological advances in the 1980s have simply resulted in more meetings of more complexity.

Currently, we know that most managers and professionals are woefully ineffective in using their meeting time productively. As we shall see in the next chapter, much of this ineffectiveness is due to a structural aspect, the dynamics of multiple information processing, a condition that won't go away by televising meetings or by distributing computer printouts faster. To get a better idea of the continuing urgency of these meeting management issues, we need to take a long look at some startling figures of the true cost of meetings in America.

The Striking Costs
of Ineffective Meetings

In the last two decades, scores of companies have practiced value analysis in an attempt to cut costs on various operations of their company. For example, total quality teams are sent out to investigate manufacturing or materials handling processes in an attempt to save time, materials, and money through a more efficient operation. While millions have been saved through these methods, a major corporate expense has been largely neglected: *the cost of processing information in business conferences*. This was once thought of as simply the cost of doing business, a given which could not be counted like excess scrap or made more efficient with machine tooling design. Yet, most managers intuitively realized that every time they gathered six or seven of their busy subordinates or associates in an hour-long conference, they were spending considerably more company money than they would by working alone or in a two-person conference. How much more seemed to escape everyone's attention, until recently. The total quality movement in American business called attention to the fact that countless areas of a business operation could be quantified and analyzed for more efficient operating — including meetings.

When a value analysis is conducted of meetings, the excessive costs documented are striking. In 1986 the authors had conducted such an analysis of one of the major companies previously surveyed. They estimated a loss of nearly $55 million dollars a year because of ineffectively planned and conducted business meetings (see Table 1-2). A similar exercise was completed in 1995 for a larger multi-products firm using our most recent survey figures of average meeting hours and current regional burden rates. Despite efforts by this company to automate many functions and downsize through attrition, steady growth throughout this 10-year period maintained a large population of 15,000 professionals at this site. Survey estimates were applied to all managers and technical professionals designated as having some managerial or team leadership responsibilities. This included approximately 500, 2,000 and 7,000 individuals at the senior, middle, and junior professional ranks, respectively. To determine the approximate cost of meetings for this company, we simply multiplied the number of employees per management level by the time (hours) spent in meetings per week by the current regional burden rate for companies of this type. Dividing the annual cost by the average meeting efficiency rate of each level obtained a loss of approximately 130 million a year! For many companies, a savings of a fraction of this amount

TABLE 1-2 The Cost of Meetings in a High-Technology Corporation

Number of Employees per Level	Hours per Week[1]	Estimated Burden Rate per Hour[1]	Cost of Time in Meetings
Senior Management (500)	12	$100	$600,000
Middle Management (2,000)	10.5	$85	$1,785,000
Junior Management (7,000)	8.4	$50	$2,940,000
Weekly Cost of Meetings			$5,325,000
Annual Cost of Meetings ($5,325,000 × 48 weeks)			= $255,600,000
Estimated Meeting Efficiency (50% of annual cost)			= $127,800,000
Loss Due to Ineffective Meetings			= $127,800,000

[1] Meeting hours and burden rate drawn from one Fortune 500 high-technology company included in Mosvick 1995 study.

could mean the difference between a vigorous climate of growth and mere survival.

These kinds of horrendous losses caused by meeting inefficiency need not be accepted as a normal and necessary cost of doing business. Through better meeting design and improved meeting skills, meeting times can be cut in half and the effectiveness of the decision-making process be improved at the same time. Every minute spent by each committee member in a mismanaged meeting is a loss of time and energy that could be spent on more productive corporate activities. One cannot hope to reclaim every lost dollar. But if organizations pay attention to analyzing and improving the single business activity upon which they spend the most collective time — the business meeting — there exists untold savings which can be turned to more productive enterprises.

Meetings: "A New Economic Indicator"*

One barometer of whether a problem is reaching truly serious proportions is when national news magazines react to the issue. Isodore Barmash, a business writer for the New York Times *writing in* Newsweek, *takes a jocular view of meeting management problems. His proposal of meetings as a "new economic indicator" suggests that this problem has finally reached the national consciousness. Most of us recognize that a good deal of truth and consequent concern lie behind these satirical remarks.*

So much has been written about the decline in our nation's productivity and so many reasons advanced that one wonders why we haven't solved the problem.

But, we haven't, and we won't unless we identify the real culprit. I, for one, know what it is; and it's as elusive as only the truly obvious can be.

Meetings.

It doesn't really matter where, be it government, business or education, but meetings are held at the drop of a memo. They are wasteful, and mostly painful. I am reasonably certain that if there were an organization called the National Commission on the Study of Multiple Encounters, its findings would be devastating. It would discover, I am sure, that there were 3.8 trillion meetings held at American companies last year. Of that number, 70 percent lasted 45 minutes or more, and about 75 percent included 10 participants or more. If the NCSME pursued its research properly, it would also find that the growth trend of meetings has exceeded major economic indicators such as the gross national product, the rate of inflation, interest, unemployment—and productivity.

Meetings, I therefore suggest, have become our national pastime, yet one is hard put to see any advantage to them other than someone's decision to hold a meeting so the group can for a time avoid doing the job it is paid to do. In that sense, meetings are relaxing. The irony is that no one does.

After a lifetime of work, I cannot remember one meeting that ended happily. With the boss walking out with a satisfied smile. Or rivals leaving with more charity in their hearts for others. Or men and women certain they received parity in the discussion. Or new employees convinced they hadn't been patronized. Or seniors feeling they hadn't been overlooked, at least a bit. Or the second-in-command believing he had gotten his due.

Sparks: Most meetings start with a promising signal. "I thought," says the boss, "that we would just get together for a few minutes to lay out our new program and get some discussion going." He smiles brightly and everyone glances around, wondering, no doubt, who will win or lose in the looming confrontation. Is it one-up time again?

"Here's what we're going to do," he continues. "But if anyone has any other ideas, I'll be glad to hear them. You already know that." Most people don't, but then there's always the chance that a gathering will produce some creative sparks; two heads are better than one, or so goes the saying.

The more motivated — or more fearful—promptly start writing. The rest sit doggedly without lifting a pencil. Peer pressure is strong, and soon they are scribbling, too. A half hour later, the meeting is abuzz and so is each participant's brain. A major source of uncertainty is the degree of democracy implicit in the meeting, and everyone's participation represents a reaction to the boss's stated desire for "everyone's input." Put up or shut up. Which is better?

Rhetoric: I do not mean to imply that all meetings are governed by insecurity or fear, just most of them. They should be eliminated and substituted with a brief one-one-one session where there is more real dialogue and less rhetoric. Phone conversations can also be substituted for some in-person meetings. There is the tendency to cut things short; facial expressions aren't visible and there is a better rein on emotions.

The trouble with meetings is that too much is considered and too little is resolved. Meetings are self-perpetuating. They last twice as long as they should. They are an excuse and are often intended to impress others with the patent effort to induce employee participation. Meetings are a euphemism, a ploy really to evaluate the three P's—people, programs and politics. Meetings are deceptive. Meetings aren't held to hear what everyone has to say, but for everyone to hear what one has to say.

And their incidence hasn't been reduced by our use of computers. Quite the contrary. Despite the fascination with millions of images moving back and forth from the video-display terminal and the computer mainframe, there is an accompanying fascination with studying the printouts. Not on an individual basis, of course, but in a multiple encounter—a meeting.

How unproductive are meetings?

Well, if the National Commission of the Study of Multiple Encounters could figure it out, the number of hours spent on meetings in the United States, based on the numbers I estimated earlier, is almost incalculable, as is the number of employees involved. It would come to trillions of man- or woman-hours annually that can be translated into lost productivity. So revealing would the findings be that they might be considered a new economic indicator—the American meetings rate, seasonally adjusted.

Of course, I can hear the cynic's standard question: "How do you know that canceling meetings will make a difference?" The answer has to be, "How do we know it won't unless we try?"

So on that score I would like to propose that we declare a national moratorium on meetings in all segments of our society and see where that takes us. It might not immediately start the smokestacks belching again. But since many meetings include refreshments, it would surely result in millions ingesting less caffeine and fewer calories. What can we lose?"

---

* Isadore Barmash, "A New Economic Indicator," *Newsweek*, September 9, 1985.
  Copyright 1985, by Newsweek, Inc. All Rights Reserved. Reprinted by Permission.

Although few managers have taken the time to cost-out the inefficiency of their meetings, they are becoming increasingly aware of the parameters of the problem in all kinds of industries. Tubb's comment on a life insurance company survey mirrors our analysis:

◆

> ... the average executive in that organization spent approximately 700 hours a year or almost two of every five working days in meetings. If any portion of this time is wasted (and estimates center at around 50 percent inefficiency for most business meetings), then this company is squandering a large amount of very costly executive salaries (Tubbs 1984, 6).

The basic point is clear: managerial time is valuable. All managers should be concerned for the cost effectiveness of their personal communication, their work group's communication, and the organization's general communication, because all have a direct impact upon the company's freedom to remain an effective enterprise. It is equally important to recognize that through proper training and practice managerial communication tasks can be carried out far more efficiently than most of us can imagine.

Summary

There are three emerging trends in the contemporary business scene that are placing a greater emphasis on the frequency and importance of efficient business meetings: (1) the need to adapt to accelerating changes in the business environment; (2) the need to work within an increasingly challenging coordination of interdependent, self-managing participative work teams; and (3) the need to embrace the new world of "virtual meetings" and computer-mediated communication as the meeting model of the 21st century.

Most organizations are ill-prepared to deal with these trends. Three surveys (Mosvick 1982, 1986, 1995) have revealed the effects of these trends on managers and technical professionals:

- They are spending nearly one-fourth of their work life in meetings. Group meetings occupy the center of their business communication world.

- Meetings will increase in frequency and complexity in the future. Managers and professionals at all levels participate in more, slightly longer meetings as they are promoted.

- Many meetings are managed inefficiently; it is reported that at least 50 percent of meeting time is wasted. Meeting management may be the single most underdeveloped management skill in America.
- Wasted group productivity accounts for major financial losses in virtually all major business, governmental, and professional groups.

This growth in group activities threatens to dominate all managerial tasks, diverting time from other important management activities. The need to curb this trend and to make it more manageable is self-evident as we face a period of accelerating change and growing complexity of business issues.

Why these perennial problems continue to plague managers' lives in light of the obvious need to do something about them raises other questions. Raising the general consciousness about the scope of the problem and the forces underlying the problem of ineffective meetings is a helpful first step. However, it is not enough. If we are to understand what we must do to resolve these problems, we must first take a closer look at the very core of the problem; the specific symptoms of ineffective meetings and the peculiar kind of information processing which goes on in the average meeting. It is to that issue to which we turn next.

2

The Way Things Work
Understanding Information Processing in Business Meetings

The Problems with Today's Business Meetings

Most meetings fail. This is a critical fact that today's manager sooner or later comes to realize. Although meetings are a fundamental management tool for making informed decisions, most are ineffective in achieving their intended results. New managers are often distraught to discover this fact; more experienced managers come to accept the limitations, often avoiding their use altogether. MacKenzie (1972) illustrates this sorry state:

> *Ask any group of managers in any country in the world to list their three most time-consuming activities, Invariably, "meetings" will appear among the three. I have asked this question of more than 200 groups, and in every case but three, more than three-quarters of each group indicated that half their time spent in meetings is wasted. The problem . . . is not being sure which half (MacKenzie 1972, 98).*

Similarly, between 1981 and 1995 Mosvick asked over 1,600 managers and technical professionals to assess the meeting efficiency of the meetings in which they participate. (Considering all the various types of meetings you attended last year, please estimate the overall meeting efficiency of those meetings in attaining their goals or objectives within the time allotted for the meeting.) Their average estimate for all levels was 49 percent! This generally dismal picture of meetings is not unique to high-technology industries. Almost identical responses are found in surveys of other diverse groups such as health care professionals, executive MBA students, state and federal officials, etc. Year after year, this broadly representative sample of American managers and technical professionals at all levels reports that meetings were only *half as efficient* as they could be!

What Are the Specific Problems with Meetings?

How can we account for the persistence of this unproductive state of meeting management in America? To answer this question we must start with the empirical survey answers. In all surveys, managers and professionals were asked to list the two most personally bothersome problems that occurred in business meetings they attended. A total of 2,431 responses were received and content analyzed into 36 specific categories. The top three problems alone accounted for one-third of the total responses; the top 10 and the top 20 categories accounted for 70 percent and 92 percent, respectively, of the total meeting problems reported.

One telling similarity between the latest survey and the previous surveys is that it produced nearly twice as many meeting problems! Management of meetings apparently remains a hot topic of the fast changing scene. Otherwise there is little change between the kinds of problems encountered by managers and technical professionals in the early 1990s and those found by their counterparts in the early 1980s.

Task-Oriented Meeting Problems — Not Interpersonal Sensitivity Problems

In a closer look at what goes wrong in meetings, nearly 1,600 managers and technical professionals were asked to respond freely to an open-ended question. What was the general characteristic of their

TABLE 2-1 Ten Most Frequently Reported Meeting Problems (N = 1305)

Rank	Type of Problem	Number of References
1	Getting off subject: Rambling, redundant, digressive talk	345
2	Inconclusive: No results, decisions, assignments, or follow-up	279
3	No goals, purpose, or agenda	264
4	Meetings are too long	256
5	Ineffective leadership: Disorganized, little control	254
6	Starts late/tardiness: Time wasted during meeting	189
7	Poor or inadequate preparation by all	188
8	Information overload: Unfocused, irrelevant information	175
9	Individuals monopolize discussion	58
10	Interruptions from within and without	56

Source: Data taken from Mosvick surveys (1981-1995) of 1,600 managers and technical professionals (scientists, engineers, and technicians).

Additional categories of meeting problems which received more than 20 references were the following: participants have no decision authority (51); too many people at meeting (33); side conversations during meeting (33); no pre-meeting briefing/postponed meeting (33); participants have hidden agendas (30); ineffective decision making process (26); ineffective speakers/communication problems (25); uncooperative team attitude or effort (24); people do not participate (22); repetitive, boring subject matter (22); and miscellaneous (61).

Many of these remaining meeting problems obviously are related to the top ten categories. Over the 14-year period of these surveys, there are two general conclusions from this data that warrant comment — the dominant task-oriented character of these meetings and the surprising persistence of these many "obvious" problems in some of our finest organizations.

responses? Of the thousands of things they could have said, there was little emphasis on problems of interpersonal dynamics. Less than 3 percent of the total response referred to the category of individual domination or hidden agendas. Only four other respondents mentioned social-emotional concerns such as "being attacked," "personality conflicts," "too authoritarian manner," or "too status conscious." This particular response does not diminish the fact that some of these concerns exist and do aggravate meeting situations. But let's not second-guess the survey respondents; let's take them at their word. These respondents have overwhelmingly presented a list of basic, procedural, task-oriented problems. The basic meeting problem in the survey respondents' experience is not that participants can't get along with one another for whatever psychological reason; the problem is that participants either do not know or do not follow simple procedural guidelines in preparing for and running meetings.

Persistent Problems

This list of problems seems quite familiar. It is probable that these same problems are mentioned about meetings conducted in a wide variety of governmental, business, and professional settings. The reason these problems have a familiar ring to them is that each of us has experienced them firsthand. Most of us have been saying these things about meetings for as long as we have been attending them.

The fact that these problems are obvious and pervade many different organizations should give us all pause. When viewed as behavior, these problems appear to be specific items which any dedicated manager could soon correct. Taken together, however, *these statements characterize modern meeting management as fundamentally disorganized, unplanned, and poorly executed.* Yet, they are statements drawn from highly competent and otherwise satisfied employees of American corporations. Why do these same criticisms seem to come up time and time again? Why do they seemingly resist all changes in management style or organizational structure? It is unlikely that they represent some quirk or character flaw in Western managers, since these same managers have proven themselves to be thorough planners and implementers in many other areas of managerial behavior. The fact that these problems seem to continually recycle over time in a variety of different kinds of organizations suggests that one should look closer at the actual dynamics of a meeting. In meeting practices, we are dealing with a somewhat different kind of managerial behavior which is deeply entrenched. Consequently, a thorough analysis and a committed effort are required for change to occur.

There are many disruptions in any business meeting. Some are an inherent part of any group meeting which involves interactive discussions. Disruptions such as tangential comments, interruptions, and misunderstandings are structured into communication patterns and are present whenever individuals interact. The business meeting, with the advantages of spontaneity, directness, and idea stimulation, contributes directly to the problem of chaotic communication by its very interactive nature. That is, many individuals contribute to the ineffectiveness of information processing through poor listening habits, weak critical thinking skills, and communication anxiety. If one thinks of business meetings as a series of speeches which are simultaneously composed, rehearsed, and delivered by several persons at once, one begins to understand the complexity and inherent weakness of the meeting process.

To overcome the chaotic nature of business meetings there must be a method of control that doesn't stifle the meeting process, especially its creative and interactive nature. This chapter presents a method that selectively structures meeting discussion in a way that keeps the meeting under control while maximizing meeting value.

Information Processing Dynamics

A key to improving meetings is knowing how to control them. The standard advice on how to control a meeting is overly simplistic: have an agenda, start and conclude on time, and appoint a secretary. While this is sound advice, it generally has little impact on effectively controlling the main meeting activity — group discussion.

A more effective method of control is derived from information processing theory, which looks at how group participants select and process information to arrive at decisions. The information that group members process includes statements and data as well as situational and personal elements that can and do influence individual perceptions. *Information processing theory best represents the communication and decision-making processes which go on in typical business meetings.* By understanding how individuals process information, we can devise better ways to facilitate group processing of information as well.

How can the information flow in groups be better understood? To do this, let's begin by examining the typical information processing functions that occur in small groups and then considering the information processing problems which are unique to business meetings. The two most common examples of small group communication that we will compare are the *presentational communication format* and the *interactive meeting discussion.*

Presentational Communication Format

Compare information processing in a speaker-to-audience situation and information processing in an interactive business meeting. First, note that in a typical speaker-to-audience situation, whatever the size of the audience, the information presented is predominantly in one direction, from the speaker to each audience member (see below). Speakers have enormous control over the information they present to their audience, the sequence and structure of the topics, and types of supporting materials they use. Speakers also have relative control over the length of time they spend on each part of their presentation. They may make

INFORMATION PROCESSING IN
SPEAKER-TO-AUDIENCE PRESENTATION

**PROCESSING IS ONE-TO-ONE

**SPEAKER IS IN CONTROL OF:
① Structure and order of information
② Length of time spent on each topic
③ Logical inferences from supporting data
④ Audience adaptation to group and individual views

logical deductions, summaries, and transitions at the exact moment that seems most appropriate for the optimal processing of the information by audience members. All of the speaker's communication strategies and persuasive tactics may be planned days ahead of time. The speaker may revise the speech and rehearse portions of it endlessly to hone it into a precise, coherent, and efficient message.

Interactive Meeting Discussion: The Billiard Ball Effect

In contrast to a presentational format, business meetings offer an entirely different form of information processing. The processing of information in a business meeting seems to resemble that of a billiard ball. What happens to a well-stated question in an open panel discussion is similar to what happens to a billiard ball when it strikes other balls on a pool table. This effect is illustrated by the following excerpt drawn with little editing from an actual conference:

Member A (Chair)	"Ladies and Gentlemen, the issue we are looking at today is this: what changes should be made in our overseas business acquisition policy in Europe? Many of you have worked there, so what do you think?"
Member B (Jim)	"Well, in my view, we cannot begin to answer this question without first examining our acquisition policy in the United States."
Member C (Jeanne)	"I agree with Jim. We are a global, transnational company. Supposedly we have broad international guidelines to apply to any region . . . let's start with our basic policy statements."
Member D (Greg)	"Now come on Jeanne, we all know that most of that is strategic plan language which isn't very helpful. We've got a problem in Europe, and let's stick to it. Every subsidiary in Europe is having trouble meeting corporate goals but Germany. . . ."

Member B (Jim)	". . . that's because Germany's economic policy is the only one strong enough to withstand the aggressive price competition of the Pacific Rim countries . . . even Japan is having a hard time competing with the five other tigers."
Member E (Nate)	"Well that's also because they have finally yielded to a little U.S. pressure, decided to spend some money on their infrastructure, and open up their markets to foreign consumer goods."
Member C (Jeanne)	"Yes, but they are still very protectionist on the big ticket items: autos, computers, electronics, heavy construction. . . ."
Member A (Chair)	(To no one in particular) . . . "Well, we all know that the U.S. was initially responsible for that policy right after World War II, so we've got no one to blame but ourselves."
Member D (Greg)	"Yeah, that was a real winner, just like General McArthur's great idea to write a no military clause into their constitution so we could financially support their defense for 50 years."
Member C (Jeanne)	". . . Ah . . . How did we get to General McArthur?"

This illustration is not particularly exceptional or bizarre. This pattern of interaction is routinely found in meetings around the globe in groups that are largely unplanned and unstructured. It is the way persons meeting together in an open discussion react to statements made by another. The initial statement is reacted to differently by each participant, who, in turn, makes comments that take the discussion in different directions, changing the topic and causing new reactions with each remark. Participants jump from one topic to another with little sequential order or apparent relation to a preceding statement. They respond at different levels of abstraction, which makes processing information more difficult, and each member contributes personal views which drives the discussion further off the track (see Figure 2-1).

Looking at the meeting as an information processing event gives us a new model of the meeting. From an information structuring and sharing viewpoint it can be said: **The Model of a meeting is a mess.** Participants, as well as leaders, contribute significantly to this information processing mess. This is done in numerous ways, sometimes out of necessity, but usually without malice aforethought and with only

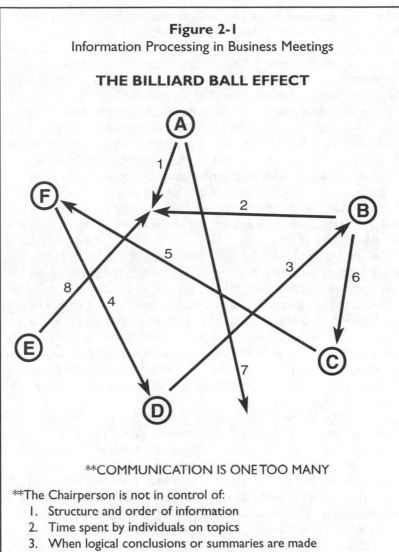

Figure 2-1
Information Processing in Business Meetings

THE BILLIARD BALL EFFECT

**COMMUNICATION IS ONE TOO MANY

**The Chairperson is not in control of:
1. Structure and order of information
2. Time spent by individuals on topics
3. When logical conclusions or summaries are made
4. Audience adaptation, since views are in the process of changing

the slightest insight of the havoc they are creating. Participants are actually the main instigators of some of the most frequently observed information processing problems in business meetings. These problems include *information queuing*, in which participants serially "store up" comments while waiting to speak, and then offer those comments, often inappropriately, after the original topic of discussion has moved on; topic jumping, or inappropriately shifting the subject of discussion to another topic; *solution jumping*, in which participants prematurely attempt to discuss solutions before adequately defining the problem; *abstraction analysis,* in which different "levels" of language are inappropriately used; *interrupting others,* too often and at length; and *inconclusive progressions,* failing to appropriately summarize discussions prior to moving on to new topics. These problems, as well as others, are discussed in more detail in Chapter 7.

In the flow of vigorous exchange, the chairperson seems almost powerless to control the structure, order, and type of information being discussed. The chairperson is limited in controlling the amount of time each individual spends on topics and finds it difficult to draw logical conclusions or summaries at the right time, if they are made at all. Unlike the public speaker who can take weeks to adapt to an audience, the chairperson must make on-the-spot adaptations to statements and feelings of several people, each having different perspectives, concerns, and verbal styles.

Meeting leaders have a far more complex and difficult job monitoring information than most of us realize. Sitting in the midst of this chaos some chairpersons simply give up and withdraw, allowing the discussion to take a meandering, unproductive course. Others resort to heavy-handed leadership techniques or adopt a symposium format in which each participant delivers a brief, uninterrupted speech in sequence. None of these is a productive alternative. Withdrawal means directionless discussion; heavy-handed authority inhibits the best analysis; and the use of a symposium format loses the advantage of spontaneous interaction.

What factors can account for the billiard ball effect? Certainly, a poor orientation to the problem in the chairperson's initial remarks contributes heavily to this random, haphazard method of communication. Another major factor is that "meeting speech" makes use of natural spontaneous speech found in everyday conversation, in which participants simultaneously choose their words and phrases in the act of speaking. This kind of speech differs extensively from the more structured utterance found in public speeches, and in the grammatically correct uninterrupted string of sentences found in written communication. Conversely, spontaneous speech is seldom formal or carefully constructed. This speech is characterized by sentence fragments, ten-second statements, frequent pauses, incomplete references, occasional errors, and many starts and stops because of interruptions (Goss 1989, 125–131). Anyone who has studied the written transcript of a small-group discussion has found that natural speech is not particularly coherent. The typical confluence of thought and speech found in a two-way conversation is compounded by the larger number of competing voices in a five- to seven-person group. In the larger group, statements and responses seldom synchronize smoothly. This verbal free-for-all is an inherent part of the meeting structures — a necessary penalty for using an open, roundtable format.

However, participants contribute to this problem in a host of other ways. Besides the previously noted tendency to engage in solution jumping, topic jumping, or analyses that are too abstract, participants exhibit other bad habits which add to this problem of information-processing chaos. Often, participants do not listen to others because they are concentrating on comments they intend to make. They regularly interrupt each other's commentary and disrupt a coherent line of thought. Because they do not employ thorough critical thinking skills, the evidence, reasoning, and sources are often poorly evaluated. In addition, participants fail to use what controls they have to limit or redirect a wayward discussion. Some of these actions are intentional — others unintentional — yet all contribute to this information-processing anarchy we call a meeting.

Monitoring Talk Time Distribution

One of the simplest ways to begin to understand the complex flow of interaction in meetings is to monitor how much group participants talk; that is, how much of the total amount of communication time that is available is used by specific group members. This communication is referred to simply as *talk time*. Our ongoing research using both participation indices and timed contributions in actual and simulated business meetings shows that chairpersons talk more often and more extensively than any other group member. In fact, there is a tendency for meeting chairpersons to talk almost *twice as often* as any other group member. Their average talk time was approximately half of the total talk time available to the group, while some participants scarcely contributed at all. The following chart approximates the proportional talk time of a typical six-person business meeting (see Figure 2-2).

Why Chairpersons Tend to Dominate Groups

There are at least three reasons that may account for somewhat greater dominance by chairpersons in business conferences. One, the chairperson usually has a relatively large amount of substantive information about the conference topic to convey. This information may be technical, but more often it is administrative because the chairperson serves as a communication link between superiors and subordinates. Two, every chairperson tends to have greater procedural duties in order to effectively monitor, guide, and clarify a discussion. Many of the chairperson's most important contributions are strictly procedural. Three, the chairperson's typically higher status gives him or her greater freedom to speak without interruption. Higher status can be a liability

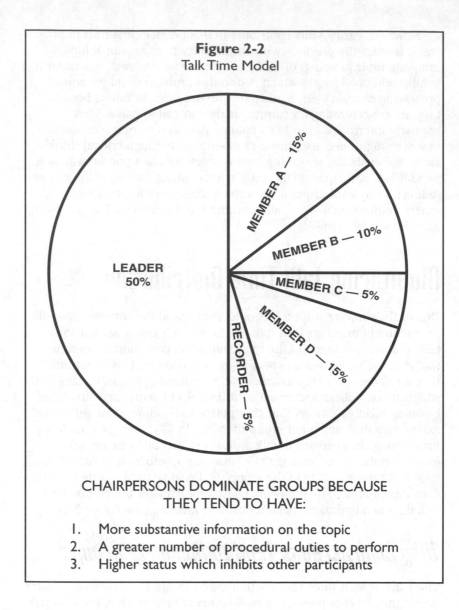

Figure 2-2
Talk Time Model

LEADER
50%

MEMBER A — 15%

MEMBER B — 10%

MEMBER C — 5%

MEMBER D — 15%

RECORDER — 5%

CHAIRPERSONS DOMINATE GROUPS BECAUSE
THEY TEND TO HAVE:

1. More substantive information on the topic
2. A greater number of procedural duties to perform
3. Higher status which inhibits other participants

and can be particularly devastating to others when it is consciously or unconsciously abused by a conference leader.

Talk time dominance by chairpersons is better understood in light of the research conducted. Harms (1974) viewed a small, seven-member group as a time-sharing system. He noted that only 80 percent of meeting time is typically available for communication because 15 percent of the time is spent in mutual silence and about 5 percent of the time is wasted when two or more participants talk simultaneously. Therefore, the available talk time (80 percent) works out to about 11 percent for each of the seven members in the group. This is sufficient time for each person to make ten half-minute contributions per hour. Equal time-sharing, however, is seldom the case, and a person who usurps greater amounts of talk time (for example, 40 percent) drastically diminishes the amount of time remaining for other members (Harms 1974, 98–99).

Observations of many business conferences lead one to agree with the statement that the first place to look for the causes of failure in a small group is how the communicators share time (Harms 1974). One indicator of a smoothly functioning group is relatively equitable time-sharing among members.

Any disproportionate amount of discussion time claimed by business meeting leaders is counterproductive to the group's initial purpose. The chairperson should want to hear the opinions and contributions of others. If the chairperson dominates the group, he or she is not attempting to attain a more equal, democratic division of talk time appropriate to modern decision making. Simply put, if managers are serious about encouraging the best thinking of their associates and team members, they clearly should not be talking so much.

What is a reasonable amount of talk time a chairperson and other participants should claim in relation to each other? An estimate of an ideal distribution profile for a six-person group is shown in Figure 2-3.

No real-life group can hope to enact a distribution precisely like this, nor should they strive to, since on every issue some individuals have more expertise and thus more to say than others. Every group, however, should aim at a reasonable division of talk time, wherein each participant has nearly an equal say in the discussion while allotting the chairperson slightly more time for the additional administrative duties.

Benefits of Equitable Talk Time

Proportionally distributed talk time offers several benefits. First, the group will have a more balanced discussion rather than one dominated by one or two individuals or by the chairperson, as business meetings tend to be. Second, it heightens the probability that the meeting time will be more productive. Since participants are invited to the meeting based on their ability to contribute valuable information and expertise, it follows that a group in which everyone takes an active role is likely to produce a higher quality meeting. Third, promoting equitable talk time demonstrates the manager's willingness to be participative, democratic, and rational in group decision making. This technique thus has important symbolic value.

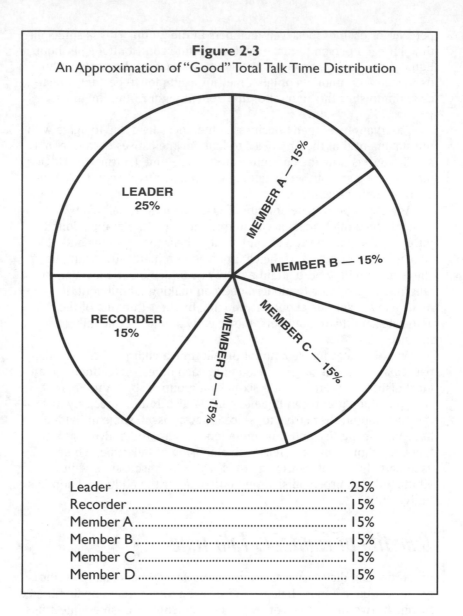

Figure 2-3
An Approximation of "Good" Total Talk Time Distribution

LEADER
25%

MEMBER A — 15%

MEMBER B — 15%

MEMBER C — 15%

RECORDER
15%

MEMBER D — 15%

Leader	25%
Recorder	15%
Member A	15%
Member B	15%
Member C	15%
Member D	15%

Talk Time and Personal Influence in Meetings

Some readers may feel that we are overly preoccupied with the fairly narrow question of sheer quantity of talk time. Managers in meeting seminars often ask, "Can't one make a case that in meetings we need fewer talkers and more listeners?" and "Don't you agree that quality not quantity of contributions is most important?" The quick answer to these questions is yes, and of course in many meetings this will be the case. However, besides the preceding rationale for group effectiveness, there are some important reasons why each of us needs to develop a personal stance on the question of an equitable slice of the talk time pie. It stems from one stubborn fact of our group research.

Our 20 years of research and observation of literally hundreds of business meetings indicates that in general, *the sheer amount of individual talk time correlates more consistently with influence than any of the following key influence factors*:

- *Position power:* The power and status of the individual
- *Communication power:* Effectiveness in verbal and nonverbal communication
- *Analytical power:* Effectiveness in critical thinking and problem analysis
- *Information power:* Stock of general knowledge and expert information on a given topic
- *Trust power:* Degree of personal credibility, trust, and acceptance
- *Group health:* Extent of conflict and polarization of the group
- *Unknown factors:* e.g., hidden agendas, alliances, and factions

Clearly any one of the preceding factors will at times be dominant with certain groups in determining influence. Lack of trust, in particular, has turned up in several studies as the most pernicious factor in a lack of individual influence and general group ineffectiveness. However, in our research with the generic "Round Table" meetings, talk time is consistently the most highly correlated with being chosen as the most influential participant by expert observers and/or group members.

There are a number of reasons to explain this finding. First, the meeting itself is not a forum for silent contemplation (though sometimes we wish it were). It expects and requires talk. This is particularly true of the steadily expanding surge of nonhierarchical groups, self-managing teams, and total quality management task forces. These new cultures are based upon participation. They expect and require a reasonable amount of problem/solution analysis, clearly expressed, to function effectively. Then too often the person who either has "nothing to say" or who "talks all the time" is increasingly the exception rather than the rule. Modern organizations hire smart, well-educated people who have a lot to say in their specialized areas if given the opportunity. Modern organizations place a high premium on technical information competence. Uninformed blowhards do not last long at these organizations.

From a process standpoint, individuals who introduce key points find that others respond to and amplify their topics through questions or statements, clarifying, extending, agreeing, or disagreeing with the topic. In a sense the topic introducer sets the agenda for the minidiscussion focusing on his or her idea for a fairly lengthy period of time. Obviously being junior in age or status inhibits one for a while, but given the growing momentum towards self-directed teams, hierarchical status prerogatives play a decreasing role in influence. The proverbial wise man of the group who says nothing until the last few minutes and then steps up with the perfect solution is a myth. It just doesn't work that way in the give-and-take of the average business meeting.

Yet, there is a prior question that we need to address: why should anyone want to be influential in a meeting? Is it not the wrong theme for these times? Clearly the need for emphasis upon "we" versus "me" is an important insight from the team movement. We all need to place more attention on the group's synergistic problem solving than on our own individual brilliance in crafting the right solution. However, we also need to understand that a desire to be influential is not an entirely selfish drive.

Over the years we have asked many groups to respond to that question: why does anyone want to be influential in group decision making? Here is a representative sample of their answers:

1 To promote acceptance of my point of view as the best for the group

2 To contribute toward developing the best group decision that includes some of my views

3 To help develop the most realistic solution — because I'm going to have to implement it

4 To prevent the group from making a very bad, costly decision

5 To help sharpen or clarify a good idea or approach of a colleague

6 To demonstrate my leadership and analytical skills; to gain visibility from my boss for future gains and promotion

7 To contribute to feeling a cohesive part of the group

8 To participate in the decision-making process however small

9   To stop Joe Blow from getting his way

10   To help the group better understand the size and significance of problems and opportunities

Although we see quite a mix of motivations that fuel our meeting involvement, it seems clear that few causes are advanced without commitment to a healthy, balanced talk time profile.

Increasing Equitable Talk Time

How can groups approximate this ideal division of talk time? As we have suggested, much of this is an individual responsibility that will be discussed at greater length in Chapter 7. However, there are three specific actions a convening manager can take to encourage a more equitable and appropriate division of the total talk time in a meeting.

Restrict Chairperson's Substantive Comments. After a short orientation speech, chairpersons should avoid extensive substantive contributions to the discussion. There will be certain times when the chairperson should contribute specific facts or opinions related to the issue being discussed, but it is important that the chairperson keep these to a minimum. Most of what the chairperson needs to say should be said in the orientation speech (see Chapter 6). After this, the chairperson should restrict contributions to procedural comments and let the group discuss the substantive issues.

Appoint a Different Chairperson. Managers are not required to lead every business meeting held within their task group. In fact, it is recommended that managers occasionally appoint subordinates or colleagues to lead their business meetings. The manager may choose to give a portion of the chairperson's orientation speech, such as detailing parameters of the problem, suspected causes, or consequences if action is not taken; however, throughout the meeting the manager should acknowledge the chairperson's prerogatives even if the chairperson is the manager's subordinate. Moreover, the opportunity for subordinates to lead meetings gives them valuable leadership experience. It is, of course, important to alternate the person assigned to this role to avoid playing favorites.

Don't Attend Certain Meetings. To give the group autonomy and force group members to act and think more independently, a manager may occasionally opt not to attend certain meetings. This practice can be introduced in a routine meeting by taking a few minutes before leaving the room to orient the group to the parameters of the problem and by giving the group a clear charge of what you expect. This practice can be expanded to include other meetings as needed.

Monitoring Information Processing: Stop and Go Signs of Interaction Controls

All leaders and participants face a real dilemma in managing meetings. Obviously, some measure of control must be exerted over the often random, chaotic information flow which characterizes the structure of an open panel discussion. On the other hand, excessive control severely limits spontaneous creativity and the cross-fertilization of ideas for which the panel discussion exists. Therefore, control cannot be heavy-handed or the very process one is trying to manage is destroyed.

How do leaders walk the fine line between sufficient control and overcontrol? How do participants contribute their opinions without infringing on the talk time of others? To better understand group information processes, one also needs to recognize some of the obvious verbal and nonverbal forms of interaction control.

Verbal Methods

Let's begin by listing some of the more obvious verbal methods by which individuals control meetings. Some use these methods deliberately; others inadvertently, with little awareness of what they are doing, or of what their particular verbal style is saying to others. By verbal methods we are referring primarily to rhetorical strategies and vocalizations, which influence the back-and-forth flow of talk in a discussion. Even at this level, however, it is interesting how many meeting participants are oblivious to the influence of these obvious devices which encourage or discourage their participation.

In most meetings, four basic verbal control methods are at work:

1 Talking frequently and at great length on a topic

2 Not allowing interruptions or turn-taking by others

3 Talking loudly; dominating a discussion by sheer volume

4 Using vocalizations as reinforcers or "stoppers"

The tendency to talk constantly and monopolize a discussion is recognized by most of us as a major pattern of communication control. It is a crude but effective ploy — at least in the short run. Similarly, maintaining the floor in an endless filibuster requires that you prevent others from interrupting or taking a turn. The point is, however, that some interruptions are quite natural and that everyone deserves an equitable share of the discussion time. The overcontroller or monopolizer ignores the right of others to contribute to the discussion.

Another method of interaction control is simply to talk louder. One learns early in life that loud, strong volume can drown out the competing voices of others. This simple technique can be observed in daily operation as conference leaders and participants try to overpower their colleagues through sheer volume. Good discussants use volume appropriately, at the beginning of meetings to command attention in bringing the meeting to order and to deflect incipient side discussions that occur within the discussion. On the positive side, the individual who has ready command of a naturally strong voice has a real advantage if it is used selectively and appropriately. On the negative side, the constant "loud mouth" who uses loud volume to squash the contributions of others is quickly tabbed a thoughtless bore.

Generally, most of us are aware that certain statements or vocalizations can be used to encourage or discourage others from talking, but we are usually not aware of how powerfully they operate. For years social psychologists have studied the effect of using simple statements of agreement in response to the statements of others, such as "uh huh," "yes," "yes, I see," or "go on," often accompanied by smiles or positive head shakes. Conversely, the effect of elements such as nonsmiling facial expressions, negative head shakes, and negative statements such as "no" and "uh-uh," have also been studied. The results of these experiments are surprising. These experiments have shown that simple exclamations are powerful reinforcers which can significantly increase or decrease the amount of time an individual spends on certain topics. This technique can even condition the repetition of such nontopical items as the number of plural words a person uses during a given period. Most of us, particularly in a free-flowing discussion, are generally unaware of how these "little" elements are influencing our verbal output. Both positive and negative feedback statements are some of the most readily available methods by which one can influence and control the interaction of others.

Nonverbal Methods

In addition to the verbal methods of control, there are a large number of nonverbal patterns which are used to control, influence, or dominate the interaction in business meetings. There is a category of nonverbal indicators called "regulators" which people use to cut off or encourage contributions by others. They include head nodding, eyebrow raising, meeting or averting of gaze, and making various facial expressions ranging from smiles to glares, which signal "go ahead" or "shut up," respectively. There are also impatient gestures such as drumming one's fingers on the table, which says "yes, yes, it's obvious" or "get on with it." There are shifts in body position and leg motions which imply impatience or frustration. A classic example of a nonverbal indicator is turning one's back to a speaker, which communicates the message "I'm not listening."

Often, individuals use these verbal and nonverbal control techniques without being aware of it; others use them intentionally, quite conscious of their effect. Unfortunately, individuals react to these control devices with little understanding of how they are being manipulated. After observing and researching countless business meetings, we believe strongly that most participants do not pay sufficient attention to the major impact of these "obvious" features of interaction. All participants need to recognize and confront rude and dominant behavior whether intended or not. Moreover, one needs to appreciate the power of the simple methods of positive reinforcement to bring forth the contributions of others, as well as to maintain general control of the meeting.

Summary

Successful meeting management requires, first and foremost, an understanding of how information is processed in business groups. It means developing a real appreciation for the natural information chaos that occurs in meetings. Understanding phenomena such as information queuing, topic jumping, solution jumping, interruptions, and the difference in levels of abstraction as natural meeting phenomena means less blaming and finger pointing and more individual action to curb these tendencies. We begin to see these tendencies as inevitable parts of the meeting process — the trade-off for the kind of spontaneous interactive exchanges we seek.

Similarly, the quality of communication time in a group is dependent on the equitable distribution of available talk time. Competitive talk time can be controlled by a dominant chairperson and influenced by a participant through common verbal and nonverbal methods.

These methods provide some insight into the sources of power and influence in a group. Therefore, leaders and participants must recognize the inherent meeting obstacles when they appear, and develop immediate and effective tactics to overcome them.

Decisions, Decisions
How Groups Make Decisions

Why do successful, experienced, and cohesive groups occasionally blunder into world-class decision disasters? Why do most of us become ultraconservative when faced with the really "big" decisions? Why are as many as 50 percent of the important organizational decisions made by default? All of these issues are hot topics in the rapidly changing world of decision making.

Before suggesting new methods to manage meetings effectively, it would be helpful to understand some of the main findings. This chapter will review recent findings in decision making, traditional methods for decision making in industry, potentials and pitfalls in the use of the standard agenda, and new influences in decision making, including a discussion of Japanese decision-making practices.

It is true that few decisions in most modern organizations are clear and simple. One is seldom dealing with clear-cut choices between alternatives. Most decision making is essentially a matter of using a comparative advantage strategy, precisely what Peter Drucker refers to in defining a decision:

A decision is a judgment. It is a choice between alternatives. It is rarely a choice between right and wrong. It is at best a choice between "almost right" and "probably wrong" — but much more often a choice between two courses of action neither of which is probably more nearly right than the other (Drucker 1966, 143).

Contrary to the view of many business critics, the hundreds of business groups which we have observed do not act like either of the two extreme versions usually portrayed: the whimsical, impulsive, seat of-the-pants decision-making group or the ultraconservative "analysis paralysis" group, incapable of making any decision because "all the data are not in." The groups we have observed, with few exceptions, try to use some kind of rational decision-making model in their deliberations. They are experienced enough to know that "all the data" will never be in and that most decisions are compromises or approximations of the ideal. Much of this is the result of the growing emphasis in the last twenty years on better-educated managers and professionals. From their education they have come to respect rational methods and have acquired some logical decision-making systems. They are also armed with a number of new tools of computerization, which helps them assemble, categorize, and interpret the ever-increasing data flow. Clearly, some of these new managerial decision makers are worth studying in their own right; they are complex theorists as well as astute practitioners who are steadily converting this art into a practical science.

On the other hand, there are many managers, young and old, who for a variety of reasons have a rather rudimentary understanding of the process of rational decision making. In general, they know how to make fairly appropriate decisions as individuals, but they have trouble transferring these approaches or techniques when engaging in collective decision making with their colleagues. The fact that their decisions are imperfect and often contradictory is attributable less to the rationality of their approach than to their lack of basic skills in managing information collectively.

One useful approach at the beginning of the decision-making process is to adopt some decision rule in sizing up the problem to be dealt with. The distinction that Koehler, Anatol, and Applebaum (1981) have made about programmed decisions versus nonprogrammed decisions may be helpful:

◆

Programmed decisions means those sufficiently familiar and repetitious to be handled by routine procedures.

Nonprogrammed decisions are considered novel, complex, or otherwise puzzling enough to require the decision maker to break new ground. Most management decision making falls somewhere between the extremes combining programmed and nonprogrammed operations. One of the characteristics of an effective decision maker, in fact, appears to be the ability to distinguish between problems for which existing procedures are appropriate and those for which new ground must be broken. it is ineffective and inefficient to deal with an exceptional problem as though it were routine, or a generic problem as though it were an exceptional case (Koehler, Anatol, and Applebaum 1981, 277–278).

The State of the Art in Decision Making

What is known about group decision making in industry is a curious blend of folklore and fact. It comes primarily from studies conducted in academic and business settings with neither setting providing a corner on truth. Because organizational phenomena must be studied amidst constant change, maintaining a current understanding about them is something of a problem. Part of the problem is the limitation on research imposed by the academic and business environments. It is an old story: businesses cannot allow the disruption to the natural patterns which permits researchers the kinds of controls they need; conversely, in order to exercise those controls academicians must resort to experiments in artificial situations and with volunteers, making it difficult, if not impossible, to transfer their findings to real-life environments. As a result, empirical research rarely focuses on what managers actually do in groups when they make collective decisions.

When empirical studies are conducted, however, the results often question the textbook model of the cool, calm, collected executive flawlessly managing the flow of information through group deliberations to an effective decision. More often than not, what is found is a somewhat harried manager who gives fragmented attention to countless pieces of information on the telephone, in one-to-one meetings, in the hall and at lunch, as well as in the formal business conference setting, all a part of the total decision-making process of which the meeting is but one part (Mintzberg 1975, 49–61; Kotter 1982).

Textbook systems have the advantage of being internally consistent, logical advice as to what good managers *should* do. However, they seldom capture the countless real-life influences of decision making or the sophisticated mixture of intuition, hard data, and risk taking that characterize many decisions. Charles Redding explains the complexity of organization communication in the following way:

—◆—

Typically, we fail to realize the communication impact of such phenomena as how much time the boss spends on Topic A versus Topic B — what priorities govern which topics get discussed first and for the longer time in meetings; what kinds of questions are raised by a certain manager; what the minutes of a meeting include and what they exclude; a colleague's facial expressions and fidgets when a topic is mentioned; who talks (unofficially, privately) with whom, about what, where, and when; which topics are never mentioned by Manager X; and much more. Nor do we typically consider as important communication dimensions of corporate life the cliques and alliances, the power blocks, and political maneuverings, the distortion and suppressions of strategic information . . . (Redding 1985, 29).

Obviously, it is impossible for any one decision-making system to be all things to all groups given the variability of decision-making factors and the many hidden agendas.

One of the more sobering statements about contemporary decision making comes from studies done by two British researchers:

◆

> No wonder it's a mad, mad world. Recent research from Brunel University's Management Decision Program into Business and Public Services show that most decisions made by most managers are largely inconsistent — with fast facts from computers, mistakes just happen faster. Brunel's research revealed that managerial decisions unwittingly contradict priorities, priorities contradict agreed policies, and agreed policies contradict what managers really believe. Depressingly, team decisions usually contradict views — they are passed by default, by domination, or from sheer exhaustion. And calling in the computer simply adds to the confusion: decision making is not merely a matter of processing facts and figures; in any case, original interpretation of the facts is frequently contradicted in the final decision (Algie and Foster 1985, 60).

Traditional Methods of Decision Making in Industry

The concerns of Algie and Foster (1985) are widely shared, although poorly understood. Yet, decision-making meetings continue every day in America using four traditional methods of decision making. The question of which method to choose is clearly related to efficient or inefficient meeting outcomes. Some methods are used disproportionately, while other methods, though widely used in the general society, such as the parliamentary procedure, have little application in typical business environments. For the moment let us briefly review these four standard methods and their basic strengths and weaknesses.

The Authoritarian Decision

The most frequent practice found in business is the authoritarian method of decision making in which a manager makes the final decision with minimal, if any, input from others. The authoritarian decision has the advantage of managerial control, and it is fast. The disadvantage of this technique is that input that might be important is not included, thus affecting the quality of the decision. Also, subordinates are excluded from participating in the decision-making process, often lowering the morale of the work group.

The Majority Decision

The practice of the *majority decision* is used most often in business peer groups or in public decision-making bodies which have incorporated the method into their rules of procedure. The advantage of the majority decision is that it uses democratic participation in the process.

The Minority Decision

Although a group may formally adopt a principle of majority rule, the dynamics of group process often result in a *minority decision* by two or three people, which is forced upon the entire group. Factions and cliques occur in all groups. There are many examples in which a few articulate, persistent individuals can dominate the thinking of the other group members. Supporting speeches are planned to trigger a bandwagon effect in support of the minority's viewpoint. The advantage of the method is that the dedicated individuals can lobby effectively to gain acceptance of their ideas within a larger group. The disadvantage is that decisions are sometimes carelessly inspected and often come back to haunt the deciding faction.

MINORITY DECISION
(CLIQUES/FACTIONS RULE)

PERMITS PERSUASION

OFTEN "POLITICAL"
DOMINANCE RESENTED

The Consensus Decision

The most notable practitioners of the *consensus decision* are found in Japanese industry, with a notable increase in North America and Europe in the 1980s and 1990s, with the emphasis upon self-managing teams and total quality management. This method is characterized by its ease of implementation. Everyone affected by the decision understands and agrees with what will be done. The disadvantage is that this decision-making method is highly time-consuming. Dr. Roy Richardson, vice-president of human resources for Graco Corporation, states that "The majority of major decisions made by boards of directors are virtually always unanimous decisions" (personal interview by Mosvick, 1 March 1995). Richardson contends that at this level of decision making any major decision has such impact that to use a method other than consensus is to invite major future problems.

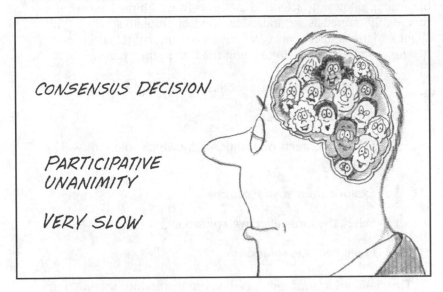

CONSENSUS DECISION

PARTICIPATIVE UNANIMITY

VERY SLOW

Although these are the four chief decision-rule schemes available to most groups, we should at least note in passing that the most frequently used decision method is a nonmethod — decision by default. Dr. Marcus Alexis, former Chairman of the Interstate Commerce Commission and Dean of the Business School at University of Illinois, Chicago Circle, estimates that as many as 50 percent of the important organizational decisions end up being decisions by default (personal interview by Mosvick, 25 October 1985). Experienced managers are all too familiar with this phenomenon. They have observed too many potentially good decisions become strangled by indecision, consigned to some bureaucratic limbo, or overtaken in one brilliant move by a competitor. Decision by default continues to thrive as one of a number of irrational decision methods too vast to catalog here. It is best seen as a sharp reminder to all that *a decision by a nondecision is still a decision.*

Let us now turn from general decision-rule schemes to the most frequently used system or process of decision making — the standard agenda.

The Standard Agenda

In the decision-making process, most business groups use some version of what has been called the *standard agenda,* an approach developed by Dewey (1910) and based, in turn, on his research into how the mind operates in problem solving. Technical professionals and managers in science-based industries find this method congenial because it follows the scientific methods in which most have been thoroughly trained as a standard method of problem solving. With slight variations, most managers have encountered this decision-making sequence somewhere along the line in their career.

1 Define and limit the problem.

2 Analyze the problem.

3 Establish criteria or standards by which solutions will be evaluated.

4 Explore alternative solutions.

5 Select the most effective solution.

6 Implement the solution.

The standard agenda remains the core method for solving problems. If properly utilized, it can be as effective as any newer method in finding solutions to most problems. It is logical, sufficiently comprehensive, and reasonably simple to understand. But not unlike other models, the problem comes in implementation: most decision groups do not follow the sequence once the fast-paced interaction begins. Let us examine the major errors in each step as reflected by American decision-making groups.

Some critics of the standard agenda point out that it is essentially a prescriptive method based upon a suspect assumption that all participants are rational decision makers. However, researchers who have experience in applied business environments tend to justify the method. As Rothwell points out:

◆

> ... the degree to which groups satisfy the four critical functions of effective decision making in a systematic manner is of central concern. (Problem assessment, criteria, merits and demerits of decision) ... Clearly, groups can be affected by nonrational influences and still reap the benefits of a systematic, rational approach to decision making ... (Rothwell 1995).

Defining and Limiting the Problem. Few American decision-making groups spend sufficient time identifying, defining, and limiting a problem in its totality. Instead, the major portion of available discussion time is devoted to arguing about the relative merits and details of their preferred solution. Consequently, premises or decisions are adopted on subpoints, which have been barely discussed because of time restraints. This increases the probability of reaching a poor solution which cannot encompass the total dimensions of the problem.

Analyze the Problem. When groups do spend any significant amount of time discussing the problem, they usually focus on the most apparent and often the most superficial dimensions of the problem. In groups, as in life, one is attracted by the latest flurry of events or the most dramatic story. Group attention tends to focus on the most recent symptom of the problem, or the one item which deviates most from the norm: the most current, striking, or controversial aspects of the problem which may or may not point to the real causes of the problem. This is not to deprecate the usefulness or correctness of quick-and-dirty analysis and quick-fix solutions. After all, quick fixes do fulfill their limited purpose well. They clearly have their place in the face of a variety of business time pressures. However, what serious problem solvers need when faced with a complex issue is a commitment to get to the bottom of the problem through comprehensive *causal analysis.* This is one feature of problem analysis which is commonly weak in American work groups.

This analytical deficiency is caused by the tendency of ignoring both definition and problem analysis and jumping to the solution. There is also the tendency of accepting the description of the problem presented by the chairperson or the owner of the problem as the correct causal analysis. This person is thought to be closest to the problem or otherwise in a responsible position to know the causes best.

We know that sound critical thinking must be utilized at every step of the standard agenda sequence if the group is to maximize their problem-solving abilities (Hirokawa 1992). An equally important explanation for weak problem analysis, however, is a lack of critical thinking skills in groups. Few managers or technical professionals have a good grasp of the critical thinking principles necessary for comprehensive causal analysis. These principles require an appreciation of both multiple causation and the basic tests of causal inferences — recognizing the difference between contingent versus principal and immediate versus underlying causes of a problem — plus a knowledge of the pitfalls of various fallacies. It is also important to have an understanding of critical thinking in action, such as the rhetorical way in which oral arguments work in a group. This is part of understanding the immediate and compelling persuasiveness of a single dramatic piece of evidence which may later turn out to be misleading and unrepresentative.

One can observe this critical thinking gap in many decisions, despite the fact that many of these decision makers have advanced degrees and spend every day reasoning and problem solving. It is as if they do not see that their own job-related reasoning skills can transfer to business meetings that are predominantly nontechnical. A director of a major research and development lab, with over twenty-five years of experience, put it this way:

I am amazed at the little carryover in problem solving skills I see in my people as they move from the bench to the meeting room. A few minutes before, they have been applying the most rigorous reasoning and causal analysis in solving some complex experimental design. Then they are asked to sit down with their colleagues to help resolve a fairly simple interface problem, say with manufacturing or marketing, and their problem solving skills seem to disappear. It is as if they had had virtually no training in defining or in getting to the basic cause of the problem. It is true that in their laboratory they work within a narrower range of familiar problems assisted by precise measurement and statistical analysis, all of which aid their decision making immeasurably. But there clearly should be more carryover of the scientific method and critical reasoning than I have observed.

Establish Criteria or Standards by Which Solutions Will Be Evaluated. In our experience with many groups in business, professional, governmental, and academic organizations, this phase is virtually never addressed. If it is addressed at all, it is in the last few minutes of the discussion as the group rushes to closure.

The criteria by which a solution will be judged as effective or ineffective should be stipulated early in the discussion. This should be done to judge whether the group solution will meet the real need and to prevent wasting time discussing irrelevant options. We have all been part of meetings similar to this one:

...After we had discussed innumerable details of a solution, we discovered, after the fact, that we had ignored an important recent company edict which imposed a big restriction on the solution: "No new funding will be available!" This discovery wiped out the entire two-hour discussion premised on the belief we could find money to hire the three staff scientists and purchase the new equipment needed to solve the problem. We were back to square one with two hours and considerable creative energies wasted.

Confusion, conflict, and wasted meeting time are needlessly provoked by not specifying the criteria. Criteria, or standards, for an effective decision usually include the following: money, general resources, human resources/expertise, company policy/customs, and ethics. In a broad sense, *criteria for a good decision become primal decision rules.* Combined with several other general and specific criteria, they constitute a major part of the whole decision-making scheme.

Few solutions are entirely devoid of financial constraints. Indeed, there are few decisions for which money is no object. The complex relationship of the money available, the probable risks, and the probable return on the investment are elements in the *bounded rationality* of most organizational decisions. These elements are, of course, less important in routine budgeting on forecast meetings where expenditures are expected and when requests meet normative budgeting estimates. They are decisive, however, when solutions must be worked out in an economic climate of company-wide layoffs and cost reduction goals or when all requests must compete for dwindling contingency funds.

General resources such as facilities, space, energy, and availability of the right kind of equipment to solve the problem must also be an obvious decision criterion. For example, specific energy or pollution control requirements for a new production line are decided constraints in locating the new facility in certain regions of the United States. Other obvious criteria to solve this problem are the quantity and quality of human resources. Human resources and expertise have become an increasingly important factor in high-technology industries. Contracts worth millions of dollars are forfeited each year by companies that have decided that an adequate number of specialized, experienced scientists to successfully complete large government projects simply cannot be found. Finding the right persons for the right solutions remains a major constraint on many businesses.

Company policy, or custom, is both an obvious and subtle "hidden agenda" item, which proves to be most influential in many decisions. Certain corporations have clearly stated principles that are part of a strong corporate philosophy, making some decisions clear and simple since certain alternatives are simply not permitted. For example, most companies have a clearly stated policy forbidding any employees from receiving kickbacks from clients or suppliers with whom they do business. Some less-publicized customs that restrict or permit decisions are nonetheless important parts of a company's culture. Criteria such as these tend to be more debatable, political, and ambiguous; therefore, they are often sources of confusion in the decision-making processes. Participants may not know, for example, that when push comes to shove and major defense contract awards come down to the wire, despite the official company policy, it is acceptable procedure to make questionable gifts to key decision makers. For obvious reasons, the quasi-legal or illegal nature of these criteria is often hidden and denied to all but a few of the movers and shakers in an organization. Hidden policies like these also occasion many closed meetings and place very stringent control on information to other groups. All of these criteria tend to compound the confusion and ineffectiveness of other decision-making groups.

Determination of criteria should be timed to take place *after* the definition and causal analysis of the problem and *before* discussions of the alternative solutions which it will influence significantly. The chairperson should touch on undebatable criteria for a good solution prior to analysis of the problem, as part of the general orientation to the task. Lengthy discussion of each criterion, however, is premature and unproductive unless one of the probable causes involves one of the major criteria directly. For example, assume that one of the reasons for high company turnover is low wages. In addition, it is also known that one of the decision criteria is that no more company funds will be available this year for wage raises. Therefore, one becomes aware in the early stages of the discussion that although the most significant cause of the problem has been identified, one must look to other supplementary methods to lessen turnover. One must be content with the knowledge that one's solution will be a partial success at best. That specific insight may be not only a great time-saver, it may spur the group on to more creative answers to the problem.

Explore Alternative Solutions. American work groups tend to spend most of their time on this phase of the decision-making process. To be the "one who solves the problems" is virtually synonymous in the American business mind with all that is good about pragmatic leadership. This is a pattern we have observed with some European groups that also tend to be compliant to the hierarchically ordered solution. The key problem, however, is that very few groups exhibit the openness or flexibility that is necessary to look at all viable alternatives. The typical strategy features a key player, usually a manager, who signals a preferred solution from the opening moments of the meeting. Although encouraging everyone to be full and frank in voicing their alternative solutions, it becomes immediately clear to the group which way the wind is blowing. Status compliance patterns soon appear and other alternatives are debated in a perfunctory manner.

On the other hand, interdepartmental meetings tend to be more open and exhaustive investigations of alternative solutions because there is usually no one person who directly controls participants' careers; "What the boss wants" is not a key to the final decision. Participants usually represent different factions, needs, and perspectives, all of which make for a frank confrontation of ideas and more ways of viewing the alternative possibilities.

Another typical strategy to consider is the bandwagon effect. This strategy is set in motion by a minority of highly vocal protagonists giving negative and cursory review of all other alternatives proposed. They often come in on cue, building the impression that there is significant opposition to every alternative but their own. They often accomplish in timing, vocal dominance, and extended arguments what could not be achieved by any reasonably objective analysis of the merits of a proposition. At the heart of this behavior is a very competitive political view of groups in operation. Individuals are out to win the conference, to get their view accepted within a win-lose paradigm. Later, we will speak to the inappropriateness of this general position; for now, it is enough to recognize that these commonly observed strategies make it difficult for any group to give each option a fair hearing.

Selecting the Most Effective Solution. Work groups have trouble with this phase of the decision process. If there has been unanimity on the decision criteria ahead of time, often the most effective solution is self-evident. In programmed decisions where a group has been working with routine procedures and familiar variables, a simple matrix comparison chart can allow even an inexperienced manager to make a good decision by adding up the comparative advantages of one solution over another. Some of the new computer-aided decision-making schemas can be most helpful in this phase (see Chapter 8). Ideally, all groups should arrive at this point with a growing consensus of the best path to take. This phase, however, often becomes the final battle between two contending factions within the group and is characterized more by acrimony than by sweetness and light.

Most managers realize that coming to a final agreement on a recommended solution is worth no more than the depth of commitment that decision makers have to the solution. To prevent this disastrous kind of paper assent, some methods try to build toward consensus from the beginning. One approach is the *ideal solution* method devised by the Kepner Tregoe management consulting firm (Larson 1969, 452–455). This approach suggests that after all group members have agreed on the nature of the problem, they should concentrate on devising an ideal solution for it. This approach exposes all hidden agenda items because participants realize that they must immediately set the parameters that will influence the final decision. They cannot change the "ideal" parameters later in the discussion to suit their vested interests. After the ideal solution has been formulated, the group is asked to decide from the real solutions available which one best approximates the ideal solution.

On this phase of the decision process, Drucker stresses the point that a group should focus on a solution that most fully satisfies the group's specifications before turning their attention to devising the compromises, concessions, and modification needed to make the decision acceptable. Choosing a solution with one eye on future compromises will result in a weaker management decision. First choose what is "right" rather than what is "acceptable." Compromises will come soon enough but should not contaminate the most desirable choice (Drucker 1974).

Implement the Solution. The selection of the best solution must be acceptable to two distinct groups: the group making the decision and the group which must implement the solution. All too often, management analysts discuss these two groups as if they were the same. More often, they are not the same groups. Anyone who has had to carry out an impossible decision made by higher managers who had no responsibility in implementing the decision, is well aware of this fact. For this reason, decision choice and implementation responsibility have been linked in most management systems, but usually not clearly enough.

Quality Plus Acceptance

So far, the entire foregoing discussion has concerned itself with the *quality* of the decision. But decision effectiveness is as much a function of *acceptance* as it is of quality. A peculiarly American oversight in decision-making strategy becomes apparent at this stage, and it is responsible for a common weakness in decision making — subordinates and colleagues resist or reject hierarchically ordered solutions. Norman Maier has stated that to be effective, a solution must not only require high quality, it must also be accepted by those individuals who must implement the decision. This approach is encapsulated in Maier's formula and explanation:

$$ED = Q \times A$$

The formula for an effective decision (ED) therefore would require consideration of two independent aspects of a decision: (1) its purely objective or impersonal attributes, which we are defining as quality (Q); and (2) its attractiveness or desirability to persons who must work with the decisions, which we are defining as acceptance (A). The first depends upon objective data (facts in the situation); the second on subjective data (feelings which are in people) (Maier 1963, 5).

Maier (1963) notes that there are generally three variations of this formula to consider: those decisions in which the quality is high, but acceptance is low; those in which acceptance is high, but quality is low; and those in which both quality and acceptance are high. For example, he cites decisions regarding plant expansions, new products, decentralizations, plant sites, price setting, cost determination, and materials purchasing as high-quality decisions that can and should be made by experts and which usually have low acceptance requirements. On the other hand, some decisions are not particularly taxing (low quality), but do require high acceptance. These usually involve treating individuals fairly and equitably, such as decisions allocating vacation schedules or distributing new office equipment. Those decisions that require both high acceptance and high quality constitute the most frequent and difficult decision problems.

The standard agenda remains the preferred decision-making process among business groups. Becoming aware of the potentials and the pitfalls of each step of this sequence is the first step toward refining one's meetings skills and improving meeting efficiency. However, one also needs to be aware of and open to new influences in decision making, which may help to improve collective decision making.

New Influences in Decision Making

In the 1980s and 1990s a considerable amount of research about applied decision making has led us to revise much of our thinking about this critical, complex process. Some of the findings run counter to some commonly held "intuitive" notions we have about the process. For example, groups tend to differ from individuals on some character-istics such as taking greater risks in decisions. Does it matter if you view the glass as half empty or half full? Apparently how you frame information and discussion makes a good deal of difference. We will take a look at some of the main findings that operate in real-life groups. Research into the process of decision making is leading us to revise much of our thinking about the most important aspects of decision making. In 1980, two psychology professors, Amos Tversky and Daniel Kahneman, presented the results of fifteen years of work in the cognitive psychology school of decision making. Tversky and Kahneman (1980) sought to answer the question, "What are some of the important influences when people make decisions?" They found that the mind is a tricky filter, engaging in a good deal of *mental framing* when coming to a decision. Depending on the frame of reference, individuals decided "yes," and sometimes "no," when faced with essentially the same set of facts.

In one of their now classic experiments, Tversky and Kahneman (1980) asked individuals what they would do when faced with these two situations: (1) You have purchased two advance-sale movie tickets for $10.00 but discover you have lost them as you approach the ticket-taker. Would you pay another $10.00 to replace the tickets? (2) As you step up to buy movie tickets at the ticket window you discover you've lost a $10.00 bill. Would you still pay $10.00 for the tickets? Most individuals refused to replace the tickets in the first case but went ahead and bought them in the second instance, even though the situations are essentially the same — the loss of $10.00.

Conservative Coming of Decisions

Tversky and Kahneman (1980) believe that better decisions can be made by understanding how small variations influence the way facts are perceived or the way those facts are presented by others. How, then, does this explain the decisions in the experiment? Apparently, the difference is because of a different **frame of reference**. In the first case, the cost of both the original ticket and its replacement are charged to one "mental account," making the total cost too high. In the second case, the loss of the $10.00 bill is not directly associated with the mental account of going to the movies. When both of the examples are presented to the same group, so that they recognize that there is no difference between $10.00 worth of tickets and a $10.00 bill, there is a big jump in the number who buy replacement tickets. One of the major facts then in any decision-making process is the person's frame of reference.

It appears that Tversky and Kahneman have uncovered a particular mindset in what they call their "loss aversion theory"; that is, the negative impact of losing is much more significant than the positive influence of winning. When individuals are faced with a major decision, they are usually more concerned with the negative consequences than the potential advantages. Rather than focusing on the positive results of the decision, their frame of reference shifts to the loss they are trying to avoid. Since the disadvantages loom larger than the advantages, they tend to become quite conservative in their decision making (Tversky and Kahneman 1980). This loss-aversion mindset may be held by one key decision maker, by a dominant clique of three people, or by the whole group. But whether the frame of reference is short-term or long-term, or held by one or several decision makers, it is a filter for interpretation which can influence all deliberations and distort interpretations of information.

Under this general condition, the potential advantages of the decision must outweigh the disadvantages disproportionately in order to elicit a clear-cut decision in which all participants are satisfied. It is highly probable that countless superior ideas die aborning each day in conference rooms across the nation because there is insufficient attention given to removing or diminishing the negative objections against a new idea.

In small group conferences, the loss aversion theory might explain why so much of a discussion centers on *immediate criticism* of any new idea. In most problem-solving business meetings new ideas seldom encounter a friendly, receptive climate. The first reaction to a new proposal is typically a series of criticisms with minimal, if any, positive reinforcement.

What are the implications of this new research for the thousands of small groups which meet each day? Fundamentally, it indicates that group participants should be spending more time ferreting out and speaking to the negative objections against a major decision to change or, as Dr. Kahneman says, "allaying the fears rather than adding to the incentive." Apparently, less time should be spent on the potential benefits of a decision and considerably more time on dealing with those objections or disadvantages surrounding the decision, both stated and hidden, since this seems to be where decisions get stuck. Kahneman and Tversky have strong support from other researchers on this point. Hirokawa (1985) found that one of the major factors accounting for high-quality group decision making was the group assessment of potential weaknesses, contrary evidence, negative qualities, and consequences of alternative choices in both the problem and solution phases. *We feel that this tendency is such a powerful decision-making phenomenon that companies should institutionalize some method of dealing with it in all-important meetings.*

Procedurally, this may mean adopting a specific group structure or process to identify and, if possible, remove the key disadvantages to a proposal. Many companies use some variation of this idea as standard practice in preparing major proposals by charging a "blue team" to research and compose the advantages of a proposal and a "red team" to analyze and state the disadvantages in an attempt to refine the proposal before submitting it to the scrutiny of the real audience or client. To further refine the proposal, an individual should play the devil's advocate. The responsibility of this role is to ensure that the "losses" be confronted, and then dealt with as an integral part of the whole decision-making process.

The real secret of this approach is to become aware of our individual or group reference framing set, to understand how this may be subtly shading our interpretation of the facts, thereby creating a biased decision. Equally important is to recognize that taking on a different perspective can provide real breakthroughs in group decision making.

◆

Dr. Tversky points out that looking twice, or even three times at how we are framing options can help us sidestep decision making traps and minimize the chances of being manipulated by others. It's important to realize that our judgments are fallible, and that what seems good from one vantage point may seem better from another ... so approach a problem from more than one perspective: if the answers you get don't agree, keep turning the picture over in your mind until you see which frame fits best (Buckley 1985, 88).

Japanese Decision Making: The Consensus Decision

In the last ten years, much has been written about different methods of decision making, each of which is argued to be the "most effective" method. A major portion of this writing has been directed at understanding the Japanese method. Many have attempted to explain how a nation with such meager resources could rise so quickly, literally from the ashes of WW II, to become the world's second largest economy. We now know that this "miracle" was due to a mix of several complementary factors: trade agreements that restricted competition allowing Japanese industry to rebuild; the widespread adoption of Dr. Edward Deming's statistical and scientific methods in manufacturing and quality control; the Keritsu as a type of state capitalism supporting and guiding long range macroeconomic decisions; and the force of the tradi-

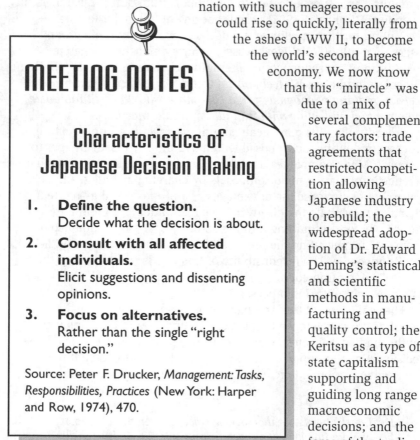

MEETING NOTES

Characteristics of Japanese Decision Making

1. **Define the question.**
   Decide what the decision is about.
2. **Consult with all affected individuals.**
   Elicit suggestions and dissenting opinions.
3. **Focus on alternatives.**
   Rather than the single "right decision."

Source: Peter F. Drucker, *Management: Tasks, Responsibilities, Practices* (New York: Harper and Row, 1974), 470.

tional Japanese emphasis upon group vs. individual achievement and decision making. Nonetheless, the Japanese consensus method contributed much to this miracle by channeling and developing the human resources of Japan. It remains a unique model of decision making worthy of our study. Drucker (1974) states that the Japanese method for making decisions constitutes an entirely different process with a different focus than the traditional American methods (see *Meeting Notes*, previous page).

As Drucker (1974) notes, the Japanese may sometimes come up with the wrong solution to a problem, but they will seldom come up with an inapplicable solution to the *wrong problem*, as often happens with many American decisions. This is because the Japanese take the time to define the problem first. The Japanese method is in many ways the opposite of the American approach to decision making: the Japanese first "sell" their ideas to all the members of an organization who will be affected by the decision. In this process, they receive suggestions for changes and modifications which further define the problem and the consequences of certain sub-decisions. Americans, who are more solution-oriented, focus on arriving at a decision and then selling that decision to their subordinates after the fact. More will be said on the method of bringing a group to consensus in Chapter 6.

Drucker (1974) examined the elements of effective decision making through a study of various complex, large-scale institutions in the United States and abroad and offers a number of novel suggestions for more effective decisions (see *Meeting Notes,* next page). Although Drucker's suggestions are by no means a systematic method, they are designed to expose and confront many of the real-life roadblocks of decision making. Drucker is principally concerned with spending much more time on problem definition; being upfront with our biases, whether they be causes, criteria, or solutions; and avoiding time-consuming discussion of nonessential topics to the decision.

Groupthink

A final insight into how groups make decisions is the notion of *groupthink*. It is best viewed as an insidious pitfall in group decision making which occurs when everything seems to be going well — members are getting along, the group is pleasantly disposed, consensus decisions are made quickly and easily. This group is ripe for the problem of groupthink.

The groupthink phenomenon, described and labeled by sociologist Irving Janis, occurs when members have such pleasant, positive attitudes toward their group that their critical thinking ability is hampered. The dominant characteristic of groupthink is a lack of

MEETING NOTES

Advice for Effective Decisions

1. Spend enough time stating and restating the initial question until everyone agrees on what the problem is.

2. Start with opinions — get them on the table.

3. Treat the opinions like hypotheses in scientific experiments: test them, don't argue over them.

4. Determine what is the appropriate way to test the opinions against reality, given this topic and the decision to be reached.

5. Establish a criterion of relevance for collecting more information.

6. Encourage dissent.

7. Withhold evaluation — appreciate diversity of perspective.

8. Develop commitment from group members at every possible point.

9. Make appropriate compromises.

10. Always ask: "Is this decision necessary?" One alternative is to do nothing.

11. Build in a feedback mechanism to check the decision's success.

Source: Peter F. Drucker, *Management: Tasks, Responsibilities, Practices* (New York: Harper and Row, 1974), 470–480.

conflict and disagreement. Consequently, group members come to an easy consensus on decisions — no one "rocks the boat" — but they may be low-quality decisions. To exemplify groupthink, Janis cites historical cases such as President Kennedy's Bay of Pigs invasion and the United States government's processing of information from Japan before the Pearl Harbor attack (Janis 1982, 245).

Other examples frequently cited are the series of decisions surrounding the Vietnam War, the head-in-the-sand response of the big three American automakers to the public demand for smaller, more economical cars, "Watergate" and more current political exposes, and the explosion of the Challenger shuttlecraft that crippled the U.S. space program for years. (Gouran, et al. 1986) In each of these major decisions, supposedly made by some of America's best and brightest, elements of groupthink can be seen at work.

In the past decade there have been several empirical studies attempting to understand the groupthink phenomena. To cite one example, Cline (1990) describes types of communication that lead to groupthink including a high degree of verbal statements of agreements without clarification, lots of nonverbal signs of agreement, virtually no statements of conflict or disagreement, and statements that directly solicited agreements from participants such as "right?" or "don't you agree?" These groups tend to be fearful of any real arguments and willing to maintain harmony at all costs. Other writers have noted that groupthink is related to the inability or unwillingness of participants to use appropriate critical thinking, and the tendency for the group to pressure nonconformists to conform to majority views.

Groupthink is not the result of conscious, individual manipulations; it is a group phenomenon of which most participants are unaware. Subtle conformity pressures, status differences, a norm of agreement, and a strong feeling of cohesiveness among the group all contribute to groupthink. Participants should be familiar with groupthink symptoms to prevent it from occurring (see *Meeting Notes*, next page).

There are several antidotes to groupthink. Although the following techniques may lead to longer meetings, the higher quality decisions that result will justify the tactics.

 Minimize potential status effects between members by requesting that the person with the highest formal status occasionally relinquish the chair of a meeting or refrain from attending some meetings.

 Develop alternative methods of gathering information which challenge the prevailing attitudes and opinions of the group. For example, collect information anonymously from group members.

 Develop a norm in which disagreement is acceptable and necessary; encourage the role of devil's advocate.

In this examination of three major phenomena that affect decision making, we have seen that there exists a common need in each to require sound critical thinking of a proposal including the presentation

MEETING NOTES

Symptoms of Groupthink

A norm of suppressing conflict
"Why do you insist on ruining the progress we've made on this issue?"

An illusion that the group is invulnerable
"Of course we're not going to get any flak from FTC about this."

An ability to rationalize away problems
"I can't see getting much competition on this; after all, our biggest competitor has just changed CEOs. It'll take them a year to get reorganized."

Negative stereotyping of possible critics of the decision
"You know how quality control people are; they'd nitpick any good product to death."

of negative objections and alternative views of the situation. *Because the consequence of lack of critical analysis can be so disastrous, we advocate that each organization must somehow institutionalize or structure in some process that guarantees this thorough, systematic examination of decisions. One of the most successful approaches is to develop a devil's advocate role required with all major organizational decisions (see Chapter 6).*

Summary

In this chapter we have examined the growing complexity of decision making in contemporary American business meetings. Drawing primarily upon the advice of experienced managers and empirical studies, we found that decision making is at the center of the typical manager's day. We then reviewed the advantages and disadvantages of traditional methods of decision making — the one-person decision; the majority decision; the minority decision; and the consensus decision. It was noted that, unfortunately, another method — decision by default — may be the most frequent pattern of business and governmental decision making. Next, we closely examined each step of the most common small-group format used in business decision making — the standard agenda. The most common mistakes in this format, which groups need to avoid in order to improve the efficiency of their meetings, were:

- The tendency to ignore a full definition of the problem and to move immediately to a discussion of solutions. Groups need to spend considerably more time exploring and defining all dimensions of the problem in coming to understand all implications of the problem and the solution.

- The tendency to ignore systematic analysis of the problem and to pay attention to the most current, dramatic, and controversial aspects of the problem. Groups need to develop sound critical thinking skills and to devote more time to a thorough causal analysis of the problem.

- The tendency to ignore the need to establish criteria or standards by which solutions will be evaluated. Groups need to do this early in their deliberations, before solutions are discussed, in order to focus the discussion and avoid the time-consuming discussion of irrelevant topics.

- The tendency to concentrate solely on the quality of the decision while ignoring the need to gain group acceptance of a decision. Groups need to recognize that there are usually several equally good decision options from which to choose. More time should be spent on selecting the option most acceptable to the group in order to better facilitate the implementation of that decision.

Finally, we explored some of the new currents in group decision making. The first concept, the loss-aversion theory, uncovered the predominantly conservative mindset or frame of reference that decision makers acquire when they face major decisions. They focus inordinately on possible losses versus probable gains. From this analysis it becomes evident that decision makers must direct more effort at dealing with the major objections or disadvantages of a proposal, since this is the major point at which key decisions get sidetracked.

The second concept, the need to develop consensus decision making, drew heavily from the characteristics of Japanese decision making. These successful practices suggest that American managers might profit by spending more time consulting with all the individuals who will be affected by the decision prior to the decision — eliciting suggestions and dissenting opinions, while focusing on various alternative solutions rather than the one "right solution." Although a perfect consensus is not practical in many situations, an approximation of consensus is a viable option which increases the probability of better quality decisions, a more cohesive group, and smoother implementation of the decision.

The third concept discussed was groupthink, which is the tendency of well-integrated long-term groups to engage in subtle conformity pressures in coming to a decision. These groups need to guard against the tendency to adopt an illusion of invulnerability and negative stereotyping of their critics, which suppresses conflict and rationalizes problems away. These blindspots can result in major policy mistakes and very costly consequences. Established groups in particular need to develop ways of gathering information which challenge the typical attitudes and opinions of the group, and to create group norms in which disagreement is not only accepted but required. The institutionalizing of a devil's advocate role in all major decisions would go far in resolving this problem.

Beneath the Surface
Hidden Variables Which Influence Business Meetings

◆

Harry's eyes glazed over as a familiar scene unfolded. Jim, the marketing manager, was at it again. Talking in his jerky, explosive, driving manner, alternately fidgeting while waiting to respond, punctuating his key points with finger jabbing and by pounding the table. Meanwhile, Hal, the project director, sat stolidly eyeing Jim in a cold manner. Sheila, the human resource manager, attempted to jump into the discussion during a pause: "We have to think about the head-count issue since the new directive...." She was cut off in mid-sentence by both antagonists. Hal glowered at her; Jim was so preoccupied with his own proposal that he hadn't even heard her attempt to enter the discussion. The wrangling went on and on. Harry leaned back and tuned out; years ago he would have jumped in, attempting to straighten out the charade, but he no longer saw the value in trying. He knew that eventually Jim would challenge Hal's authority on the matter, and sure enough that's what happened: "Enough, that's enough," Hal stated, in a loud, harsh voice. "Jim you'd better spend more time coming up with a better proposal before you think you can tell me how to run my job. We're dismissed. The rest of you report back to me in writing. We'll meet again on this when I call you."

This meeting dialogue, typical of many business meetings, was nonproductive because of a number of hidden variables. In this case, the clash reflected sexist and ageist stereotypes and a basic conflict between two dominant personalities: a Type A and an authoritarian.

All of this had little to do with the proposal before the group but everything to do with a predictably poor solution to the problem.

The Influence of Individual Factors

Today both researchers and managers/professionals tend to use the language of system analysis in talking about groups in terms of inputs, throughputs, and outputs. Although in this book we concentrate on key factors that occur during meetings (throughputs) to obtain the best solutions (outputs), we cannot ignore important factors that need to be taken into account before the meeting starts. Some of the more important inputs are personality and other individual factors.

How important are personality and other individual factors in small-group interaction in organizations? The answer to that question is usually dependent on the setting and the orientation of the people making the judgments. But despite the strong influence of the particular business culture and the other group interaction elements, individual factors and personality continue to play an important role in how and why some meetings are successful and others are not.

We shall not attempt to oversimplify this issue by presenting the usual "three handy categories" in which we can typecast all of our colleagues seated around the conference table. All of us recognize that individual and personality factors interact in far more complex ways than that. We know that it is difficult to sort out the long-term effect of these factors on a group's functioning. However, it is equally nonsensical to deny that virtually everyone makes evaluations of others, both in and out of groups, based on personal perceptions of how various stereotypes or personality categories project.

One must be aware of the risks in attributing motives to others. For example, one is usually wrong in attributing "the entire drop in sales revenue" to the authoritarian personality of the sales manager. However, we have all encountered a sufficient number of "pure authoritarian types" to give some credibility to both this kind of statement and to the stereotype underlying it. Or, as one colleague put it talking about an unpopular regional sales manager, "No, he's not responsible for 100 percent of the sales decline . . . try 150 percent!" Yes, authoritarians are still out there, barking sharp, incoherent orders at their subordinates, and glaring at everyone except their boss. Most of us do not have time to fathom the reasons for this behavior. Besides, understanding someone's past is less important than realizing that this is a consistent line of behavior with which other group members must deal.

Personality Perception and Stereotypes

How one perceives the personality of others is weighted heavily by one's own cultural, familial, and disciplinary orientations. Within these orientations, perceptual blind spots develop which many individuals try to ignore or deny; yet, the influence of these differentiators is obvious when one begins to interact with others. For example, three major determinants — age, sex, and race — are highly influential in attributing motives to and judgments about the person across the table. It is rare when these factors do not form some subconscious basis for such insidious judgments as, "Nearing retirement, playing it safe, going for the cautious, least-risk strategy," or "Articulate and pretty, but shallow on substance; agrees with everything but can't lead," or "Sharp dresser, energetic, socially astute, but won't be accepted by others." We will discuss only a few of these influences in this chapter, primarily to demonstrate the complexity involved when assigning reasons for the behavior of our fellow small-group members. Physical attributes are a good case in point.

Physical Attributes. Often, we are less aware of the attributions we make with regard to physical size and appearance than with the determinants of age, sex, or race. However, most of us attribute motives to others based upon a variety of physiological stereotypes we have learned as part of our cultural conditioning. The inferences we make about a person, based on stereotypes associated with body types and extremes in weight, height, and general size, operate as hidden persuaders in groups as they do in everyday life. For example, many Americans, imbued with variations of the Protestant ethic, overladen with our society's emphasis on slim and youthful appearance, often make some immediate judgments about corpulent individuals. These individuals are often associated with being overindulgent, undisciplined, and self-gratifying. But on reflection we see that our cultural values are showing. For instance, in India, a rotund individual may be viewed as "handsome" and associated with success and good health. Similarly, many of us ascribe the causes of individual behavior in groups to the fact that an individual is too short, too tall, or too muscular, conveniently forgetting the scores of instances in which these stereotypic assumptions have proven baseless.

There is a body of research, however, indicating that there may actually be some difficulty in separating factual and fictitious perceptions. An investigation of this phenomenon has uncovered significant (but not surprising) evidence that being a good-looking person gives one several advantages in virtually all walks of life (Berscheid and

Walster 1969). People attribute all sorts of successful virtues to good-looking people: better informed, better able to lead, better able to get along with others.

These personality traits can help one a great deal in small-group interaction. On the other hand, whether the individuals to whom these fine traits are attributed actually possess these qualities is not so obvious. But, as any social scientist will point out, perception is reality. Within limits, if one thinks that something is so, and acts accordingly, the effect will be the same. For example, if a subordinate is considered lazy and is constantly criticized for bad work habits, the individual will often come to dislike his or her job and be unmotivated about performing it well.

Whether evaluating physical attributes or personality variables, one needs to exercise special caution in making judgments about personalities similar to one's own. The tendency is to engage in the "halo effect, "which is simply a case of positive overgeneralization; more good things are attributed to an individual than that person deserves. Several research studies show that there is a tendency to rate subordinates or colleagues as more competent if their values closely match those of the supervisor. Equally unfair, of course, is to overgeneralize the negative traits, letting one negative performance of a subordinate forever cloud the perception of that person's ability to carry out an assignment.

Intercultural Factors

As we have become a global economy the acceleration of intercultural business contacts has naturally spilled over to the conference room. Increased meetings sponsored by multicultural corporations and trade organizations like the European Union, NAFTA, and the Pacific Rim Associations have heightened our awareness of intercultural meeting problems. What effect does this infusion of intercultural factors have in these meetings? To answer these questions we have lots of anecdotal experiences, but unfortunately little empirical, business-based research on what happens when representatives of different nations confer. As Brilhart and Galanes note, "While much is known about how Mexicans and Arabs behave within their own culture, almost nothing is known about how Mexicans and Arabs behave when they work *together* in the same small group" (Brilhart and Galanes 1995).

Each year there are some useful publications that help prepare expatriate managers or short-term visitors on what to expect when working in a particular country (see next page). These insights are difficult enough to utilize when working one-on-one with someone from another culture. What is particularly difficult is applying these cultural tips when the business meeting is composed of members of seven different nations.

In particular we recommend:

 International Dimensions of Organizational Behavior, by Nancy J. Adler (1992), and Geerte Hofstede's *Culture's Consequences: International Differences In Work Related Values* (1984).

 Understanding Cultural Differences, by Edward T. Hall and Mildred Reed Hall, 1990 Intercultural Press, Inc.

 Global Communication and International Relations, by Howard Frederick, 1993 Wadsworth Publishing, Inc.

Some of the best work drawn from real-life business environments has been done by two European researchers, Andre Laurent and Geerte Hofstede, who have produced some research generalizations with long-ranging implications. Laurent was one of the first to point out that most of the management research was done by Americans, for Americans, reflecting essentially an American world view. Laurent researched the behaviors and philosophies of managers in nine European nations, the United States, Japan, and Indonesia. He asked managers from each country to describe their approach to more than sixty common work situations. He found a great deal of variation among countries.

To note a sample of his findings, in response to the statement, "**The main reason for hierarchical structure is that everybody knows who has authority over whom,**" he found wide disparity in country managers who agreed with that statement (e.g., 18 percent in the United States, 45 percent in France, and 86 percent in Indonesia). Most Americans felt the main need for hierarchy was to organize work and problem solving, not to affirm status and authority. However most southern European and Asian managers agreed with the statements.

Similar differences were found on other questions. For example, responses to the statement "**It is important for a manager to have precise answers to most of the questions that subordinates may raise about their work**" found only 10 percent of his Swedish sample agreeing with the statement, while 46 percent of the German, 66 percent of the Italian, and 78 percent of the Japanese samples agreed with the statement (Laurent 1983). One can see how such basic differences in management philosophy can, on occasion, cause many communication breakdowns in international conferences. As Adler states:

---◆---

Most American managers believe that managers should help subordinates discover ways to solve problems, rather than simply answering their questions. By contrast the French generally see the manager as an expert. Most French managers believe that they should give precise answers to subordinates' questions in order to maintain their credibility as experts. When an American manager tells French employees, "I don't know the answer, but maybe if you talk to Simon in marketing he will know," the French employees do not assume that they have received appropriate problem-solving help, but rather assume that their boss is incompetent (Adler 1992).

Some of the most impressive research on cultural differences is that of a Dutch researcher, Geerte Hofstede, who conducted a study of 160,000 employees and managers of a large American multinational company, covering 60 countries that included both Eastern and Western cultures. Hofstede was able to unequivocally answer a key "cultures" question: "What type of culture is the more dominant in determining employee attitudes or behaviors — the national culture, the organizational culture or occupational culture?" Hofstede's research, all within one strong organizational culture, found that national culture was the clear winner. It explained 50 percent of those differences, far superior to all other demographic factors such as professional culture, age, gender, or race in explaining these differences (Hofstede 1980, 1988).

Will standardization and globalization of industrial techniques and technology eventually do away with these cultural variations? Apparently not. Three studies show that foreign employees working within foreign multinational companies maintain and even strengthen their cultural differences, i.e., the Germans become more German, Americans more American, etc. (Adler 1992).

Some of the main clusters of attitudes and behaviors that Hofstede, Hall, and other researchers were able to isolate give international managers some useful broad expectations about colleagues from various cultures. Knowing where your meeting colleagues fit in on the continuum of any one of these cultural factors provides many cues for your interaction with these individuals.

1   *High-Low Context Communication.* Whether a meeting participant comes from a high-context or a low-context communication country is quite important. Hall (1976) found that low-context cultures such as northern Europeans (e.g., Germans, Scandinavians, Swiss) prefer everything to be spelled out in clear, unambiguous language. In contrast, Asian nations such as China, Japan, and South Korea find much meaning in the contexts of

the communicative situations. They tend to prefer ambiguous messages with several possible interpretations to preserve harmony, save face, and allow more transactional possibilities.

2 *Individualism/Collectivism.* Do your colleagues represent a collectivist culture committed to group-centered, conformist, traditional values and consensus decision making, or are they a highly individualist culture, such as the American culture that values self-sufficiency and individual decision making?

It is also useful to know that most people from collectivist cultures are also high-context communicators, while most people from individualist cultures are usually low-context communicators.

3 *High-Low Power Distance.* This factor refers to the extent that various nationalities accept power or status differences as legitimate. Are your colleagues from an egalitarian culture like the people of Israel, New Zealand, or the United States who prize equity and fairness in power sharing, or are they from countries like Mexico, India, and the Philippines whose inhabitants tend to accept rigid hierarchical systems with large power differences as appropriate?

4 *Uncertainty Avoidance.* This factor refers to how comfortable a particular culture is with unpredictability and uncertainty. Do your colleagues represent countries like Great Britain or Sweden that tend to have a high tolerance for ambiguity, dissent, and deviance, or do they represent nationalities like Greece, Japan, and Belgium whose citizens go to great lengths to avoid ambiguous situations? How might this factor affect meeting interaction? Lustig and Cassota (1992) suggest that high power-distance cultures value authoritarian, directive leadership, where low power-distance cultures value participative, democratic leadership. If, for example, an American group leader tries to use a participative leadership style with most Latin American groups, he or she would probably be seen as weak and inept (Adler 1992).

Cultural Stereotypes. What we believe to be appropriate management practices in our own culture, and the stereotypic assumptions we hold about the attitudes of our intercultural colleagues, present related sources of confusion in international meetings. Just how seriously should we treat these cultural stereotypes? Fairly seriously it turns out. As Andre Laurent noted, while most Americans, true to their individualist values, try to deny that any stereotypes exist, most Europeans treat them as real entities — natural, national character distinctions that guide interaction when you deal with 'those people' (personal interview by Mosvick, INSEAD, Fontainbleu May 1992).

Mosvick found strong confirmation of this view in exploratory interviews conducted with 62 mid-level managers in Europe and the United States from 1992 to 1995. These managers represented four different multinational firms located in the United States, France, Belgium, Germany, the Netherlands, and the United Kingdom. All managers were well educated and had worked in another country for a year or more, supervising employees of varied European, Middle Eastern, or Latin American backgrounds. One interview question related directly to the functioning of cultural stereotypes. For example, "In your experience are there any characteristics of the (Germans, French, Americans, etc.) which you feel are dependable predictors of their behavior in meeting?" Although a few respondents qualified their answers by saying, "Of course, these are only stereotypes," nearly all respondents (85 percent) answered with firm conviction about their cultural observations. Here are some typical examples:

> "The Germans are hard to work with and they are very tough negotiators. They want every detail written out precisely, but once they put their signature on the agreement you can depend on their word."

> "The French are very thorough, quite abstract and concerned with the principle of the thing, and they never rush the negotiations. They are precise and analytical but very gracious and enjoyable to work with. However when they finally sign an agreement, you can expect to renegotiate various details many times over in your relationship."

> "The British can be unexpectedly blunt and direct at times and they exercise a power move as subtly as anyone. While I don't think any national type has a corner on good analysis, the British do have a natural language advantage which gives them negotiating power over other nationalities."

While there was quite high agreement concerning what different nationalities (e.g., American, British, Germans) thought of other

We've Got to Start Meeting Like This

specific cultures, more interesting was the fact that these cultural stereotypes were alive and well, working as an introductory framework for interaction with "foreign" meeting mates. Perhaps the single most important thing all international conferees can do is to identify their own cultural stereotypes.

We all have cultural stereotypes which we carry around with us. We "size" people to fit these cultural boxes. There is research that shows that various ethnic groups are characterized with a significant amount of agreement. For example, Americans are seen as materialistic (67 percent), Germans as industrious (59 percent), and English as conservative (53 percent) (Karlins, Coffman & Walters 1969, 1–16). Global judgments about different ethnic groups often stem from experiences which seem to contain a little truth. This attitude is nowhere more evident than in the comment from an international manufacturing manager in one of our seminars: "Why is it that I have never worked with a German or an American of German ancestry who was not well-organized, punctual, perfectionist, hard-working, some- what humorless, and a bit critical or judgmental?" In response, we asked him if it was not true that he worked primarily with engineers. Finding this to be the case, we then suggested that those personality traits might as well be associated with the discipline as with the nationality. He remained unconvinced. This mindset is typical of a broad array of cultural stereotypes. They are often self-fulfilling prophesies.

Whether Americans are in fact more materialistic (or pushy, or aggressive, or insensitive — take your pick) than are people from Europe, Asia, or the Middle East, or if this perception is an artifact created by Hollywood, is quite open to debate. Nevertheless, cultural perceptions influence our judgment and that of our international colleagues when we sit down to do business.

Age Stereotypes. As the United States grows older demographically, the issue of aging is raising its graying head as a component of behav- ioral stereotyping. Whether reading from Aristotle, Shakespeare, or Gail Sheehy's *Passages,* and their similar "ages of man," there is universal recognition that there are differences in perspective and behavior that cluster around different stages of life, as well as obvious differences in how one lives, acts, and learns at different periods. Mosvick (1966) found, for example, that older (ages 37–55) aerospace technical professionals learned principles of human relations signifi- cantly better if they were presented as part of a logical and interrelated theory and system. Younger technical professionals tended to ignore the theoretical system, regarding it as a hindrance; they learned these principles significantly better if they were presented as a series of handy techniques or formulas, a "quick and dirty" learning approach with emphasis upon immediate application of "what worked"

(Mosvick 1966). Yet, we have all encountered younger professionals who could make sense of a managerial technique only if it was part of some larger theory, and we have all known older professionals whose learning style was as oblivious to the merits of theory as that of any hard-charging young engineer's.

Each year the research on aging and the workplace seem to expand the capability and productivity of older professionals. Yet, if the ongoing research on aging demonstrates anything, it is the inherent mistake of engaging in this special kind of social stereotyping. For example: Are older professionals more cautious decision makers or is this just another misconception based on a stereotypic assumption? Some of the research on this question is flatly contradictory. While we should be aware of how judgments about age affect our motive analysis of others, we suspect that patterns of aging alone tell us little about a group's capacity or incapacity to function well. Most groups would probably fare better by trying to assess a person's full individuality in explaining his or her behavior.

Professional Stereotypes. In working with more than 25,000 technical professionals over the past thirty years, we have observed that group interaction is influenced not only by the level and type of education but also by the type of positions which the individual has occupied. The French call this *professional deformation*; that is, an individual takes on the attributes dictated by the patterns, attitudes, and technology of the job. For example, before the recent quality circle revolution, the quality control manager's principal daily behavior consisted primarily of criticizing everything and everyone about errors in standards. Eventually, this constant preoccupation with criticism produced an individual who habitually projected this negative judgmental behavior in all settings. Over time, one takes on not only the vocabulary and jargon of one's work group, but also the group's way of approaching problems and its view of other groups. Consequently, when a marketing executive sits down with a manufacturing manager and a research and development scientist, there is predictable conflict which goes beyond personality or gender.

Often, the extent to which problems are seen through the lens of occupational specialties is underestimated. In a classic test of this assumption, twenty-three executives were asked to read a long factual case study about a steel company and report what they thought was the major problem the new president of this company should deal with first. Of the twenty-three executives, six were from sales, five from production, four from accounting, and eight from miscellaneous departments such as public relations and research and development. As might be expected, virtually all of the executives viewed the problem in terms which reflected *their* major interests: those in public relations and industrial relations saw human relations as the problem;

sales executives and accountants saw sales as the problem; production people felt that the production issues were the problem (Dearborn and Simon 1958, 140–144).

Nonetheless, generalizing about groups such as technical professionals should be done cautiously. Research indicates that the disciplinary orientation and education of the individual in a group should be considered when discussing technical professionals. Allen (1977) points out that lumping engineers and scientists together when talking about technical professionals is a mistake. Allen (1977) clearly states that engineers are not scientists, that engineers are oriented more toward managerial positions, that they approach problem solving differently, that they are less concerned than those in science with what one does in a given position, that they are more concerned with certainty of rewards, and that they place comparatively less emphasis on independence, career satisfaction, and the inherent interest of their specialty.

Compared to scientists, engineers are willing to sacrifice some independence for more material goals, and they assume that their success will depend upon practical knowledge, administrative ability, and human relations skills. Engineers also have different patterns of communication, different patterns of using people as information sources, and different approaches to solving problems. Further, engineers are generally more like managers in personal orientation and behavior than they are like scientists. The scientists, for example, devote 75 percent or more of their time to communication, but most of this time is spent on reading scientific literature. The engineer spends more time on personal contact and is more dependent on colleagues in problem solving than the scientist. In sum, the communication patterns of engineers and scientists are both quantitatively and qualitatively different (Allen 1977, 39).

Status. Another predominant variable that affects group processes is the relative status of group members. Higher status individuals command control of the group and its discussion more easily, while lower status individuals often have difficulty making any impact on the group whatsoever. This is often the case, unfortunately, regardless of who has the most accurate or relevant information on the topic being discussed.

Higher status permits a group member to talk at length without interruption by submissive subordinates. Higher status also allows the chairperson unequal access to an on-going discussion via verbal and nonverbal cues which signal, "I have the right of way."

In many cases, status can be read nonverbally. Individuals who are lower in status tend to project nonverbal signs of compliance and submissiveness. McKenna and Denmark concluded that when persons of low status in business talk to their supervisors, or to anyone in a higher position, they tend to adopt a deferential body and facial set. The pose includes smiling and nodding, holding the arms close to the body, and keeping the legs close together. Women were found to adopt this pose more often than men. This behavior only becomes a problem when a person carries the posture around from meeting to meeting and, in effect, always signals a low-status presence even in situations when it is neither appropriate nor accurate (Parlee 1979, 16).

Status and power can be derived from where a participant sits in a meeting (Korda 1975). Some seating positions tend to be more influential than others, most notably the end of the table or next to the chairperson or other high-status individual. Studies done by researchers who have observed small groups tend to agree on the following:

1 Seating position that gives greater visibility determines the flow of communication which in turn influences who emerges as the leader.

2 Individuals who dominate discussions tend to choose central seats (those at the ends, and the middle seats on either side of a rectangular table). They receive more communication from others and tend to talk more.

3 Individuals who choose the corner seats of a rectangular table contribute the least. Researchers found that people who avoided the central or "high talking" positions were more anxious and actually stated that they wanted to stay out of the discussion (Barron 1985, 154).

This evidence suggests that the act of perceiving another person's personality, or of attributing motives to another person, is a complex undertaking. This research highlights the many different perceptual blinders which develop from notions about age, sex, race, physical attributes, and cultural biases which often cloud one's judgments. Above all, this research illuminates the central problem in the use of stereotypes: they are used to make unreliable judgments about individuals and groups.

The Influence of Personality

In addition to the individual, cultural, disciplinary, and professional orientations which influence our patterns of interactions in small groups, there are some general clusters of behavior or personality traits that are also influential. By *personality* we refer to those unique patterns of traits and behaviors that set an individual apart from others and which are relatively stable over time. Individuals are remarkably consistent in presenting the same kind of general behavior and attitudes to the world. Although the general view of personality today is one which is less rigid and which recognizes more evidence of change and flexibility, there remains strong evidence of the relatively unchanging nature of the human being's general perspective and behavior over time.

There are many different types of personality traits, some of which are called different names by different researchers. Not all of these traits have an impact on small-group interaction. What follows is a brief discussion of some of these key personality traits which can be identified when they are exhibited by interacting in groups. Provided our labeling is reasonably valid, identifying these traits may help in interpreting individual behavior while diagnosing group needs.

Introversion-Extroversion. Perhaps the most common observation made of others is the degree of introversion or extroversion they display in the group. To be a shy person in America imposes burdens in many areas, but in no area more significant than in small-group interaction. Effective group accomplishment requires harmonious and active interaction. Members must commit themselves to a certain level of oral communication and involvement. As might be expected, those who have severe communication apprehension are poor candidates for productive meeting members. The most common attribute that hinders an individual's effectiveness in a small-group meeting is shyness. The shy individual states his or her opinion less often and with less force. Fewer contributions translate to less influence in the business meeting. The shy individual is interrupted more often and tends to back down when topics are debated.

The silent, introverted participant requires special efforts on the part of the chairperson, if indeed that individual's contributions are to be elicited. Prior to the meeting, it is essential to brief these individuals on what they will be expected to report on in the meeting, to give them as much security as possible. During the meeting the chairperson must be most vigilant to catch the introverts' muted talk signals: the heightened eye contact, the half-open mouth, the beginning of an exclamation, or a half-hearted gesture for recognition. It is unwise to put introverts on the spot by asking them directly, "What do you think about this?" unless you know definitely that they have a good fund of information on the topic.

In contrast, an individual who is naturally more assertive often has an inherent advantage in the interpersonal communication of group discussion. That person is more likely to have his or her opinions heard and more likely to control the discussion of the group, thus strongly influencing the meeting outcome. In Western culture, those who have low communication apprehension and who exhibit self-confidence, or who are naturally more expansive and verbal, tend to be more effective in meetings. Some extroverts, however, border on being compulsive talkers. Meeting chairpersons must quickly recognize those tendencies and firmly muzzle those acts early in the meeting. At times, heavy-handed tactics are required, such as interrupting, summarizing the extrovert's contributions, directing questions to other members of the group, and protecting others from their interruptions. One strategy of last resort is to apportion and enforce speaking time to each person on major sub-points of the agenda.

Type A/Type B Behavior. The personality construct which has received much attention in recent years is Type A behavior. This behavior is characterized as hard-driving, pressured, competitive, impatient, and aggressive. Type B behavior, in contrast, represents patterns of behavior that are easy-going, relaxed, sociable, and relatively noncompetitive. It is estimated that about 40 percent of the population in the United States falls into the Type A category and about 60 percent into the Type B category (James, Campbell & Lovegrove 1984, 129–134). This construct is most useful because it is easy to recognize consistent, nearly compulsive behavior with specific symptoms (see *Meeting Notes,* next page).

In reading the list of behavior traits, one can easily see why a Type A personality can be counterproductive to the effectiveness of a group. While the Type A persons may be successful in some positions, small-group interaction in particular seems to bring out the worst in them as Barron (1985) indicates:

◆

> *Type A's tend to be more impatient with others and grow angry when these persons hold them back in any way. Similarly, Type A's generally report feeling less comfortable around other persons than Type B's. When given a choice, they prefer to work alone rather than as part of a team. Type A's seem to resent being told what to do more strongly than Type B's .... Finally, Type A individuals tend to be more irritable and aggressive than Type B's. Thus, they are often more likely to lose their tempers and get into arguments with persons around them (Barron 1985, 154).*

How should one deal with Type A behavior when it emerges in meetings? The key to dealing with Type A behavior is understanding that Type A's usually don't realize the scope and impact of their behavior. It is often necessary to take them aside and speak directly about the unacceptability of behavior such as constant interruptions, rushing the deliberations of the group, and introducing needless tension through overaggressive and irritable behavior. During a meeting, when a Type A is in the midst, participants and chairpersons alike must be especially vigilant of this behavior and take measures to curb it. Remember that Type A's are usually achievers with a record of accomplishments which

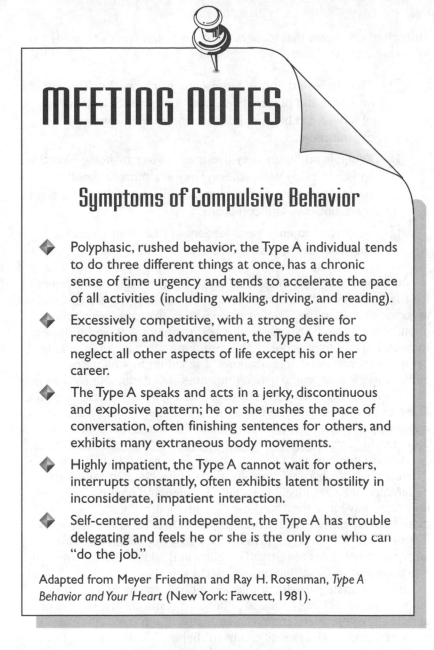

MEETING NOTES

Symptoms of Compulsive Behavior

◆ Polyphasic, rushed behavior, the Type A individual tends to do three different things at once, has a chronic sense of time urgency and tends to accelerate the pace of all activities (including walking, driving, and reading).

◆ Excessively competitive, with a strong desire for recognition and advancement, the Type A tends to neglect all other aspects of life except his or her career.

◆ The Type A speaks and acts in a jerky, discontinuous and explosive pattern; he or she rushes the pace of conversation, often finishing sentences for others, and exhibits many extraneous body movements.

◆ Highly impatient, the Type A cannot wait for others, interrupts constantly, often exhibits latent hostility in inconsiderate, impatient interaction.

◆ Self-centered and independent, the Type A has trouble delegating and feels he or she is the only one who can "do the job."

Adapted from Meyer Friedman and Ray H. Rosenman, *Type A Behavior and Your Heart* (New York: Fawcett, 1981).

can be channeled into productive group effort. Type A's are as intelligent and committed as the next person, but they are simply not well constructed for working as a team member in groups.

The Authoritarian Personality. Much has been written about the authoritarian personality since the concept was first introduced some thirty years ago. The personality measure designed to identify authoritarians shows that those who receive high scores have the following characteristics:

 They believe that it is natural and correct that there should be status and power differences among people, that the use of power and hierarchical decision making is proper in organizations.

 When in authority, they use their power by being directive and controlling with others. They are more inclined to conform to rules and regulations; in a subordinate role, they are submissive and compliant.

 They tend to emerge as leaders in situations requiring a more demanding autocratic style.

Authoritarians seem to embody a primitive "strong man" theory of leadership. They believe in and need a hierarchical structure in which to locate their identity. Like the successful bureaucrat (which they often become), they also need rules and regulations to secure their roles and justify their actions. They are naturally happier in strictly defined structures and organizations. The extent to which true authoritarians exist in the general business population is not known. One would suspect that authoritarians are a species nearing extinction as contemporary organizations rely more and more upon teamwork and cooperative interdependent efforts. Whether or not they are disappearing fast enough from the business scene is open to debate.

How do you deal with the authoritarian personality in conference? In some respects, because they are so comfortable with traditional hierarchies, they are ideal organizational men and women. However, they often have problems working in contemporary matrix management groups without clearly defined power and authority relationships. It is especially difficult for them to work in groups with complex and ambiguous problems requiring flexibility and adaptation in leadership functions and problem-solving approaches.

In subordinate participant roles, one needs to worry less about authoritarians' behavior because, like good staff officers, their efforts are usually appropriate and compliant. Give them the chairperson's reins, however, and a radical change of behavior often occurs. Once legitimized in the role of "leader," authoritarians feel empowered to be as demanding, controlling, and directive as a military officer. Other participants soon resent this dictatorial behavior.

Obviously, this style does not mesh well with the notion of shared leadership functions or equalitarian views of decision making. If someone consistently displays this type of behavior, it is unwise to appoint such persons to a chairperson role. If the person is already in a managerial or chairperson position, direct personal counseling on the expectations of the group concerning the leader behavior is often in order; and this counseling must come from the person's supervisor if it is to have an impact. In the actual meeting, it is very difficult (and often political suicide) to confront this behavior, if you are the authoritarian's subordinate. Peer-level colleagues have a considerable advantage in making this type of intervention successfully; they should first counsel privately, but then, if necessary, make it clear publicly that certain kinds of behavior are unacceptable in participative decision-making settings.

The Machiavellian Manipulator. A disruptive meeting personality that is closely related to Type A's and authoritarians is the manipulator. This category is adopted from the sixteenth-century politician, Niccolo Machiavelli, who advised would-be rulers to adopt ruthless, amoral strategies to gain power, and to manipulate and use other people in any way necessary to attain personal ends. If you look at the latest books on the newsstand that deal with power and intimidation, or if you simply observe the scramble for power within your own corporate setting, you will find these ideas still quite relevant today.

A personality assessment measure devised to test to what degree individuals are manipulative shows that a large percentage of people receive high scores (called "high machs") on this scale (Barron 1985, 157). Just as the authoritarians interpret hierarchy, structure, and power as "natural," the high machs interpret manipulating others as the way the world works. To them, to suppose otherwise is to be naive. To high machs, the small group is just another means to their ends, another arena in which to demonstrate their talent.

One would suppose that an individual who operates with such patently obvious techniques of self-interest would be quickly shunned by the group. There are, however, many reasons why this does not happen: many groups are short-term, dissolving before the harmful effects can be clearly tied to the manipulator; the many distractions in small-group interactions make it difficult to detect manipulation in action. Because they are often experts at these techniques, the manipulators are shrewd and persuasive.

Specifically, how do high machs operate? Barron (1985) describes their major tactics:

First, in contrast to most individuals, high machs show a pattern of cool detachment in their dealings with others. While most persons give way to their emotions and let their hearts rule their heads, ... high machs almost never do. Instead, they work coolly and pragmatically toward the goals they are seeking. . . . They may pretend to be experiencing strong emotions. But this is all an act. Other

people mean little to them.... Second, high machs appear to be both resistant to influence from others and very skilled in exerting such influence themselves. Thus, they are not easily swayed by opponents. Rather, it is they who usually do most of the persuading. ... Finally, ... high machs do not allow themselves to be affected by factors that strongly influence most persons — considerations such as friendship, loyalty, keeping one's promises, or morality (Barron 1985, 157–158).

How does one deal with the Machiavellian manipulator? In small groups with a longer life, such as standing committees, staff groups, or quality circles, most group members eventually come to know the manipulator. In short-term groups, however, the best defense is the understanding of the general nature of manipulators and an ability to quickly detect their presence. What makes this advice difficult to follow is the apparent inconsistency of high machs' behavior (presenting compliments and agreement one moment and power tactics the next) which keeps meeting participants off balance. Fundamentally, high machs are very arrogant and blatantly self-centered — lying, cheating, and distorting issues while using people and objects to their end. Here one must fight fire with fire, since the career you save may be your own.

These are four basic personality profiles that seem to provide the greatest number of problems for small-group leaders and participants. At this juncture, some readers will be quick to observe that the average person in a typical conference has no time to check out all of those variables before interacting. True enough; however, some processing of any or all of those factors is occurring, often unconsciously.

Usually, too many other tasks confront the involved participant to allow enough time for extensive motive analysis. In long-term groups, however, after one has had sufficient opportunity to observe consistent problematic patterns of behavior in one's colleagues, one should spend some time pondering whether certain personality traits are at the bottom of these group problems. Whether this behavior is observed in a one-time meeting or in meetings over a longer period of time, some behavior is so blatantly selfish, uncooperative, and destructive to the group that it must be confronted at once. To sit back and indulge overaggressive, domineering, and manipulative behavior is to become an enabler who sanctions further destructive acts.

The Influence of Gender

One of the most powerful myths that affects a woman's role in business meetings is the notion that males and females differ greatly in personality. The research clearly indicates that men and women are more alike than different in not only general personality traits but in general management behaviors as well. Similarly, no given style, whether predominantly male or predominantly female, is inherently better in small-group decision making, although many writers have suggested that the woman's power sharing, process-oriented, collaborative style may better fit the requirements of twenty-first century organizations. Our view is that in America it is increasingly less accurate to talk about typical men's or women's communication patterns since many of the most publicized findings of the 1970s and the 1980s reflect the gender stereotypes of those periods that are quickly fading as a result of educational campaigns at all levels of our society. While there are some communication behaviors that tend to be gender marked, they are primarily cultural, not biologically driven, and, therefore, amendable to the new instruction about roles. The good news is that we can educate and are educating ourselves about what is appropriate and reasonable gender interaction.

Then too, the way some research conclusions are derived are sometimes problematic. Business communication behavior is often situational and at odds with conclusions derived from experiments of interpersonal laboratory groups, studies of intimate family interaction, or studies of child development. What we know about boy/girl play patterns at age eight may have very little to say about the behavior of experienced, educated male or female managers at age thirty. Researchers can take little more than a brief snapshot in time, often with contradictory findings. For these reasons we find it more useful to talk about "powerful" vs. "powerless" communication behavior that may apply to either gender equally.

Some behaviors are obviously more important in task-oriented business group interaction than in relational or interpersonal communication groups. In business meetings, influence is often determined by the amount and quality of participant contributions. Consequently, in keeping with our focus, we will examine only those communication behaviors that are most critical in influencing typical business meetings (in mixed sex rather than same sex groups that have different dynamics). We will look at the most current mid-1990s findings on the better established generalizations of genders in such areas as talk time, turn taking, and interruptions, language style, and nonverbal communication.

Talk Time, Turn Taking, and Interruptions

One of the more thoroughly established research generalizations is that in mixed sex discussions men talk significantly more than women

(Borisoff and Merril 1992) and interrupt women far more frequently than women interrupt men (Mulac et al. 1988).

While we have no doubt that this generalization remains a general norm, it is one that is clearly situational. Verbal dominance is usually strongly influenced by nongender factors such as the person's position or status and the participant's degree of expertise on a specific topic, whether the discussion takes place in a business meeting context or in a voluntary association. And, as we have seen, individual personality traits and related expressiveness remain significant factors throughout one's life.

In our observation of numerous business meetings at all levels of management, we are seeing as many exceptions to the "norm" as examples of it. Current research is beginning to catch up with these changing gender patterns. For example, Maybry found that in some instances women talked as much or more than male colleagues (Maybry 1989). Men and women who have made it to managerial levels have managed to understand and apply the level of assertiveness appropriate to the business culture. Our greater concern is for those younger associates, male and female, who either have not learned or resist understanding the business meeting context.

On the one hand we have also too often seen the "powerless style" in action. We have observed that in numerous business meetings some men tend to take their turns, while some women tend to wait to be *given* their turns, when contributing to the group's discussion. In a fast-moving discussion, it is easy to be bypassed if you are not verbally assertive. An individual who does not make contributions is thought not to have any significant opinions to offer to the group and is therefore viewed as an unproductive or unnecessary member of the group.

The dominant norms in most business cultures often favor behavior which is assertive, dominant, and decisive. The business meeting is no exception. Often such behavior might be considered inconsiderate, overly aggressive, and unproductive by some participants who withdraw to avoid interaction. For many individuals, the tendency to interrupt or slight the contributions of others in meetings is often unintentional; i.e., a product of how they have been socialized to interact in groups. There is sufficient evidence to categorize this as predominantly a male socialized communication pattern, but clearly either a male or female can be an abuser or enabler in these communicative transactions. Even if unintentional, ideas and valid contributions made by women are often lost when their comments are interrupted or ignored. Group productivity suffers from this loss of input. One of our workshop participants, a 45-year-old marketing specialist, who has an MBA and works for a Fortune 500 corporation, summarizes her response to the problem in the following way:

The issue is a lot more complex than most managers realize. Most women must still tread a fine line between behavior which can be interpreted as pushy and that which is legitimately assertive. It is relatively easy to document blatant discriminatory behavior in the workplace. It is a lot more difficult to put up with the subtle day-to-day discrimination which takes place in committee meetings and conferences. I know that a lot of the squelching of women's comments is not intentional; but today I don't care what the motivation is because no one stamps on my lines. I just don't allow interruptions when I'm talking from anyone until I have had my full input. I try to keep my comments clear, short, and factually based, and now my male colleagues know my style. They know that I won't put up with overriding verbal behavior. In a way, I think I have helped to improve the interaction of the whole group, but that wasn't my primary motivation. I was out to defend my right and duty to equal expression because I know if I don't do it, no one else will.

One of the more troublesome aspects of mixed group interaction is how stereotypes and projections come into play. A typical finding is that identical messages of men and women will be interpreted differently, usually with a male bias, with females seen as more bossy, dominating, and emotional (Butler and Geis 1990). A similar study found identical messages to be "clearer" if attributed to a male (Seifert and Milhem 1988). Other preconceptions about gender roles tend to limit influence and status in group interaction. Rothwell emphasizes the restriction placed upon women in noting:

In mixed sex groups men are normally assumed to be the task experts whereas women are assumed to be the relationship experts.... This puts women at a disadvantage in the group ... assuming the lower status role of keeping the peace while men carry out higher status roles of making important decisions (Rothwell 1995).

However, sometimes our preconceived stereotypes swing the other way to the discredit of men. Burrel and her associates compared trained and untrained mediators of both sexes and found no differences in the behavior of trained mediators. However, the men, whether trained or not, were perceived to be more controlling (Burrel 1988).

As can be seen, getting a proper perspective on gender influences is a complex process since it is so easy to fall into simplistic categorizing about all men as verbal dominators and women as passive victims.

The more successful managers we have observed have gotten beyond these mental traps. They clearly do not condone obnoxious behavior, but they do seek to understand the motivation for it (as a culturally different way of expressing) as the first step in mediating potential interpersonal conflicts.

There does seem to be reliable, cumulative research that points to the existence of gender different uses in and attitudes about communication that are expressed in different styles. For example, several researchers point to male communication behavior as more competitive than female behavior in both same sex and mixed sex groups. One reviewer found that "men's talk" tends to be more direct, succinct, personal, and task-oriented whereas "women's talk" is characterized as indirect, elaborate, contextual, and affective (Mulac et al. 1990). Again we need to point out that these statements like all generalizations may say absolutely nothing about your opposite sex colleague, particularly in a business or organizational setting. However, given the general consistency of personal behavior over time, it would be surprising if many of these patterns did not carry over to some extent to business meetings and conversations.

One of the more popular recent books on this subject is by Deborah Tannen who takes the view that to deny communicative differences between the sexes is destructive for both parties since "pretending that women and men are the same hurts women, because the way they are treated is based on the norms for men. It also hurts men who, with good intentions, speak to women as they would to men, and are nonplused, when the words don't work as they expected, or even spark resentment and anger" (Tannen 1990).

Tannen states that most women typically engage in "rapport talk" used primarily as a means to establish connections and negotiate relationships, whereas most men use "report talk" primarily as a means to preserve independence and to negotiate or maintain status in a hierarchical social order (Tannen 1990, 77).

In this same vein, one of the more thorough recent reviews of gender behavior found that interruptions function differently for men and women. Men apparently interrupt primarily to control the discussion unlike women who interrupt primarily to communicate assent, to elaborate on an idea offered by another group member, or simply to be a part of the conversation (Stewart et al. 1990).

Rothwell agrees with Tannen in his assessment of the clash of these different styles;

Again, the temptation is to brand men as jerks for trying to dominate conversation, and to brand women as subservient for letting men dominate. Tannen offers a different perspective. As she explains, men who approach conversation as a context in which

*everyone competes for the floor might be treating women as
equals expecting them to compete for the floor like everyone else.
If women have something to add to the conversation they will fight
for the floor, so goes the reasoning from the male perspective.
Since women do not view conversation as a contest and have little
experience fighting to be heard, they are less likely to compete for
the floor leaving men to assume, erroneously, that women have
nothing important to say. So women feel frustrated, even abused
because men appear to accord little value to their conversational
input, and men feel unjustly accused of insensitivity
(Rothwell 1995).*

Successful managers of the 1990s hold similar attitudes that frame
their interaction. They are clearly aware of the differences in style and
talk out style conflicts rather than let interpersonal tension build to a
destructive flash point. They tend to have genuine respect for the
individuality of all colleagues, with good appreciation of the special
strengths that any gender style might bring to the conference table.
Increasingly we will see research findings such as those of the Duerst-
Lahti's study of successful, high-status business men and women.

*She observed that, contrary to the findings of others, women were
not frozen out of conversations. The women talked more often but
for shorter periods, gave more indications of verbal support, and
freely challenged the men. They had power in the group, and their
ideas and proposals were included in the final product. They
seemed to have mastered the use of power just as effectively as
the men (Brilhart and Gallanes 1995).*

It is one thing to say that the norm of a business meeting is a male
norm. It is another to say that this norm should continue unchanged.
Various writers have made a claim that women's communicative
patterns offer a superior model to follow in a team culture. Helgesen in
her book, *The Female Advantage: Woman's Way of Leadership*, emphasizes women's "natural" inclination to develop and use a web of
relationships, to respond to people and problems with flexibility and
adaptiveness, and to rotate leadership and be more supportive, cooperative, and democratic.

Perhaps the more acceptable position is to recognize that the best
of both gender tendencies should be incorporated into the new meeting philosophy. At present it is hardly a two-way street, with many
women clearly disadvantaged. This does not mean that women must
become male meeting clones or that men must apologize for every
directive and decisive tendency. Each of us must develop an individual
style that is personally appropriate with some accommodations to the

context of meeting dynamics. We suggest that the rules of the game are being steadily redefined every day by women and men who appreciate how effective a more respectful, collegial, collaborative style can be building cohesive and productive teams.

Powerful and Powerless Speech

One's choices of words, stories, and slang; a particular accent; and different vocal qualities all say a lot about one's background, attitudes, and philosophy. The intensity and emotion in one's voice, the unique pattern of inflection and pitch, and the level of verbal complexity one uses to supplement or complement verbal expressions all contribute to a unique language style.

Let us look briefly at some of the specific characteristics of language use that can be labeled more or less powerful or effective vs. powerless and ineffective at meetings. Given the different backgrounds of each of us, some of these differences, such as one's degree of directness or qualification used in normal speaking, can be quite important in personal effectiveness in business meetings.

Directness. Various studies find that in America, Northern Europe, and in most English-speaking countries, powerful, effective language is marked by directness vs. indirectness, by clear declarative statements vs. tentative statements. For example, saying, "This is what we must do" vs. "Don't you think that this should be done?" is generally interpreted as more powerful, influential discourse. Rightly or wrongly, individuals whose every contribution is tentative and nonfluent give the impression that they are unsure of their position. Group members often disregard ideas expressed in such a half-hearted manner. They may also attribute these ideas to others in the group.

This pattern was first examined in what has been termed "traditional women's speech." Dr. Lillian Glass advises women to avoid the emotional-state verbs: " 'I think,' 'I believe,' 'I assume,' 'I guess,' 'I hope' are tentative phrases. Don't start sentences with them. Begin with 'I know' or 'It is' instead" (Scott 1985). We think that this is good advice for men as well as women. Other research on powerful and powerless speech has identified a common element used by individuals under stress or uncertainty which they called "the hesitation": "My father . . . uh . . . is in the business. He works with . . . uh . . . insurance claims on this sort of thing. Uh . . . he's an underwriter" (Bradac and Mulac 1984, 307).

Conversely, anyone using overly directive language in a predominantly female group may often sound intimidating and threatening, even when such a meaning is not intended. Directness of expression is more than a matter of gender style; it is also a question of accuracy in the use of language. Women and men alike should inspect their language to discover where they are using tentative and weak expressions out of habit. More direct and assertive expressions should be substituted whenever possible. Confident people speak confidently; people who know what they are talking about usually sound as if they know what they are talking about. They convey this impression not through a loud, domineering style; rather, they speak firmly and clearly with little indirectness or ambiguity in their language.

Qualification. Another difference between powerful and powerless speech is found in verbal qualification, such as upward inflections and tag endings. Some individuals end their sentences with a question mark instead of a period. (Currently in the mid-1990s we seem to have a linguistic plague about where everyone seems to be talking in whole paragraphs of upward inflected endings? As questions?) One person, for example, might say "Find out for tomorrow's meeting," whereas another person would be more apt to say "Could you find out for tomorrow's meeting?" Or "We need to do this now," versus "We could possibly do this, if we have sufficient authority, unless we find another alternative." The latter phrase is wordy and less direct. It moves so cautiously from one qualification to another, that there is no force in the statement. Likewise, constant use of tag lines such as "Could you?" "Do you mind?" "Is that all right?" are characteristic of tentative individuals who are politely asking permission rather than asserting themselves verbally.

A balance of polite and assertive language style is desirable but overly qualified speech used by anyone — female or male — tends to be ignored in today's business environment. Such language may seem more courteous and respectful of others, but it is generally less effective in business meetings. If your verbal profile is predominantly one of qualification and indirectness, you are highly unlikely to be an influential member of a group.

Nonverbal Communication

Each of us gives off a host of nonverbal signals every day. Experts tend to agree that as much as two-thirds of our total meaning is derived from nonverbal communication. Not all of them are gender related, and many of them are beyond our control or, at times, even our awareness. Although the world of nonverbal signs is vast, a few signals, however, mark successful or unsuccessful interaction in business meetings. Most of these signals have to do with avoiding a negative or low-status presentation in meetings.

Women in general are clearly superior to men in their ability to sense and interpret nonverbal behavior. One researcher examined sixty-four studies over a six-year period and found that in 84 percent of the cases women decoded nonverbal communication better than men did (Rosenthal 1979). Does this decoding ability translate into job or task advantages in the business meeting? It is difficult to say for certain, but doubtless many women have found this extra sensitivity to nonverbal signs to be a valuable attribute in business.

Space. In business and governmental organizations high status was often signified by allocating individuals better located, larger offices than those in lower echelons of the organizations. Having the large, richly furnished corner office at the top of the tower said it all. It usually included a large, impressive meeting table within the office to give "the boss" the home field advantage. Indeed, researchers have found that most of us work better in our own territory where we are more comfortable and in greater command of resources like staff support. This finding is worth pondering in planning certain critical meetings. Calling the meeting in your home turf may give you special advantages that you may or may not want to exercise. Much of these trappings of power are going away as organizations begin to challenge the very need for a rooted space. Temporary, modular electronic equipped purely functional offices are in vogue. They are often the site of three or four person team meetings, increasingly accompanied by one member plugged in through his car phone. We have already discussed some of the implications of where you sit in the meeting room as dimensions of your general influence. However, we also need to be aware of what our bodies are saying at meetings. Body orientation itself can serve as a block of meeting interaction. As Scheflen found, your body orientation is a fairly good indication of how open and accepting you are to other individuals. Leaning toward others projects a sense of liking, of belonging, and interest; leaning away from others usually indicates dislike, disinterest, or rejection (Scheflen 1972).

One nonverbal characteristic that is gender-oriented has to do with the use of space around an individual. Men tend to spread out and use as much space around them as possible, whereas women take up as little space as possible; i.e., sitting more "closed" and using fewer arm movements. Whether it is consciously intended or not, the expansive use of space is a more dominant behavior, in effect saying: "I am more powerful and thus deserve more territory."

Not only do women tend to sit in a less expansive manner, they tend to allow their territory to be invaded more often than men do — usually by higher-status males. The Eakins (1978) say that "it appears that women's territory is perceived as smaller by both males and females. Women may be more tolerant of, or accustomed to, having their personal space breached by others. This may also be an indication that they are considered to be of lower status by those with whom they interact" (Eakins and Eakins 1978, 170).

Eye Contact. In America appropriate eye contact is quite central to any interpersonal interaction including business meetings. Avoidance of gaze is usually interpreted negatively as apathetic, dishonest, rude, or anxious behavior (Andersen 1992). The length of eye contact is always problematic since obviously cold, unsmiling staring can be interpreted as challenging, competitive, or dismissive. Normally, eye contact will not be absolutely steady but will naturally fluctuate. Individuals usually engage in eye contact at the beginning of a new utterance, then allow their gaze to wander for a few seconds as they concentrate on organizing their on-going discourse, after which it tends to return to the person or persons to whom it is directed. The focus of eye contact is also a telling sign of group leadership. In reviewing video tapes of hundreds of small group meetings, we have found that in approximately 90 percent of the cases, one can detect the most influential member of a group with the sound turned off simply by noting the person who is the primary object of gazes from most of the group. While other cultures (Japanese, S.E. Asian, American Indian, etc.) dictate eye contact avoidance as a mark of respect, in American and European culture, the rules for eye contact in business meetings are no different from those in any other setting. Direct, fairly constant eye contact is a sign of interest, respect, and involvement.

Facial Expression. In any communicative situation, facial expression is probably the single most important element of meaning because it usually provides the underlying tone or context by which we interpret verbal meaning. Business meetings are no exception, so it is also important to know what our faces may be signaling to other meeting colleagues. In American culture, there is a general expectation that facial expression of both men and women should be mildly pleasant. Overly serious or negative facial expression is usually read as a sign of hostility, disagreement, or noncooperation.

Probably the most important generalization about facial expressions concerns smiling behavior. One smiles for a number of reasons, but a dominant reason for smiling is approval seeking. A smiling expression indicates a compliant, willing-to-please attitude. When seeking approval, both sexes smile more often; but the results of research show that women smile more, in general, than men, even when they are not seeking approval. Few of us have pathological needs for constant approval, but many women attempt to present a happy face to everyone, whether they feel happy or not. Social psychologist Nancy Henley calls the smile "the women's badge of appeasement" that placates the more powerful male (Leo 1985, 82).

It does not seem as if smiling would be a problem in business interactions, and usually it is not. But smiling can inhibit one's meeting effectiveness by projecting the image of constantly seeking the approval of others present. When the smile is relatively fixed and constant, it can also make the wearer seem to be frivolous, immature, or relying inordinately on physical attraction or charm. The Eakins (1978) state that the smile can be indicative of "the social status of women and be used as a gesture of submission as part of their culturally prescribed role" (Eakins and Eakins 1978, 156). For these reasons, consultants have become quite direct in their counsel to their female colleagues in business: "Stop nodding and smiling and agreeing so much. We do entirely too much of that, and it lessens our effectiveness" (Scott 1985, 8C).

Summary

In this chapter we have attempted to deal with the hidden factors which influence a person's behavior in small-group conferences. We have seen that before we utter one word to our colleagues at the conference table, we are predisposed to act and speak in certain ways by a host of influences. That's natural; we couldn't interact without this motive attribution process. What is unnatural is that sometimes motives or characteristics we assign to others are not accurate. They are artifacts of one of a number of stereotypes we carry around with us. Whether these reactions come from stereotypes about culture or race, about physical attributes or professional orientation, or from status or gender assumptions, is less important than that we each must personally recognize them and deal with them immediately in the conference. Few of us will be completely successful in this venture; however, we can interact with one another more productively once we have removed the negative debris of irrelevant prejudices and extraneous factors from our meeting efforts.

Some factors, like personality traits, aren't as hidden. Some personality factors are so blatantly evident that everyone realizes the source of various acts in a meeting. We cited four personality profiles that are particularly influential in business meetings: the introvert and the extrovert, the Type A personality, the authoritarian, and the Machiavellian manipulator. Each of these personality types can destroy the effectiveness of any small group if left unchecked. The negative behaviors they exhibit need to be monitored and curbed when they arise. To that end, we included some specific techniques to counter behavior which is detrimental to the group.

We have given special attention to the increasingly important issue of gender influences in business meetings. Here we examined some of the myths and realities about gender differences in work groups and how differences in gender specifically can affect small group meetings. We noted a number of verbal and nonverbal communication behaviors which are associated with successful and unsuccessful meeting interaction whether used by male or female: to speak clearly and confidently and to fend off interruptions; to use a language style that is clear, direct, and assertive rather than hesitant and overqualified; and to develop techniques of nonverbal expression and use of space which will facilitate successful group interaction.

Through this discussion we have suggested the need to become consciously competent in recognizing and dealing with the hidden variables which influence meetings, which is no small feat. Few of us have the time to engage in motive analysis or personality assessment while tracking the discussion on a cognitive level in the midst of a fast-paced, richly diverse information flow found in most meetings.

Nonetheless, it is a mark of an experienced meeting manager that he or she has developed an ability to "listen with a third ear" for those extraneous nontask factors which spell the difference between an excellent meeting or a disastrous one. Good meeting managers not only know where those behaviors are coming from, they know exactly how to use specific skills and techniques to deal with them. As Part One laid the groundwork for an understanding of the many factors of small-group business meetings, Part Two is designed to spell out the roles, strategies, and skills for planning, conducting, and implementing effective meeting management.

PART 2

Meetings: Doing Them Better Tomorrow

Preparing for Success and Avoiding Meeting Problems

[N]othing is ever really buried in a meeting. An idea may look dead, but it will always reappear at another meeting later on. If you have ever seen the movie "Night of the Living Dead," you have a rough idea how modern corporations and organizations operate, with projects and proposals that everybody thought were killed, constantly rising from their graves to stagger back into meetings and eat the brains of the living.

— Dave Barry, *Claw Your Way to the Top**

Planning and Conducting Meetings That Work

Everyone has a favorite horror story about meetings and Dave Barry is no exception. There are, of course, hundreds of ways that meetings can

---

* Dave Barry, "How to Succeed in Business Without Really Succeeding," *Minneapolis Star and Tribune Sunday Magazine*, July 6, 1986, p. 12; prepublication excerpt from *Claw Your Way to the Top* (Emmaus, PA: Rodale Press, 1986).

go awry, but we will focus only on those problems reported by our 1,600 managers and technical professionals. As you review those top ten meeting problems, you will note they are chiefly characterized by poor planning and follow up and poor command of time and lack of control during the meeting allowing off-topic, irrelevant discussion. In fact getting off the subject is the single most commonly reported meeting problem in business meetings. Those problems may not be as exotic as quasi-therapeutic analysis of meeting problems, but they are the real nuts-and-bolts problems that all meeting managers must resolve. We will explore these and related problems by looking first at planning business meetings and then at conducting a meeting to avoid these major pitfalls.

Essential to any effective meeting is adequate preparation. Too many business meetings are thrown together, casting serious doubt as to what will go on in the meeting and what is expected of those who attend. Ironically, meeting preparation does not take excessive time.

The meeting planner's goals should include the following:

- To coordinate and focus group efforts
- To choose the best structure for information processing
- To give participants clear behavioral expectations
- To save time and reduce needless conflicts

These issues should all be of concern to the meeting convener prior to the meeting.

In this chapter we will discuss the essential steps necessary in preparing an effective meeting. These steps will include: (1) the purpose, general objectives, and the problem of pressure due dates; (2) the type of format and leadership style to fit the task; (3) who will (and will not) participate and who will serve as chairperson; (4) how and when participants will be briefed on their task; (5) the time, place, and duration of the meeting appropriate to the task; (6) how the "tentative" agenda will be assembled and distributed; (7) how proceedings and results will be recorded and by whom; and (8) who will have responsibility for implementation steps and action items.

Purpose and General Objectives

Write down the purpose of the meeting in one clear sentence. Try to make it as specific as possible and include the expected outcomes in phrases such as:

To decide upon a marketing plan and determine individual implementation responsibilities for all members of this group. To be completed by July 1.

There are three general goals that most task-oriented groups should be concerned with in planning a meeting. Business meetings are by their nature devoted to a task, so these same three goals are important to both leaders and participants. The chances of achieving these objectives increase with better meeting preparation. These three main purposes are productivity, maintenance, and commitment to decisions.

Productivity

Business meetings are held to produce effective decisions. We may call this a "quality result" or an "optimal decision." Whether this end result is a major policy decision or a minor production schedule decision, the hope is that it is the best decision possible given the available information and time constraints of the group. Group effectiveness will most often be judged by the effectiveness of the decision after it has been implemented. Proper planning can make the optimal decision easier to obtain.

Maintenance

In order to reach high-quality decisions, group members must maintain satisfying and facilitating relations with one another in the process of decision making. This factor is increasingly important as a result of the massive shift to work teams and self-managing teams in the 1990s. All must therefore work to prevent disruptive interpersonal conflicts which might diminish optimal group productivity. High-tech industry is filled with groups composed of bright, independent, high-achieving experts who produce low-quality results because they cannot work together effectively. Planning can help the group to work together by making it clear what is expected of the group and each individual.

Commitment to Decisions

In most, but not all, groups it is important to gain a commitment by all to the decisions made by the group. Some groups have the luxury of making decisions which others, not themselves, must implement.

However, decision commitment is particularly necessary if the group members will be implementing the decisions. A group decision is worthless if it is undermined in the implementation phase by members who had reservations about the decision as it evolved in the group. A true consensus of support needs to be achieved. A meeting that is well organized in advance will increase the chances of a smooth, effective decision-making process; therefore, it is easier for group members to feel a commitment toward both the group process as well as whatever outcomes are achieved.

Meet only for a specific purpose and accept routinely scheduled meetings with one major qualification: staff meeting dates can be reserved but only with the agreement that a meeting will be called if there is sufficient business (with enough cancellations to enforce that understanding). Above all, attach specific due dates to the accomplishment of a group objective. Without the pressure of due dates, the discussion will wander and valuable time will be squandered.

Meeting Format and Leadership Style

One of the first decisions in preparing a meeting should be the type or style of meeting you want to have. We will examine the main types used predominantly in business in this section and additional meeting formats used for special needs in Appendix A. Meetings are held for different reasons. To get the most out of your meeting, decide what you want to gain from it and select an appropriate meeting style to achieve that purpose. The amount of decision-sharing responsibility you allow participants is a critical early decision by a meeting convener. This will determine if your meeting will have a consultation, recommendation, or delegation style and structure to it. By selecting and communicating the proper meeting style, the manager makes clear the scope and extent to which participants may share in the decision process.

The Consultation Meeting

These are usually ad hoc groups rather than standing committees. They are usually called on short notice for one or two hours and are often one-time occasions. For example, a supervisor may gather his key subordinates to consult on a specific decision. It is the supervisor's intent to obtain the group's immediate suggestions on a specific issue or problem. Constraints and parameters of the problem are outlined and the leader participates with the group in exploring problems and/or solutions. Although the supervisor or team leader actively participates throughout the discussion, an effort should be made on his or her part to listen and not speak in order to optimize the group's suggestions. Participant input is spontaneous, usually without the benefit of lengthy consideration, but valuable nonetheless in helping to shape a manager's decision. There is little group autonomy in these meetings. The supervisor usually chairs the meeting, and it is clear that the supervisor owns the problem and is responsible for the final decision.

The Recommendation Meeting

This meeting is more formal, lasts longer, and features independent deliberations by the group. The manager appoints a committee with the expectation that they will meet two or three times over a period of time. The manager meets briefly with the group to outline the problem and makes it clear that, after orientation of the problem, the group will be left to their own independent deliberation concerning recommendations to be reported to the manager. It is also made clear that while the group has the autonomy to choose their own leadership and decision process, the appointing manager still retains final decision power. This implies the manager may be forced to reject any and all of the committee's recommendations. In this meeting, participants perceive that their ideas will have greater influence. Some of the most important policy guidelines in many companies are often initiated by committees of this type from lower levels of the organization. Such committees have a lasting impact in a company as the convening supervisors come and go. Because of this, participants often take their committee assignment seriously and consequently have stronger feelings of participation in the group process and final recommendations.

The Delegation Meeting

In this meeting, the manager delegates complete decision-making responsibility to a group of trusted subordinates. Such a meeting is less frequent because of managerial pressures and fears about losing control. Subordinates often have enough experience, however, to analyze and resolve significant problems affecting their responsibilities with minimal guidance from their management. No act demonstrates so powerfully the trust and respect which managers place in their subordinates than does the delegated decision. It is unfortunate that such delegation often involves trivial decisions to be made. Once a manager decides to delegate a decision, he or she needs to let the group work out a solution without intervention or later modification on the manager's part. One of the worst errors a manager can make is to delegate a decision and then intervene in the decision process.

Degree of Decision Sharing: *Be Clear!*

Group	Action	Leader	Decision Ownership
Consulting Group	"Advise Me Now"	Manager	Manager
Recommendation Group	"Meet and Make a Recommendation"	Group	Manager
Delegation Group	"You Decide"	Group	Group

Don't Forget to Report Back on Your Final Decision

There are a host of other meeting purposes which are more specialized. An effective meeting organizer will select a meeting format that meets the needs of the situation. These additional formats are discussed in greater depth in Appendix A.

One of the commonest mistakes made with meetings is to use only one type of format to fit many different meeting tasks. Know your meeting format options. Is your main purpose to share new information with your group without encouraging a good deal of interaction? If so, choose a straightforward briefing session and a more directive style of leadership. Keep the meeting short (20 to 30 minutes) and to the point. Is your goal to generate a number of solutions for a problem you have already well defined? if so, choose a format such as the creative ideation format which allows the group freedom to exploit a creative, nonjudgmental method of operation under a minimal leadership style. Is your task to rank or identify key priorities among a large number of problems? If so, choose a nominal group method which efficiently allows the group to agree upon a general ranking (from one to fifteen items) in a brief period of time. Is your goal to share expert opinion with a group followed by a group discussion of the ideas presented? If so, choose a hybrid meeting format such as a symposium style of presentation with three experts talking for ten minutes each, followed by a roundtable discussion under a more consultative participative leadership style. Remember, *choose the right method and leadership style to fit the specific group task.*

Participants and the Chairperson

Concerning participants, sufficient thought needs to be given to who should attend and why each person invited *needs* to be there. Having individuals present who should not have attended or who don't know why they were invited can quickly make a meeting frustrating and unproductive for everyone. Poor meeting invitation practices crop up in the best-run companies. As consultants, we have often observed large, unwieldy meetings of more than twenty persons — when one third of that number would have sufficed for the decision task. It is not uncommon to observe meetings in which everyone is invited except those individuals with the real decision power concerning a certain decision. Few initial meeting planning choices can prove so costly and time-consuming as that of inviting the wrong people to a meeting.

Make an attempt to get away from a typical format and participant list which encourages an open-ended discussion of any and all topics. Such an approach tends to make the meeting time excessively cluttered and disorganized. Instead, focus your meeting purpose by targeting specific individuals who need to be invited, and plan for shorter, tighter meetings in which everyone knows the overall purpose and his or her own specific role when the group convenes. This may seem to imply a greater number of meetings. However, if they are more effective, the total time spent in meetings will be less, and resentment about participating in meetings will also diminish. Participants should be invited to attend a meeting if:

 They have direct responsibility and authority over the topic of discussion, or

 They have information which is necessary to make an effective decision regarding the topic and which cannot be easily obtained elsewhere, or

 They will have the responsibility of resolving or implementing the recommendation of the group.

Group Size: A Key Variable

Do not forget to give serious consideration to the size of the meeting since it is such a crucial variable. It affects virtually all aspects of group interaction. The size issue becomes increasingly important as industry removes middle management levels and extends the span of control to greater numbers of direct reports. The representative

Harrison/Hofstra University Study (Hosansky 1989) reported alarming average numbers of people at typical meetings.

TABLE 5-1	Average number of Participants at Meetings
Business Function	**Number of People**
Manufacturing	22.7
Finance	19.9
Sales/Marketing	16.5
Human Resources	13.5
General Management	13.1

If these are primarily "telling and selling" meetings where full group feedback is relatively unimportant, larger group size may not be as significant a barrier. However, if we are concerned with the interactive roundtable meeting that seeks everyone's active involvement, then we have problems. We know that all sorts of bad things happen when meeting size exceeds seven to nine people.

- Participation rates widen dramatically: the gap grows between the few (two to three) who talk a great deal and the rest who say virtually nothing, thereby significantly limiting the goal of equal participation.

- The healthy dynamics and cross-stimulation of ideas of the interactive meeting is lost: meetings take on the formal, constrained authoritarian character of a one-way briefing session.

- The anonymity effect is heightened. People are not only inhibited from participating by the large-size groups, individuals literally can not actively participate because of talk time competition and, consequently, feel anonymous and uncommitted to decisions.

- Managing the meeting effectively becomes increasingly difficult for chairpersons and unsatisfying for group members who can not get their ideas on the table and have their "say."

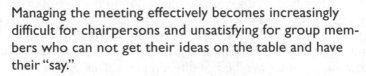

Rothwell makes an important point when he states that "Complexity increases as the size of the group grows, both in terms of group relations and potential interactions. As we add individuals for 2 to 8 the possible number of interactions between the group members increases exponentially from 2 to over 1000" (Rothwell 1995, 39).

What is the ideal size? A number of studies have examined this question. Studies by researchers like Hackman (1987) and Sundstrom et al. (1990), who study independent work teams, have found that the answer to this question is **the smallest size capable of performing the task effectively.** In general, the experts say the best group size is an uneven group of five or seven individuals (uneven to prevent deadlocks); groups of five members are considered ideal. Groups of fewer than five members may not have a broad enough mix of expertise to handle the task efficiently. Groups of more than seven members have other complications noted above.

Some companies call attention to the importance of this decision via a meeting notification format, which forces meeting planners to distinguish between *essential* and *optional* attendees. (See Appendix B, Form 3). Essential individuals are those who are expected to make a contribution at the meeting. Others with a "need to know" are invited to attend at their option but with clear expectations they will not participate.

Finally, spend some time selecting the chairperson. The manager charged with the task is usually the designated chairperson, but this choice should not be automatic. There may be other reasons to select another person, e.g., to give a junior manager more leadership opportunities, to allow a group freer deliberations without the inhibition of a higher status manager, etc. It is also important to choose a person whose general leadership style (authoritarian/directive, consultative/participative, nondirective) fits the task.

Participant Briefing

After the meeting organizer has decided who should attend a particular meeting, the attendees need to be informed. Whenever practical, each member should be personally contacted and the meeting purpose and individual expectations briefly explained. When it is not practical to contact all members, be sure to contact the key individuals who need to be properly oriented to the meeting objectives.

Each person invited needs to be specifically informed as to why he or she was asked to attend, what they should be prepared to present or bring, and the overall anticipated outcome. If the person needs to be present for only a part of the meeting, indicate at what time and for how long so that he or she may plan accordingly.

Whenever possible, written notices should be used to reinforce oral notification. Written notices are most effective in legitimizing and formalizing individual meeting expectations. Instead of just sending an announcement to a list of individuals, indicate after each participant's name — as appropriate — what is expected of that person in the meeting. For example:

Jeff Bridges — Problem Statement

Betty Schumberg — Cost Analysis

John Coleman — Impact on Operations

Participants can often be given advance questions to think about prior to the meeting. Such a technique can be used to shape expectations for what will be discussed and how it will be discussed.

Brief each participant either in person or on the meeting announcement. Do this at least a few days in advance, if possible, to give everyone sufficient lead time to prepare adequately. Participants have every right to request this information, and managers should readily supply it if they are interested in structuring an efficient, effective meeting. Nonexistent or inadequate briefing remains one of the most frequently reported faults of meeting conveners in our survey. It is also one of the key steps which gets skipped most often under time pressures.

The Meeting — Time, Place, and Duration

Another overlooked, yet critical, detail of meeting preparation involves abrupt and inconsiderate scheduling of the meeting. It is not enough to simply announce a time and distribute a memorandum to attendees, as is common practice in many businesses. If each member has a specific reason for being present, then an attempt should be made to accommodate everyone's schedule. Where coordination presents an impractical task, rank the importance of having each member present and be sure that key attendees can be present. Have other members assign a substitute — as appropriate — to facilitate their purpose for being asked to attend.

Regarding the specific time of the meeting, a number of conventions may influence our choice. Emergency events dictate meeting times more often than most of us would like. When afforded sufficient lead time, however, there are good reasons to hold meetings at 9:00 a.m. or earlier — most people are supposedly more creative during this period. There are also very good reasons to schedule meetings at 10:30 a.m. and 3:30 p.m. because of the built-in closure that comes with those time slots. At 12:00 p.m. and 5:00 p.m., participants are more likely to want to wrap up the meeting so that they may leave for lunch or home.

Concerning location, most meeting settings are sufficiently numerous, pleasant, and of adequate size. They are not, however, sufficiently removed from distractions and interruptions (one reason why meeting in the boss's office in competition with telephone and secretarial interruptions is not a good idea). Rooms with round tables are preferred but virtually nonexistent unless you want to meet in a company cafeteria. Some tasks require an off-site meeting if the goal is to combine business with socializing or to engage in intensive marathon deliberation free from routine and predictable home-office interruptions.

How long should you meet? Aim at not longer than one hour for most problem-solving meetings, but longer if the task requires more extensive work. However, do note that participant efficiency will diminish greatly after two hours, so plan breaks accordingly.

The Tentative Agenda

Standard procedure for most business meetings today involves a meeting agenda. A good agenda can be used to keep the group on track — in both subsubject and allocated time. Good agendas also have a structure for each topic to help curtail rambling, open-ended discussion. A subtopic structure also provides benchmarks for summary and consensus, which is useful in providing impetus for the group's efforts. Place as much relevant information about the meeting on the agenda as possible. General time estimates should be placed by each topic so that everyone can help keep the meeting focused accordingly. The person chairing the discussion and/or providing essential information should be indicated on the agenda wherever possible.

We strongly advise that agenda preparation become a routine procedure, based upon a form, to ensure that all necessary information is included for every meeting. It should be possible to get a form standardized for all meetings in your organization (see sample in Appendix B), as many firms have done.

The agenda should be distributed in advance of the meeting to clarify and confirm attendance and expectations of everyone involved. Bring additional copies to the meeting in case participants or their substitutes have forgotten theirs or substitute members are sent.

Some kind of an agenda should be distributed ahead of time to get the group focused on how they will attack a problem. An agenda represents an important collective agreement on how the group sees the problem and which elements they should discuss in what order. Don't distribute an open agenda and ask participants to add issues to

it. Those memos always get lost in circuit and no one sees the whole
structure of the agenda. Take the responsibility on yourself as the
convener of the meeting. Do not use the agenda to engage in information overload or as a vehicle for personal polemics. Limit the agenda to
four to five main points plus a reasonable number of subpoints, and
label it as a "tentative" agenda. One of the chairperson's first actions
should be to ask for changes and additions to that tentative agenda so
that the group can come to a genuine structural consensus before they
delve into the details of problem solving.

Recording the Proceedings and Results

There should be clear agreement that all important decisions of the
group be recorded and distributed in the meeting minutes. A willing
recorder should be chosen by the chairperson prior to the meeting,
allowing that individual some time to prepare for this special role in
addition to his or her usual participation. This individual should not be
the chairperson, who has more than enough to do in running the
meeting properly. The recorder should be an individual who has the
ability to articulate the consensus of the group (not what was said by
everyone, but *the main items which the group agreed upon*). This
individual should also have an ability to condense these points clearly
and faithfully in a brief one-page memorandum of meeting minutes.
(See Appendix B for a full discussion of the recorder's role and duties.)

Implementation Steps and Action Items

Whether this is determined prior to the meeting or within the meeting,
it is important that some one person have clear responsibility for each
item. To designate an "actor" charged with making something happen
provides a feedback loop which carries out the basic purpose of the
group — to solve the problem. All action items or implementation
steps agreed upon by the group should be recorded. These notes
should indicate whether these steps are to be carried out by members
of the same group deciding the problem or by members outside of the
decision group. These specific assignments should be published as part
of the meeting minutes. This simple act prevents needless and often
rancorous misunderstandings about who has responsibility for which
action items. It also provides a published reminder to the person
whose task it is to complete a particular responsibility before the next
meeting.

Mistakes to Avoid in Meetings

With appropriate preparation some of the most important meeting problems should have been addressed (poor preparation and follow up and lack of goals, purpose, or agenda). Problems of a somewhat different nature are the kind of problems which occur during the meeting.

Prepare the Orientation Speech

Much of this preparation falls to the hands of the planning group or chairperson. This is especially true of the orientation speech, which we contend is one the single most important acts of effective leadership and group functioning (see the discussion in Chapter 6).

Planners and chairs need to remind themselves of the typical state of mind of participants at the opening of their meeting, suggested by these research conclusions compiled from four different studies:

 Approximately one-third of the participants invited to a meeting have no functional or decisional reason to be in attendance.

 Approximately one-third of the participants have no idea why the meeting was called or what the main issues under discussion are.

 Approximately one-third of the participants needed to make the decision on meeting issues are not in attendance.

Approximately one third of the participants feel that they have little to no impact on the decisions made in the meeting.

The probability that each of these findings does not refer to the same one-third of participants presents a real challenge to the chairperson. An orientation speech is not a substitute for a sound meeting briefing, but lacking the former for whatever reason, it is the next best thing.

The chair needs to give a clear purpose and direction for every meeting. The lack of an orientation speech contributes powerfully to an unstructured and chaotic discussion.

No Orientation Speech

The importance of the chairperson's orientation speech has been sufficiently emphasized in Chapter 6. The chairperson needs to give a clear purpose and direction for every meeting. The chairperson who begins the discussion in a vague, unfocused manner simply invites the kind of structureless meeting our survey respondents deplored. Participants have a right to this kind of information at the beginning of a discussion. If it is not forthcoming from the chairperson, they should persist until most of those items (i.e., significance, due dates, problem boundaries, procedures, etc.) are clearly spelled out.

Even if a meeting is called on short notice, such as an emergency meeting, goals and expectations can still be clearly communicated in the chairperson's orientation speech. Routine meetings, such as staff or committee meetings, also need to have a clear purpose for each session. Often, routine meetings lose a sense of purpose because although group members reserve the time on their calendars, they have few preconceived notions about what will be discussed or how they should prepare. Consequently, such meetings lose a sense of importance and urgency, and the time is spent in a less productive manner (such as more socializing or increased talk with less action). This sets a poor example for effective meeting management, one that can easily become the norm for all meetings in the organization if left unchecked. The chairperson must take the responsibility to give purpose and importance to every meeting.

Meeting Too Long

Meetings run too long for a number of related reasons, including not starting on time, not adhering to time estimates, and running overtime. These factors indicate a general lack of an established and mutually agreed upon priority for the value of the group's time.

Starting Late

Meetings that begin late are more apt to have time problems for the duration of the meeting. If the meeting begins late because the chairperson is not ready, his or her credibility is likely to be damaged for the entire meeting. If the meeting begins late for other reasons, the chairperson must evaluate the reason and weigh it against the importance of starting on time.

Usually, meetings begin late because the chairperson is waiting for group members to arrive. This might be an acceptable reason if the individual whom the group is waiting for has a vital role in the presentation or final decision that the group will make. More times than not, however, the meeting is delayed waiting for individuals who have a lesser role. Not only does beginning late waste the time of the group, it positively reinforces the latecomer ("I'm important enough that they didn't begin without me"), while it negatively reinforces those that have arrived on time ("What's the use in coming on time? We never begin as scheduled"). The messages that are being sent to all participants should be thoroughly considered before deciding to begin a meeting late.

As a chairperson, it is best to begin on time whenever possible and establish a reputation for leading prompt and professional meetings. Chronic latecomers may make a special effort to arrive on time for your meetings if you are consistently prompt in beginning them.

Not Adhering to Time Estimates

Respecting time constraints must be an important consideration throughout the meeting. The nature of group discussion, especially if the topic of discussion is important to participants, invites a lack of concern about time constraints. Participants get caught up in discussing a topic and time slips by unchecked. Of course, the group should take an adequate amount of time to discuss each topic. Prolonged discussion, however, should not be at the expense of other equally important topics, nor should the length and amount of detail of the discussion come as a surprise to any group member. If discussions on subpoints do run overtime, either the time estimates were underestimated or the discussion was not effectively limited. It is not necessarily bad for a group to discuss a topic longer than planned, but the group should make that choice and then revise the agenda, rather than simply continue the discussion at the expense of other topics.

Another variable that unnecessarily extends the amount of discussion time is the "over-talkers," individuals who say more than they need to, repeat themselves unnecessarily, speak at greater length than is necessary, and speak when they have nothing substantive to add to the discussion. Since influence in the group comes in part from the frequency and length of contributions, participants may overstate their ideas in order to have an impact on the group's decision. This is a difficult variable to monitor. Group members should be aware of the problem and be made to feel comfortable in monitoring the relevancy of each other's contributions. The chairperson can set the example and ask that comments be brief and to the point. Remarks will tend not to be repeated if topics are concluded when they seem to have run their course. A poorly run meeting usually runs overtime in both the discussion of specific agenda items and the overall meeting length, undermining the effectiveness of the entire meeting.

Running Overtime

If the meeting runs overtime, it may be because it was not planned well to begin with or because adequate monitoring of time did not occur throughout. Unfortunately, it is often at the end of the meeting, when the group is out of time, that participants first become concerned with time constraints. This is an inexcusable fault, which is reinforced when the meeting is allowed to continue beyond the scheduled conclusion time. Conclude on time and learn from the experience to better plan and monitor time usage the next time you meet. If the discussion is crucial, proceed with it only after obtaining permission from the group and allowing those who must depart to do so gracefully. At all costs, avoid a hasty conclusion in which decisions are reached without adequate consideration or a consensus from the group. Decisions made because the group is out of time are apt to be of poorer quality, with little or no group commitment. Such practices are what make meetings so ineffective and frustrating for participants.

If you can see that your meeting will run out of time, take the last five to seven minutes for a clear and orderly summary of what has been decided and what remains to be decided. It is better to have covered half the agenda well than to rush through the entire slate of topics, creating more confusion than initially existed.

Getting Off the Subject

Getting off the subject is the most commonly reported meeting problem in business meetings. It usually exists when a meeting lacks structure, when there is extensive topic jumping or group members prematurely jump to a solution, and when irrelevant discussion occurs.

Lack of Structure

Meetings which are unstructured, which do not systematically progress from point to point in an organized way, are difficult to keep on track because there is no common plan or perception as to what should be covered or how it should be covered. This usually occurs because of a variety of reasons, which we will review in this chapter. The main reason discussions get sidetracked once the meeting is in progress, however, is a lack of discipline in "tracking the discussion." Poor discipline in tracking the discussion appears to be everyone's weakness, not just the chairperson's. It refers not only to the need for proper summaries after each point, but also to the needed emphasis upon crystal clear structure and progression throughout the entire discussion (see Figure 5-1).

Figure 5-1
Structuring the Flow of Information

DISCUSSION

Problem Analysis: Recognizing, locating, and defining the problem and several components.

INTRODUCTION

Chairperson's Orientation Speech
    Background of Issue Causes
    Consequences
    Relevancy
    Admitted and Preempted Matter

Appointment of Recorder

Discussion of Final Agenda Format

Determination of Criteria for "Good" Solution

Agenda A

Begin analysis of causes of problem

Recorder Summary

"Therefore we are agreed that three main causes of the problem are: (1) ... (2) ... (3) ... "
Be certain that you have properly concluded the discussion of point A to the satisfaction of all before going on to point B.

Agenda B

Begin solution analysis by listing alternatives

Recorder Summary

"Thus far we are agreed that there are four basic alternatives in solving the problem. They are (1) ... (2) ... (3) ... (4) ..."
Again, be certain that the group has fairly well exhausted alternative solutions and that all ideas are in before going on to the next agenda item.

CONCLUSION

Chairperson requests total recorder review of main items of consensus

Chairperson checks group satisfaction on decision

Chairperson makes certain all action items to be done by individual group members are recorded and circulated

Agenda C

Testing and evaluating alternative solutions with regard to criteria for best decision. Choosing the best solution.

Recorder Summary

"After looking at all alternatives in light of the criteria, we have agreed to recommend the following solutions: (1) ... (2) ... (3) ..."

Topic and Solution Jumping

Most groups jump from one topic to another at an alarming rate. The average group shifts topics every 1.5 minutes (Bales 1950). In addition, research confirms a long-suspected tendency of groups to jump back and forth on topics (Fisher 1974). Changing topics is a natural occurrence in the dynamics of a typical discussion, however, and needs to be monitored by all group members in order to avoid being excessive. This is especially true in heated or salient discussions. There will always be some backtracking and repetition of topics as group members develop a different perspective or feel a need to reconsider a specific issue. Some topic jumping and recycling is inevitable and, at times, desirable — as when attempting to consider new perspectives on a problem. Both the chairperson and all participants must strive to keep the number of topic shifts within reasonable limits. Minimizing topic jumping requires vigilance and intervention by everyone in the group. A group awareness of the tendency to shift topics unnecessarily will help reinforce group compliance. Any member of the group should be able to say: "Wait a minute, can we take a moment to complete this topic before we shift to that issue?"

To a lesser extent, the group also needs to monitor the degree of topic shifting between subpoints. Topic jumping from one major point to another major point, however, is obviously more serious than topic jumping from one subpoint to another subpoint. An occasional out-of-place comment is tolerable if it does not divert the attention of the entire group for a prolonged period.

Topic Jumping = Recycling, Backtracking, and Repetition

TOPIC A → B → A → C → D → B → E → A → C → D → F, etc.

"Average Group Shifts Topics Every 1.5 Minutes!"

Solution jumping occurs when the group tries to solve a problem before adequate definition or analysis of the problem has been made. Americans are particularly guilty of this habit. Nourished in an extremely pragmatic "can do" culture, which has conquered challenges from the western frontier to landing on the moon, Americans usually define a problem as "something that can be solved." Other cultures (such as the French) define a problem as something that either can be solved or for which there is no solution. Americans tend to propose a solution for a problem as soon as the chairperson stops talking and invites comments. This is common practice even on complex problems where additional information and analysis is obviously needed; thus, the mistaken solution is often inappropriate and costly. The urge to solve the problem expeditiously is overpowering. It is also infectious; a resolution is quickly attempted, and in so doing other members are invited to jump on the bandwagon and offer premature solutions as well, compounding the difficulty of properly assessing the problem.

Solution jumping, like topic jumping, requires immediate intervention and correction by the chairperson or other group members. To obtain the best solution, all group members must develop the habit of using the methods that emphasize the orderly and appropriate processing of information. These methods involve the use of suspended judgment, critical reflection, causal analysis, and clear internal summaries.

Irrelevant Discussion

While irrelevant comments may not shift the discussion, they do contribute to unfocused conversation and excessive tangential excursions. As noted, a well-planned chairperson's orientation will avert a significant amount of irrelevant comment. All group members need to relate their comments to the discussion and ask for clarification when another person's comments seem to be unrelated to the discussion. Repeat violators should be tactfully confronted by the chairperson during the meeting or on a one-to-one basis during a break, as appropriate.

Meeting Without Goals or an Agenda

Meeting without goals or an agenda is an invitation for all the afore-mentioned problems to occur. Meetings need to have agendas, and the chairperson needs to give a clear orientation speech for each session.

No Agenda

The need for a clear agenda should be well appreciated at this point. An agenda is an essential prerequisite for any effective business meeting. A lack of one suggests poor planning. A tentative agenda should be distributed in advance to meeting participants and revised as needed at the outset of the meeting. Having the plan for progress explicitly endorsed by all group members helps to assure their coopera-tion in reaching the goals of the meeting in an effective and timely manner. Without such steps, the meeting is more likely to be rambling and unproductive. Even with spontaneous or routine meetings, the group should have clearly stated goals and an agreed upon plan for reaching those goals.

Inconclusive Meetings

Meetings are often inconclusive because they lack effective summaries, or because no decisions or assignments are made at the conclusion of the meeting.

A Lack of Summary

Inconclusive progression, or a lack of summary, refers to the tendency of groups to move on to another topic before they have fully or conclu-sively summarized the first topic. As previously discussed, effective information processing requires a discipline and procedure throughout the entire meeting. Subpoints must be summarized and decisions need to be made by the group during the entire meeting, not just at the meeting's conclusion. An effective chairperson does not let the discus-sion ramble unchecked, but instead notices when new and relevant information concerning the topic has been exhausted. The chairperson then cuts off discussion, summarizing areas of agreement and dis-agreement and moving the group toward more productive tasks.

Inconclusive progression tends to be one of the most common problems in all groups we have observed — staff, problem-solving, and interdepartmental groups alike. In coming to understand the flow of information in a group, it is important to see that internal summaries serve a critical and often understated function in keeping the discussion focused and on track. If summaries are neglected, it is inevitable that the group will use their time inefficiently through needless backtracking and repetition of issues.

Inconclusive progression is a special case of topic jumping. We treat it separately because the lack of clarity and closure on what a group has decided about the major points on its agenda can seriously confound group efforts. Why? Because the conclusion or agreements arrived at about the major subpoints of an issue usually constitute the logical rationale for the final decision about the entire issue. If the consensus concerning each of these subpoints is unstated or poorly articulated, there is often much confusion, disagreement, and resentment at the "announcement" of the group's final decision. Time after time, we have observed members moving from one issue or subpoint to another like this:

◆

Well. . . . I guess that sort of covers the main questions concerning the benefits options . . . Why don't we move on to the next topic on the agenda, the OSHA compliance report. . . .

With internal progression like this, it is predictable that the final summary will be equally vague and imprecise. Group members will leave the meeting wondering what was decided or, more likely, falsely assuming what was decided and basing subsequent actions on those false assumptions. Chairpersons and participants alike need to remind each other how important it is to fully conclude each subpoint before going on to another topic. Although this is often a task delegated to the group's recorder, it is the responsibility of every member of the group. Insofar as possible, there should be a clear statement of both the *substance* and the *degree of consensus* on each major subpoint before the group is allowed to move on. Here is an example of the kind of internal summary groups should strive for in their discussions:

◆

I think I've got this straight but check this over . . . So far we have generally agreed on three main points concerning the benefits options. First, four out of the five representatives, Ben excluded, generally support the company's cafeteria benefits plan. Second, we all tend to be unclear on what relationship, presently, if any, this has with flex-time and four-day week options. We need additional input from HRD and Legal on this issue. Third, all of us are really concerned that we not get locked into a wrong decision; that is, we want a longer period to reconsider and possibly revise our benefits mix. . . .

At this point, the chairperson should be expected to check the consensus on each of these points carefully and to allow further discussion on any subpoint before restating the final version of the group's consensus. Only after this sensing of agreement can the chairperson move on to the next point.

This recommendation means that the average meeting leader must take much more time and care than usual in nailing down each topic before moving on. What needs to be emphasized is the systematic and diligent attention to gaining consensus on each major subpoint of the agenda.

No Decisions or Assignments Made

In order for a meeting to be conclusive, decisions need to be made clearly. This includes the decision to delay or not decide an issue. Usually, the decisions involve subsequent action items for group members to implement that will place the decision into motion. If the assignments are not clearly made, no action will be taken or conflicting actions might occur. The chairperson has the responsibility, with assistance from the recorder and task monitor, to see that assignments are clearly made.

Disorganized Meetings

Meetings become disorganized because of excessive interruptions, information queuing, and abstract analysis on the part of participants.

Excessive Interruptions

The information processing flow of the meeting is probably disrupted more by excessive interruptions than by any other factor. Interruptions present something of a dilemma. On one hand, a source of strength of any group interaction is open and spontaneous interaction and crossfertilization of ideas. Too much structure in a business meeting limits this creative interaction. On the other hand, extensive interruptions can severely damage the continuity and development of ideas in the group's discussion. We have all been in discussions where the thread of the discussion was lost and where little progress on key issues occurred because of constant interruptions.

Interruptions are particularly devastating when members of the group are shy or inhibited. Such individuals may possess relevant expertise, but if they are hesitant in interjecting their contribution into

FREQUENT INTERRUPTION
= "A SLAP ACROSS
    THE FACE"

LEADS TO:
① LOSS OF GROUP
    PRODUCTIVITY!
② LOSS OF
    SELF-ESTEEM!

the discussion, someone else is likely to interrupt. In fact, many meetings are dominated by one or two individuals in this way. Usually, the person interrupting has a louder voice and more aggressive communication skills. The immediate effect of such interruptions, from the standpoint of group productivity, is that key ideas are lost or needlessly postponed. Because shy people are less likely to defend their positions, ideas of other group members are repeated and given undue consideration. The overall result is a less productive meeting.

The long-range effects of interruptions are more subtle but possibly more damaging. Repeated interruptions tend to shape a role for the shy, but knowledgeable, group member. Over time, members of the group tend to ignore, dominate, and interrupt any and all remarks attempted by the more reticent person. This then becomes a norm for the way the entire group treats anything said by the shy individual. Other group members infer that if such persons will not defend their positions, the ideas they have are not worth much and, therefore, can and should be squelched at will. This pattern in turn eats at the self-esteem of the shy group member and reinforces further withdrawal from participation to the point where some reticent members simply no longer function in the group.

It does not matter if interruptions are motivated by genuine enthusiasm for one's comments or by rude and deliberate dominance tactics — the net effect is the same. For the person who tends to get "stepped on," all interruptions should be treated as a slap across the face. The person who interrupts is saying, "Be silent. Your ideas do not count. My ideas are superior." Although a vigilant chairperson should shield group members from these attacks, in fast-paced interaction, interruptions often go unchecked. It is best to encourage participants to defend their own opinions, as well as the right of others to fully express their thoughts and ideas.

In a healthy discussion group, there will always be a certain amount of spontaneous interruption. A certain level of interruption is permissible; but when it happens too often or is too abrasive, direct action should be taken with the person who is interrupting. Usually, simply raising one's voice while continuing to talk sends a nonverbal signal to the interrupter that you will not allow an interruption. If the interrupter ignores this signal and continues to attempt to interrupt, you should say directly and firmly to that person, "If I may be permitted to complete this thought," or words to that effect. This simple assertion not only allows you to finish, but it gains you increased respect and makes the group more aware of this dysfunctional behavior.

Information Queuing

This is a natural group information-processing event, which occurs quite simply because everyone cannot talk at the same time. Participants must store up their contributions and "wait on line" for an opportunity to respond to a previous statement. By the time a person does get into the discussion, those comments might be irrelevant. This is a natural phenomenon, indeed a necessity, for which no specific person is to blame. Information queuing occurs, in part, because everyone cannot respond to the preceding comment at once, but also because some participants are not assertive enough to make their comments when their ideas would be of greatest relevance. The problem also occurs frequently when individuals do not listen to the comments of others, but instead assemble their own thoughts for a speech or rebuttal which, when delivered, is disconnected from the group's immediate discussion. The chairperson and participants must be aware of all these tendencies and attempt to do three things: strive to give everyone orderly, equitable access to the discussion; remember to reintroduce key ideas which have been temporarily tabled; and require that all participants demonstrate the relevance of their comments to the current train of discussion.

Abstraction Analysis

This term refers to the level of language (high or low abstraction) that individuals use when they are discussing a subject. Many discussions are like ships passing in the night; individuals talk about topics at quite different levels or perspectives and broadcast various messages which simply do not connect with one another. For example, someone may be discussing the "big picture," while others are trying to pinpoint the details of a problem. The level at which individuals discuss a problem depends on a number of factors — their background, training, cognitive complexity, and verbal styles. One person may talk about an issue in very specific, concrete terms, while another person discusses the same topic at a highly abstract, theoretical level. This mix in levels of abstraction is particularly evident in interdepartmental groups composed of individuals from different departments and levels within the corporation, such as manufacturing, research and development, or data processing. Three representatives may discuss the same topic but from three very different perspectives, in three different specialized languages, each reflecting the culture and biases of the department represented. These different perspectives take time to understand and process; this comprehension lag often results in communication breakdowns, since individuals are simply not on the same wavelength.

ABSTRACTION LEVEL JUMPING

"The Theoretical Logico-Decutive Model Is Systemic ... etc."

"Here's What Happened to Uncle Jim"

What can a chairperson or any other participant do when a fellow group member makes a major jump in the level of abstraction? If the shift is toward a high-level abstraction, such as discussing the topic in theoretical terms or large organizational focus, two questions can immediately be asked: "How does this relate to what we were just talking about?" or "Can you give us a specific example of how this theory applies to our discussion?" Both questions attempt to lower the abstraction level by having the speaker make the relationship with the topic under discussion more concrete. The basic advice for the chairperson or any other group member is simple: Make the discussion as clear and concrete as possible; cut through the fog of jargon and special language; and keep the whole group on the same level of abstraction.

Most business meetings operate efficiently at a middle level of language complexity. Meetings are called primarily to solve problems, not as occasions for individuals to display the complexity of their thinking or the extent of their vocabulary. Contributions in business meetings need to be concise and efficient; all members need to say what they have to say in the shortest, clearest manner and at the lowest reasonable level of abstraction. The person who launches into macroeconomic views or a system analysis perspective with regard to a topic under discussion has the responsibility of showing why it is relevant to talk about the issue at that level. Like over-engineering a machine, over-abstracting a problem is not very useful in problem resolution and decision making. In business discussions, it is often needlessly confusing to the information flow of the group.

Corporate Policies on Meeting Management

To be most effective, meetings need the support of the organization. You can use much of the advice presented in this book for your own meetings, but some advice will be easier to put into practice if there are clearly established expectations and practices regarding meetings in your organization. Many companies have written and unwritten guidelines for meeting procedures. Such guidelines help to standardize the meeting activity and thus produce more effective and productive meetings. The following are some items that an organizational policy regarding meetings should address: scheduling of meetings, timing and notices, use of agendas, interruptions, physical aids, and follow-up.

Scheduling of Meetings

Meeting time is a scarce resource in virtually all organizations. There can be a significant impact upon many meeting-related problems, however, if the organization maintains some kind of company policy regarding the scheduling of meetings. Various organizations have developed, with the advice of behavioral scientists, company-wide guidelines for time usage. An example of such a schedule follows:

 8:00 a.m.–9:00 a.m. — QUIET TIME. Borrowing from time management specialists, the first hour of the day is designated as quiet time. This time is devoted expressly to uninterrupted individual work for planning, analysis, or review.

 9:00 a.m.–10:00 a.m. — INDIVIDUAL MEETINGS. This period is reserved for fifteen- to thirty-minute meetings with one or two individuals, for telephone calls or computer conferences. Many work groups also find this a convenient time for their weekly or biweekly staff meetings between supervisors and their subordinates (but only to be used when necessary).

 10:00 a.m.–12:00 noon and 1:30 p.m.–3:30 p.m. — GROUP MEETINGS. These periods are allocated primarily to group meetings. They are periods when all personnel can be expected to be on the premises and available for the larger, more costly, group meetings. Lunch periods may also be used on occasion for group meetings.

 3:30 p.m.–5:00 p.m. — MISCELLANEOUS TIME. This is the day's "swing period" used for individual work not done previously or group meeting as necessary.

Exceptions to the above general schedule abound in all organizations, and specific times are less important than the fact that a general company policy exists with regard to periods for group meetings. Once some standard, company-wide expectations exist about when meetings are scheduled, everyone can plan time more productively.

Developing Meeting Management Policies

It is important that each organization develops its own policies since these policies should reflect and incorporate the unwritten customs, work rhythms, and standard operating procedures of its own culture. A set of prescriptions that work well in one type of industry will fail miserably in another type of business.

It is equally important that this not be done by administrative fiat. Some form of consensus decision making should be used in the process of arriving at these policies. Only those policies that receive broad support from representative groups should be included in order to elicit team ownership and consequent ease of implementation.

Listed below are the meeting management policies of one large pharmaceutical company, some which might be helpful in getting you started in this process.

Meeting Management Policies

1   All associates are expected to log in their daily and weekly schedule on our company networks to afford meeting schedulers efficient access to personal schedules in fixing appropriate meeting times.

2   All meetings of one hour or more require our standard meeting notice form with a clear agenda and other meeting information.

3   All meeting participants have the right to be briefed on expectations of their role in the meeting. This can be done via the standard meeting notice and by phone, e-mail, or fax as appropriate, but it must be done as expected procedure.

4   Starting and ending on time is important. All participants are expected to be in the meeting room to start the meeting at the designated time and, barring emergencies, not five to ten minutes later. Similarly, meetings should conclude at the designated time.

5   Most managers, team leaders, and conveners have some decisional responsibilities that can not be delegated and that must be respected; however, it is the company expectation that all major decisions should be made under some kind of consensus process.

6   It is expected that all participants will conduct their interaction with due respect for the dignity of each individual. There is no place for dismissive, derogatory, or abusive interaction.

7   Conflict of ideas is expected and welcomed as the best way we can arrive at sound decisions. All participants are expected to exercise critical thinking in examining alternatives to proposals. In all major decisions the group should appoint one designated critic or "Devil's Advocate" who has chief responsibility in this area.

8   All major meetings require meeting minutes that should be accurate, comprehensive, and available to all participants within two to three days of the meetings. When possible, meeting minutes should be posted on the local network.

9 All participants are expected to evaluate the effectiveness of their department and divisional meetings at least once a year via the company evaluation form; appropriate action should be taken, if necessary, to make meetings more time-efficient, effective, and satisfying to participants.

10 Individual performance in meeting management constitutes a significant percentage of one's overall job performance. Consequently, effective participation and leadership of business meetings will be included in the discussion evaluation at each job performance review period.

There are undoubtedly more and better meeting management policies that fit the organizational roles and behaviors of each of your organizations. Resist the tendency to be too specific or too broad. The most successful policies simply document and articulate well-established informal procedures for everyone to understand.

Summary

In this chapter we have first examined important procedures to use before and after each meeting and, second, ways to avoid the most common types of problems that occur during the meeting. One of the most important aspects of effective planning is to be clear on what type of meeting you need — a consultation meeting, a recommendation meeting, or a delegated meeting. Make your selection fit the specific task before the group. Decide the purpose and type of meeting you want, and select an appropriate meeting format to match those needs from those listed in Appendix A. Decide who should be present and communicate what you expect from them. Schedule an appropriate time, place, and duration for the meeting. Prepare a "tentative" agenda which summarizes your expectations and send it out prior to the meeting to all participants. Make changes as appropriate at the beginning of the meeting, but then insist that the group follow the plan they agreed upon. Select someone to record proceedings of the meetings as they occur including who will be responsible for "action" items after the meeting. Finally, when chartering a new group, remember to prepare a series of statements that clarify the ground rules of decision sharing. Complete planning is without question one of the most cost-effective components in the entire range of meeting management activities; it is the first vital step in changing the meeting practices where you work! So use the comprehensive meeting planners' checklist in the Meeting Planners' Packet in Appendix B.

We next addressed the most frequent meeting problems as reported by nearly 1,600 managers and technical professionals in surveys spanning 1981–1995 (Mosvick 1995). We saw that many of the common problems were directly related to lack of proper planning and preparation for the meeting and that many of the problems were interrelated. Among the problems examined, *meeting without goals or an agenda* was found to be caused primarily by a lack of planning prior to the meeting and an inadequate orientation speech by the chairperson at the onset of the meeting. *Meeting too long*, another major complaint, was caused by starting late, not keeping to time estimates, grossly misjudging the amount of time needed on each subtopics and allowing the meeting to run overtime. The problem of *poor or inadequate preparation* referred both to the prior preparation of the participants for the meeting as well as to the preparation of details of the meeting facilities. The cause of *inconclusive meetings* centered on the lack of effective summaries during and at the conclusion of the meeting, and a conclusion in which no decisions or assignments are made. *Disorganized meetings*, the last of the major meeting problems that we discussed in depth, were believed to be caused mainly by excessive interpersonal interruptions, which had a negative impact on the quality of the decision and a long-term impact on participants' roles as well; information queuing, in which comments are stored for later, often untimely and irrelevant expression; and abstraction analysis, in which participants discuss a topic at cross-purposes via different levels of language abstraction.

We concluded with a discussion of the need for company- or corporation-wide policies to improve the context of meeting management including scheduling of customary meeting periods, and presented an example of the meeting management policies of one corporation as a guideline in developing policy for each organization.

6

Real Leadership
The Leadership Role in Business Meetings

The best leader is the one about whom, after the group has finished, someone says, "Who was the leader?"

— *Attributed to Lao Tze*

How the chairperson and participants view the leadership role is an important ingredient in the effective functioning of any meeting. Groups often flounder because the chairperson adopted one role (usually authoritarian) while the group expected another. The leader — that person who called the meeting — must show initiative in knowing and demonstrating more about his or her leadership role. In this chapter we will examine myths about meeting leadership, participative meeting management, the steps and importance of the chairperson's orientation speech, leadership responsibilities, bringing the group to consensus, and when and how to conclude a meeting.

Findings about Group Leadership

The single most important finding about meeting leadership is that it is situational; that is, different groups with different members performing different tasks will need different types of leadership styles. There is no conclusive evidence that any one leadership style is generally superior in business meetings. It is of greater value to ask, "What type of leadership behaviors seem most effective in the business meeting?" To answer this question, we need to ask another question first: "What are the manager's objectives in calling the meeting?" Managers may call meetings to inform subordinates of a decision, to clarify and instruct them on how a decision should be implemented, or to gain their commitment in carrying out a decision made by others. Predominantly, however, *managers call meetings to gather informed opinions from expert subordinates or colleagues to help make decisions for which the manager is responsible.* If managers could make those decisions by themselves, there would be no need to waste the time of their employees and the money of their employer. Managers need to tap the expertise of their subordinates for recommendations and to have them serve as sounding boards for their ideas.

If, in fact, managers really do need their subordinates to make effective decisions, it calls into question a number of leadership myths about meeting management. Let's examine three such key misconceptions.

Three Leadership Myths

Myth 1: Group leaders must be the most knowledgeable person present.

They must know the most on the topic, and they must demonstrate this informational superiority during the conference.

Myth 2: Leaders must not share leadership.

They must act in a dominant and directive manner so there is no question about who is boss, and control is clearly maintained.

Myth 3: Leaders cannot permit dissent.

They cannot allow for disagreement by subordinates because it would jeopardize their overall managerial control.

While most managers recognize these three notions as a legacy from the heydays of hierarchial organizations, it is surprising how these myths continue to drive meeting leadership behavior through both large and small organizations alike. Given the context of modern business meetings, leaders must adopt attitudes that are the direct opposite of these statements, as we shall explain.

Leadership Knowledge. Given the complexity of business decisions in today's technology, managers seldom have all the facts about a business problem. The exponential growth of total information and the consequent thrust toward occupational information specialization compounds the problem. Market intelligence, field test information, specialized counsel, computer simulation, collegial advice, subordinate requests, and company directives assault the modern manager every day at ever-increasing rates. This information overload makes it impossible for one person to have command over all or even the most significant information related to a pending decision.

Think of a manager's knowledge as a single piece of a puzzle. Although the manager's contributions are by no means insignificant, they are but one perspective among many valuable contributions made in every meeting. Usually, the manager's input represents a different level or kind of knowledge. While a manager's technical knowledge of a specific product or process may be superficial or dated, his or her operational experience and intuition are invaluable. Leaders who overemphasize their own contributions usually do more harm than good by inhibiting subordinate contributions. More important, heavy attention placed on the leader's opinions and biases early in the meeting sets a bad leader-centered pattern which may prematurely discourage equally feasible options for an effective decision from others.

A different attitude is needed by meeting leaders. Leaders should consider participants as coequals, each to be respected as having information and judgment at least equal and often superior to the leader's. This attitude will better set the appropriate tone for effective meetings.

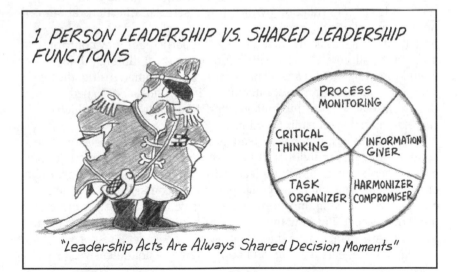

1 PERSON LEADERSHIP VS. SHARED LEADERSHIP FUNCTIONS

PROCESS MONITORING

CRITICAL THINKING

INFORMATION GIVER

TASK ORGANIZER

HARMONIZER COMPROMISER

"Leadership Acts Are Always Shared Decision Moments"

Sharing Leadership. Many managers who abhor authoritarian methods in daily operation often display dominant leadership styles when conducting business meetings. Such managers are often overprotective of their role: seldom sharing chairperson functions with others and reacting sharply to perceived dominance by group participants. In part, this feeling is understandable since the average meeting at times requires a strong leadership style to monitor and direct progress. A strong leadership style, however, should apply primarily to meeting procedures and mechanics, not to substantive or creative contributions. Leadership is and should be a series of *shared functions* among all participants. The following example illustrates this point:

◆

> Fred, a manager, was holding a meeting about a new product design. Early in the meeting, John, the production supervisor, commented critically on the remarks of the design engineer, Tom. One remark led to another concerning Tom's "compulsive" overdesigning tendencies and John's poor supervision of quality tests and production crews. At that point, Steve, a marketing analyst, remarked that the discussion sounded a lot like an inquisition, a comment which evoked much laughter from all, including the two name-callers. It released much tension and allowed the group to review the conflict more rationally.

The most important leadership act in that meeting, which kept the group from being bogged down, was humor. Leadership functions, such as the one displayed in the example, are performed by different participants at different times. In some meetings, a group member serves a leadership function by directing a series of questions about a proposal which disclose flaws in analysis, unreliable data, or a low probability of success. In such a case, that participant may contribute more to the success of the meeting through critical thinking than would the designated leader. The person who summarizes the discussion or the group's progress, integrates different ideas, or expedites a timely close to the meeting makes significant contributions which serve as crucial leadership functions.

It is folly to assume that all leadership functions can, or should be, conducted by one individual. It is far more reasonable to conclude that *all members* should contribute leadership acts with encouragement and endorsement from the formal chairperson. Of course, even in a democratically run meeting, most leadership acts will usually be performed by the formal leader. But how the leader reacts to the leadership acts made by *other* participants is the important point. The leader's response should be open, encouraging, and appreciative — not defensive.

Dissent and Negative Information. One of the authors once had the unfortunate experience of observing an engineer being fired by his manager in the middle of a conference because of the subordinate's dissent. This instance is an extreme example, but one which is a dramatic reminder that most managers dislike dissent from subordinates. This attitude, unfortunately, leads eventually to managerial isolation and poor decisions.

The place of dissent and a manager's receptivity to disagreement has been a much-discussed topic of decision making. The crippling effect of avoiding negative information discussed in Chapter 3, remains a persistent sobering organizational problem.

Most managers acknowledge a need for disagreement from subordinates. Managers may even state the importance of dissent in meetings with subordinates. They may know that meetings should be viewed as an opportunity to encourage the kind of disagreement and critical thinking that produces good decisions. Because managers feel pressure to display control before a group of their subordinates, however, the tendency of superiors is to react harshly to open disagreement in meetings. Their reaction violates the basic objective of the meeting: to collectively scrutinize ideas in order to attain the best decision possible. A team of "yes-men" cannot reach this goal. In addition, subordinates tend to withhold negative information and embellish their own work in order to appear in the best light. The combination of the supervisor's sensitivity to criticism and the subordinates' tendency to exhibit the "good news complex" (so named because of the king who killed a messenger bringing bad news) inevitably results in poorly informed, improperly analyzed decisions.

Peter Drucker cites three basic reasons why dissent is needed:

1   Dissent safeguards the decision-maker against becoming a prisoner of the organization, particularly against anyone who is a special pleader (all of us).

2   Dissent alone can provide alternatives to a decision. Any decision without an alternative is a desperate gambler's throw, no matter how carefully thought through it might be.

3   Dissent is needed to stimulate the imagination, to develop the creative solution, and to get away from the fallacy of the one right decision (Drucker 1974, 473).

The gap between what managers say and do about dissent persists. Decade after decade, the problem surfaces, propelled by the dynamics of power and the upward mobility aspirations of each new generation of managers. It seems to resist all types of training and management development.

Group leaders need to institutionalize dissent to assure that constructive criticism, negative information, and disagreement *are encouraged and expected in group deliberations as the rule rather than the exception*. One way to guarantee dissent in meetings is to assign one of the participants to be a dissenter. Establishing the role of devil's advocate is a simple, workable answer to this meeting problem. In this way, one group member is assigned the specific job of arguing against the proposal; this individual makes sure that all contrary evidence, questions, and criticisms about a proposal are placed before the group for analysis. Legitimizing this role, as well as rotating the assignment of the position, is one of the best techniques for encouraging dissent in all decision-making meetings. The chairperson can also facilitate dissent by listening carefully, restricting interruptions, and refusing to take sides in a dispute until all evidence is presented.

Proper attitudes held by leaders about leadership in business meetings are necessary to create the environment for free, open participation in decision making. Overcoming leadership myths is a start to more effective meeting management; leaders must also learn to adopt a meeting style that maintains control, yet allows for adequate group participation.

Individual vs. Group Performance

The strong surge towards work teams and collaborative decision making is fueled not only by organizational downsizing and total quality management approaches. There is a growing body of research literature that points to the general superiority of collaborative group work. Some research supports an intuitive conclusion that in some circumstances individuals will outperform groups (Forsythe 1990). However, when we look at broad emerging patterns of managerial or technical group work, there is much more evidence to support team collaboration.

Rothwell cites much recent research to show that groups tend to outperform individuals under at least three conditions: (1) when the task requires a wide range and variety of knowledge and skills; (2) when the group is relatively nonexpert in dealing with the task; and (3) when the task is complicated and all members of the group are relatively expert on the task. Much of this he attributes to the strength of more viewpoints, especially in the consistent superiority of group vs. individual remembering of key facts. He notes that a group of experts is especially effective when members are highly motivated and trained to work as a team, citing one study (Michaelson et al. 1989) which found that groups outperform their best expert member 97 percent of the time (Rothwell 1995).

Cooperation and Competition

Eventually all would-be team leaders and associates must come to grips with the fundamental issues of cooperation and competition if their group is to succeed. In our approach we continue to place the major workload on the chair of the group because he or she is such a crucial model from whom the rest of the group takes their cues. But this is clearly a shared responsibility; a cooperative leadership style will be only marginally successful when interacting with a group of intensely competitive "me-oriented" members.

The highly successful team-oriented management practices in such countries as Sweden, Germany, and Japan first forced America to question its individualistic work patterns. Various writers were quick to point out the pervasiveness of competition in American culture as rooted in our unquestioned belief in individualism and self-sufficiency. They were, after all, the values that tamed the frontier and "made America great" — a near state religion derived from meritocracy and market capitalism.

Much of this emphasis is understandable because it is a product of a long system of socialization by our schools and the larger culture. When we reflect on this issue, it is striking how few instances the average student is instructed in the values or techniques of group collaborative work (e.g. some aspects of sports, plays, and club projects). Attaining the highest grade point average is far more strongly reinforced in American society than is aiding a group in accomplishing some worthy project. Consequences of the inculcation of these core values play out every day in all forms of management communication ranging from simple two-person conversation as one upmanship games, to the elaborate strategies to "win the conference" at all costs. Like most major cultural values, this drive and its unquestionable "rightness" are so pervasive and deep they are beneath our awareness. For example, most Americans simply cannot understand why Japanese workers are embarrassed to be singled out and congratulated for their individual achievements. Because the costs of mindless individual competitiveness are so great, and the potential for collaborative work is so vast, no modern manager can chance ignoring this question.

Some of the best recent work on this basic question has been done by Johnson and Johnson and other associates in the field of education (Johnson and Johnson 1991). Here is a capsule version of some of their key findings on this issue.

---◆---

They found sixty-five studies conducted by other researchers that showed the superiority of cooperation over competition on achievement and performance and 108 studies demonstrating the same clear advantage of cooperation over individual work. Only fourteen studies contradicted these remarkably consistent results. Twenty-one additional studies conducted by Johnson and Johnson (1987) found that cooperation, not competition, clearly leads to higher achievement. As David Johnson ... concludes, "There's almost nothing that American education has seen with this level of empirical support" (Rothwell 1995) [Emphasis by authors].

It should be made plain that none of this critique is meant to question the undeniable contributions made by individual effort. Individual research, critical thinking, and common sense have saved and will continue to save countless meetings from disaster. However, both individual and group excellence is required for effective meeting management. The problem is that the way organizational work is accomplished is headed at a blistering pace toward collaborative group decision making. During the next few years of transition as organizations reinvent themselves, managers must be prepared to deal with a broad range of views concerning the appropriate balance of individual competition and collaborative interaction.

Given the powerful cultural support for individualism and competition, changing meeting attitudes will not be a simple task. It will require systematic training in cooperative discussion techniques, with both leaders and participants committed to respectful, reasoned interaction and to group, not individual, reward systems. As we have noted, the first step is for meeting managers to start where they are in developing collaborative techniques with their groups to whatever extent possible.

Hierarchical Leadership versus Participation Needs

To maintain control and accountability, organizations have been structured historically to reinforce authoritarian management styles. The almost exclusive profile of organizations has been that of a hierarchy that maximizes specialization of function, division of labor, and accountability of individuals in carrying out tasks. Major decision making, power, and influence flow downward through the organization. We can be encouraged by the fact there are swift currents of change at work in North America, Europe, and Australia. As we have discussed, enabling technology, total quality management, and global competition have driven these changes toward more horizontal team cultures. Clearly the need for employee involvement grows greater each year as better educated men and women with higher expectations of power sharing enter the market. But how fast and how far this revolution is moving are matters of conjecture.

Despite these hopeful trends, most organizations tend to remain benign dictatorships. They are not designed as democratic, fully participative institutions. Few have been reengineered from top to bottom to facilitate full consultations and participation in the organization's most critical decisions. Even in organizations with thousands of equalitarian teams at work, the most far-reaching decisions are usually made by a handful of individuals at the top of the organization. This fact has numerous implications in the ongoing interaction between supervisors and subordinates, which often make for a host of problems including poor morale, low self-esteem, and needless conflicts — all of which find their way into the business meeting.

How does this basic conflict affect business meetings? The business meeting is a microcosm of that conflict. We suspect that any time an individual or a group arrives at a decision that ignores the opinion or suggestion of an expert member of the group, there are negative effects. We are most concerned, however, with the needless conflicts, perceived manipulation, and miscommunication that result when participants have unclear notions about the extent of their decision-making responsibilities. The kind of distrust that results when ground rules are unclear affects not only the decision under consideration, but also the effectiveness of business meetings in general. When participants have unclear expectations of the group task and their share of the decision-making prerogatives, they cannot produce the best results. Participants often feel betrayed, confused, and negative about the worth of business meetings and resentful toward the person running the meetings. Since the small-group business meeting is the key forum in which this confrontation is played out, it offers both an opportunity and a potential pitfall for effective participative management.

Involving Participants in Meetings. Clearly participative decision making as found in such organizations as General Motors' Saturn Division is the wave of the future. More and more managers and professionals are members of this growing base of these progressive organizations that have thoroughly institutionalized this process. However, even in old-style organizations there are countless task forces and committees that provide potential opportunities to demonstrate participative leadership style. The participative style of meeting management combines aspects of directive and democratic behavior in the group setting. It is a compromise between the contending needs of the organization and the needs of individuals in the organization. This style is simple and direct about the questions of shared responsibility in decision making. It gives meeting participants "psychological participation" and helps to develop better decisions with better commitment from all involved.

Whether meetings are routine staff conferences, technical coordination meetings, or policy decision meetings, all involve shared decision making. Often the meetings involve a number of smaller decisions made over a period of time. Even when decisions are piecemeal, however, the need for individual participation is still important. Individuals may have strong sentiments about relatively minor pieces of a plan or project because they represent an opportunity to demonstrate their expertise and experience. Individuals become emotionally invested in the outcome of smaller decisions as well as the major ones.

Decision Sharing and Management Attitudes. When involving subordinates in decision making, the leader must make the decision-sharing role of participants absolutely clear. If the scope of the subordinates' decision power is not made clear, a number of negative consequences follow. An example illustrates this point.

◆

Some years ago, a committee was formed in one division of a large multinational company and was charged with defining the policies and procedures for making new product development groups more effective. They were led to believe that if they reached consensus on these proposals, their recommendations would be rubber-stamped by higher management. Members of this committee met diligently because they were vitally interested in increasing the flow of new product ideas. After four months of work, much of it on their own time, their recommendations were forwarded to top management. The committee members were proud of their achievements, and they assumed that their recommendations would become official policy.

Instead, they were rudely shocked to learn that top management had already adopted other recommendations which ruled out most of their suggestions. The other recommendations had not been communicated to the group because some upper executives felt the adopted recommendations were privileged information. To aggravate matters further, most of the remaining recommendations were dismissed out of hand with little additional study. Among the recommendations dismissed were two that the group felt to be crucial in importance, and which later proved to be so.

The consequences of this action were predictable. The committee felt that they had been abused by top management — that neither their ideas nor their dedication was appreciated. As the news of these events spread, other personnel were reluctant to participate in committees because they felt that their ideas would not be taken seriously and that these efforts would be a waste of time. Morale among the work groups plummeted, affecting many other employees. Cohesiveness in work groups and commitment to the company diminished as well. Several members of the committee quit their jobs or requested transfers to other divisions. For two years thereafter it was difficult to find managers or technical professionals who would participate in new product teams.

Such instances occur with alarming frequency in organizations. Sometimes miscommunication is caused by difficult-to-predict management changes. Often, miscommunication is inadvertent: a manager intends to involve subordinates, but does so after the fact. Other managers distrust any type of participative decision making, but go through the motions because of a directive from above. Subordinates perceive the real attitudes of these managers quickly and, after a few frustrating efforts, soon play along by going through the motions without genuine effort or involvement.

Some managers deliberately subvert the participative process by ignoring recommendations, shifting goals in the middle of the group's work, failing to give credit to the group for good ideas (which are often claimed as the manager's own), or simply neglecting to give feedback to the group on their recommendations. Any manager can easily sabotage the meeting process and thereby "prove" that participative management just doesn't work. The huge amount of personal and financial loss incurred by these methods is incalculable. When other clear options are available, such practices are fundamentally bad management.

New Groups — Old Groups

There is surprisingly little written in real business environments about the importance of the age of small groups. Yet we all know intuitively that how we manage or participate in a meeting differs greatly if the group is a staff group that has been meeting for one-to-two years with essentially the same members, an interdepartmental group of relative strangers who will meet perhaps three times on a short-term mission, or a new product team to be launched on a longer-term mission who will meet for 15 or 20 times during the year. Leadership strategies will differ for different types of groups with different histories. Obviously, managers and team leaders can and will make mistakes at any phase of a group's life, but few periods offer as many potential pitfalls as the day one charters a new long-term group. Many researchers would say that the relative effectiveness of the group is best predicted by what is said in the broad orientation to the mission of the new group.

Chartering a New Group

When a manager forms a new group or committee, he or she needs to orient the group by stating expectations and the extent to which the decision-making role can and will be shared with subordinates. The following four important statements need to be made, which will go a long way toward clarifying the decision-making expectations you have of the group.

Acknowledge That the Manager NEEDS the Group's Input. Some implicit assumptions need to be explicitly stated by the chairperson. Leaders need to tell the group that their expertise is recognized and necessary for optimal decision making to occur. Group members need to be assured that the group would not have been convened if the manager could have solved the problem alone and that they have expertise which is crucial for the best decision to be obtained.

State That No Decisions Have Been Made. Managers should acknowledge that, although they may have some biases with regard to the final decision, they have not made up their minds or taken any preemptory action, and they will attempt to be open and objective about recommendations. Managers should be careful about tipping their hand about a preferred solution because such comments will surely influence the thinking of other group members.

State That the Manager Will Ultimately Decide the Issue. Ultimate decision-making accountability is the inescapable consequence of decision accountability in business. Groups need to be reminded that the manager *might have to reject* some or all of the group's recommendations. It is important that the group know this up front so that they are not later disappointed if their suggestions are not heeded. Such rejection is the manager's responsibility and prerogative.

Promise to "Close the Loop." Managers should report back to the group what has been done with the group's recommendations. One of the most frequent complaints of business meeting participants is that they never know what happened to their recommendations. Subordinates should be given a brief rationale as to why some recommendations were adopted while others were postponed or abandoned. Not all members may agree with the ultimate action taken, but they at least will have the satisfaction of understanding the reasons behind the manager's decision.

Emphasize the Importance of Dissent. As was mentioned in the last chapter, dissent should not only be allowed, it should be encouraged. From the very start, the group must be instructed to think critically in order to make the best use of the meeting resource and time. State that you would like a consensus on the group's final recommendations, but in the process of obtaining those recommendations, you want ideas critically reviewed, assumptions examined, and objections raised to obtain the highest quality decision.

The Chairperson's Orientation Speech

The chairperson's orientation speech is the single most important act of the business meeting. This three- to five-minute speech at the onset of a meeting can work small miracles. Properly prepared, it can even salvage a poorly briefed or misdirected group. It is far more than mere "introductory comments." It is the foundation stone to the entire decision process. What is the orientation speech? It is a systematically prepared, fully rehearsed, sit-down speech of not less than three minutes nor more than five minutes (most problems require at least three minutes of orientation; anything over five minutes sets up a pattern of dominance and control by the chairperson). Although the speech should be delivered in a rapid and direct manner with a sense of urgency, its purpose and impact revolve more around the specific kind of substantive information the orientation speech contains. The goals of the speech are to accomplish four specific objectives and one overriding objective:

1 To fully orient the group on the *purposes and procedures* to be used

2 To provide a *comprehensive information* base upon which the group will build

3 To get rid of most, if not all, of the *unnecessary and extraneous discussion*

4 To obtain clear group agreement on how the group should proceed

The overriding goals of this speech are to *cut the meeting time in half and increase the probability of a better decision.*

Chairpersons should prepare their speech using the display in the *Meeting Notes,* on the next page, as a checklist. We'll review the steps of that display one by one.

Procedural Overview. State the general problem as clearly and briefly as possible. Indicate your general *objectives* for this specific meeting. For example, is the meeting called simply to list a number of current problems, or is it centered on one major problem? Do you hope to solve the problem in this one session, or is this session devoted primarily to defining and understanding the causes of the problem with later meetings to be devoted to finding solutions? Now that the participants know what kind of a meeting to expect, are they equally clear about the *procedures* you feel are appropriate? For example, do you intend to lead off with two three-minute reports from manufacturing and quality assurance, followed by an open-panel discussion of the rest of the agenda items? Do you want and expect everyone to contribute something on some agenda items? Do you intend to stick to a time schedule for each of the major agenda items — for instance, using the first hour for brainstorming, or the last half hour for making implementation assignments? If so, state the schedule specifically to the group.

Information Base. The objective here is to assemble and state the hard facts, the indisputable data, and the trends and evidence, which everyone should know as the information base for the entire discussion. These are the basic facts, what is known of the problem, which should occasion no debate whatsoever. This information base should address four specific subpoints as warranted:

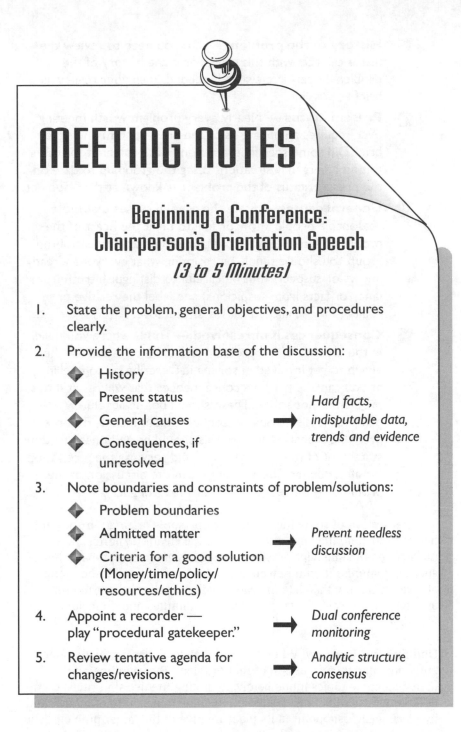

MEETING NOTES

Beginning a Conference:
Chairperson's Orientation Speech
(3 to 5 Minutes)

1. State the problem, general objectives, and procedures clearly.

2. Provide the information base of the discussion:
   - History
   - Present status
   - General causes   → *Hard facts, indisputable data, trends and evidence*
   - Consequences, if unresolved

3. Note boundaries and constraints of problem/solutions:
   - Problem boundaries
   - Admitted matter   → *Prevent needless discussion*
   - Criteria for a good solution (Money/time/policy/ resources/ethics)

4. Appoint a recorder — play "procedural gatekeeper."   → *Dual conference monitoring*

5. Review tentative agenda for changes/revisions.   → *Analytic structure consensus*

- ◢ **History of the problem** — Do you need to review the historical facts with this group, or is the history of the problem largely irrelevant? If needed, keep your review as brief as possible.

- ◢ **Present status** — Nearly every problem worth meeting over requires an update as to the present status, however brief. Did some specific event bring this problem to light? Is this an emergency situation? Bring the group up to date on the present status of the problem as known at that moment.

- ◢ **General causes** — State the general causes that most reasonable people know or feel to be at the heart of the problem. Don't be afraid of biasing the later analysis of the group. You should simply be restating what everyone already knows or suspects (but be careful to distinguish truth from fancy, or facts from suspicions) and label the relative probability of those alleged causes as tentative.

- ◢ **Consequences if unresolved** — This is where you build in the urgency of the problem and the motivation for the group to get involved in solving it. Describe, as compellingly as you can, the negative consequences that will result if this problem is not solved. These should be the absolutely predictable disastrous consequences, but include other less probable scenarios as well. This should be an honest, truthful statement of the case, which should serve as the motivation for all group members to engage in the discussion of the problem — the first step toward resolving it.

This section of subpoints of the chairperson's orientation speech is designed to state the facts of the case in the clearest, shortest, and most coherent statement possible. The chairperson can prepare this speech, compress it, and rehearse it well ahead of time. If the group is allowed to supply this data instead, it will take them about ten times as long to get it said. So save yourself ten minutes and do it right the first time.

Defining the Territory. When you rationalize a problem, you coherently organize the discussion of that problem. By excluding and including some topics immediately, by noting the decision rules, or criteria, which will allow discussion of some items and not others, and by placing each subpoint in its place relative to the larger problem, you clarify the discussion greatly. Remember, the chief objective of this phase of the discussion is to eliminate the part of the discussion that would naturally occur unless this step is taken. This step reduces the meeting to *one-half the time of a typical meeting.* It is vital that the chairperson do this in a concise, well-organized manner rather than allow the rest of the group to contribute these items. They can do so, but typically they will do it in a haphazard and very time-consuming manner. Each of the following subpoints should be covered as the situation warrants:

Problem boundaries — If this is basically a marketing problem, say so. Do not allow the group to even think about wandering into discussion problems of R & D or the responsibilities of manufacturing. Cut members of the group off *before* they go off on tangents or an irrelevant discussion. Any group or task force will wander needlessly into remote areas of the problem unless the boundaries of the discussion are firmly marked off. Some natural limits usually exist. Therefore, it is important to look for them and limit the discussion in some way, even if it is a matter of suggesting that some issues be discussed in this meeting while saving other issues for later meetings.

Admitted matter — Think of this subpoint in a limited sense as "paying what is due." In the development of any problem there is usually a set of facts, an historical interpretation, or a strategy strongly championed by some faction, which was ignored initially but later turned out to be right. Do not allow the group to resurrect these old battles. Admit the error ahead of time and give credit where it is due by citing their earlier wisdom. Then be equally firm in refusing any further discussion of the issue. Do not allow participants to waste valuable time by reworking a dead issue. Credit the issue honestly, for example: "I know all of us agree that if we had followed Ed's advice three years ago this division would not be in this crisis — and it really is too bad we did not. But that particular solution is not applicable today. It is water over the dam, and no amount of self-flagellation is going to solve the current problem. So let's not hear about what we should have done; let's concentrate on a new solution to this present crisis." If the chairperson does not make such a statement, Ed or one of his supporters will predictably take twenty minutes of the group's time to belabor the point that the group was wrong — and not be satisfied until everyone has admitted the mistake. Acknowledge the mistake early, and save twenty minutes of valuable discussion time.

■ **Criteria for a good solution** — The criteria, or standards, for a good solution are some of the primary decision rules of what gets included or excluded in most discussions. Few issues have no constraints whatsoever. Time, money, and resources are usually the major constraints; ethics and policy somewhat less so. Since we have thoroughly discussed these points in Chapter 3, we need only emphasize the aspect of timing here. Normally, this subpoint should only be mentioned briefly in a problem analysis discussion because it usually comes to center stage during the solution-finding phase. The exception to this is where a criterion, such as very short lead time, might be the single biggest factor in the decision. If so, it needs to be cited immediately; for example, " . . . we must remember that this defect must be corrected and the product shipped out the door in fourteen days, so any analysis or suggested solutions not based on that fact are irrelevant and a waste of time." Decide on the main criteria for a good decision and state them as firmly as the situation will allow. Above all, do not allow a group to waste thirty minutes discussing the causes of a problem or a specific solution which should have been ruled out by some standard or criteria during the first minutes of the discussion.

Appointing a Recorder. This is an important, although minor, step on your orientation checklist. This detail may be taken care of before the discussion, immediately at the beginning of the chairperson's speech (when the procedures to be followed are outlined), or at the last minute before the group plunges into the discussion. The group should be informed, however, of the presence of a recorder, and the group (and sometimes the recorder) should be oriented as to how he or she is expected to interact with the group. For example: *"The recorder is certainly expected to contribute his (her) point of view but is empowered mainly to check the group's progress on each point; to listen, to record, and to state the specific items we agree on pertaining to each major point of the agenda before moving on. If you disagree with his (her) interpretation or summary, straighten it out before we go on. Remember, he (she) will also be charged with writing up the meeting minutes, so make sure those summaries are stated just the way the group wants."* This kind of speech sets the stage for the dual monitoring of the conference procedure by both the chairperson and the recorder. It reminds the group of the importance of specific summaries for keeping the discussion on track.

Note: Ideally, the first three parts of the chairperson's orientation speech should not be interrupted. The specific parts should be so carefully composed that the major reaction of the group is a nodding of heads in assent or an occasional comment of agreement. The last two steps move out of the uninterrupted "speech" phase into a brief negotiation phase, where some comments from others are necessary.

Agenda Consensus. This is an important, but often neglected, step of the orientation speech. As we have already emphasized, any agenda distributed prior to the meeting should be labeled "tentative," in capital letters. At this subpoint, ask for changes to the tentative agenda — revisions, deletions, and additions to the first document. Although asking for changes is an important symbolic statement demonstrating an openness to participative methods, this is not the main reason for seeking them. The main reason for seeking changes is to gain a consensus from all members as to how the problem should be approached, structured, and analyzed. This is relatively easy to do at this early stage, before disagreements begin or discussion positions become polarized. The chairperson should elicit suggestions from all concerned participants and then democratically revise the agenda according to their wishes. After asking the group three times for additional changes, the chairperson should humorously, but firmly, warn the group that this schedule of agenda items is carved in stone and will henceforth be revised only as a result of extraordinary circumstances.

Although these measures are elaborate, they are designed to prevent one person or one faction from persuading the group that the agenda approach to the problem was wrong and that a different sequence of topics should be discussed, which would mean an additional thirty minutes of discussion. It is obviously worth spending from two to three minutes renegotiating the analytical structure for a consensus versus wasting thirty minutes or more by starting over with a revised approach. Take those few minutes to get the group's consensus on their itinerary, and then make them keep to their commitment.

At this point, hopefully, the chairperson has been speaking in a fluent, urgent manner for three to five minutes. In this short period, the group has been completely oriented. The purpose of the meeting, the procedure to be followed, the information base of the problem upon which to build the boundaries and constraints of the problem, and the structure by which the group will proceed in their deliberations have been stated. Because the group now sees the problem in its entirety, including the consequences if nothing is done, they are also better motivated to discuss the problem with some urgency. In a very brief period of time, the orientation speech has *programmed* the group to become an efficient problem-solving group. If group members have requisite expertise and have made some effort to prepare for the meeting, the group will be one of the best-managed and most productive of the countless meetings participants have attended.

In one major act you have launched a group that is well prepared to process information efficiently and have established yourself as the *person in command*: a precise, fluent, and direct speaker who is broadly informed in all aspects of the subject, including important decision-making procedures and protocols. For all of the above reasons we believe that *this is the single most important act of any business meeting*. But let's not forget the other important reason for this speech. By following the orientation speech checklist and judiciously speaking to each informational need, you are not only improving the decision-making capability of the group, but you will have saved a significant amount of time as well. The chairperson's orientation speech is the single most important step in supporting the claim that *most of the meeting time can be cut directly in half and the cost of that time allotted to more productive ventures.*

Additional Burden on the Chairperson

Undoubtedly, the more harried businessmen and businesswomen in our readership will point out that this procedure places an additional burden on the chairperson. Yet there is no way around this problem. The orientation responsibility has always been a part of the chairperson's task; however, in the past its importance has been overlooked by most researchers and ignored by most chairpersons. As a result, leaders of countless meetings have virtually foredoomed their groups to a series of frustrating, misdirected, and needlessly long meetings. Yes, it does take considerably more time for the chairperson to organize this speech — checking certain facts, causes, or company policy that may be relevant — and then to organize and *rehearse* this speech so that the large amount of diverse information can be absorbed by the rest of the group. The real question, however, pertains to quality: Do we have enough smarts to take the time to do it right the first time, or are we content to continue to take more time and resources to do it right in a second or third meeting? That is, if we have a second or third chance.

After a long period of observing and studying business and professional groups in action, we were compelled to significantly reposition these "little introductory comments" to a place of the very highest priority in meeting management. Our survey results, in addition to the experience of virtually every reader, confirms the state of relative ignorance with which most participants come to a meeting. But they are not to blame; it is not their fault. Generally, they are intelligent, expertly informed individuals who are motivated to contribute their expertise and perspective to help solve a problem. Who is to blame then? The chairperson and no one else. For this reason we have amplified and structured the subpoints of the orientation speech to meet the real information processing needs of most groups. We feel that we are not overstating the need in elevating these "introductory comments" to a new and absolutely vital orientation process. If there is one single insight to be gained from this book, it would be this: *Understand and use the chairperson's orientation speech to improve your meeting effectiveness.*

8 GENERAL LEADERSHIP FUNCTIONS

Leadership Responsibilities

An effective leader must be tuned in to many different aspects of the discussion. These range from recognizing emerging interpersonal difficulties between two members to catching major topic jumps to monitoring the critical thinking of the group. With experience, the average manager learns to listen at several levels and learns when to take remedial action. In the meantime, leaders can fulfill several basic functions to facilitate group interaction and develop that sixth sense and third ear. Howell and Smith (1956) were two of the first in this field to emphasize these basic functions:

Build a Permissive Climate. Managers will not generate valuable input from their groups when fear dominates the organizational climate. Managers with comparatively higher status who interrupt, dominate, or signal subordinates nonverbally that their contributions are not acceptable, defeat the whole purpose of the meeting. To encourage an open,

BUILD A PERMISSIVE CLIMATE

objective flow of ideas, it is not enough that the manager refrain from intimidation tactics. *Building a permissive climate requires that the manager specifically make positive, reinforcing statements about participant ideas.* It also means setting a personal example by accepting criticism of one's own ideas without reacting negatively and by listening instead of speaking most of the time.

AGENDA = ROAD MAP TO GOALS

FOLLOW A PLAN

Follow a Plan. It is important to have an agenda with which everyone concurs as a starting point. However, the group also needs to follow that agenda and to use some systematic method to review their accomplishments at the end of their meeting. A plan of virtually any kind provides a real measure of psychological comfort for groups. Making the agenda and meeting format understood by all is vital in disciplining the usually chaotic information processing of groups. If the agenda is not printed, display it on a board or on a visual aid. If members are unclear about the format being used or their responsibilities, orient them quickly and precisely at the beginning — then stick to that format.

GIVE OR GET ACCURATE SUMMARIES

"LET'S DISCUSS THE NEXT POINT."

"Before we go on to the second point, let's review what we have agreed upon concerning the first point."

DECISION

"UNSTATED ASSUMPTIONS LEAD TO BAD DECISIONS"

Give or Get Accurate Summaries. A group must receive clear summaries of all the major subpoints of the agenda as the conference progresses. It does not matter if the chairperson elicits these summaries or if another group member volunteers the internal summaries. What does matter is that the summaries be systematically stated, debated, and restated until all participants are in agreement before moving on to the next subpoint. This deliberate procedure is absolutely essential in "tracking the discussion," thus preventing needless duplication of effort or the loss of good ideas.

Give or Get Clarification of Vague Statements. Ambiguity may be a mainstay of high-level diplomatic negotiation, but it has little place in the average business discussion. Few things can stop progress in a meeting faster than a vague or ambiguous statement. Typically, members will interpret the statement in terms of their own experience, which leads, in turn, to endless disagreements of "what was meant" and needless backtracking to straighten out the intention. A simple request for clarification, if not forthcoming from members, should be supplied by the chairperson: "Wait a minute, Jim, I'm not clear what you mean by 'decision simulation.' Could you give us an example of what this might mean for our department?" If answers still remain vague, persist until the intended meaning is clear.

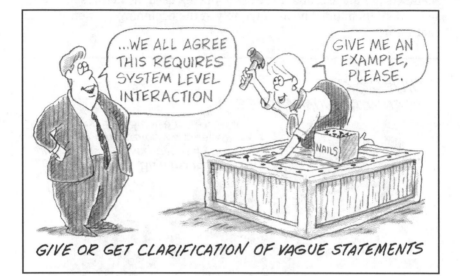

GIVE OR GET CLARIFICATION OF VAGUE STATEMENTS

Promote Evaluation of All Generalizations. It is surprising how often unsupported generalizations occur in meetings. Many of us will uncritically mention a so-called "basic axiom" which we feel to be indisputable but turns out on later examination to be nothing but a long-cherished personal belief with no basis in fact. Our ears should prick up when someone says "all of us know" or "it is an uncontested fact that" or "it's common sense." The problem is that many of these unsupported and often irrational generalizations become accepted building blocks for a larger decision which may as a result become a major disaster. The chairperson should promote evaluation of all generalizations by saying such things as, "Could we just examine that generalization for a second, Bob? Does anyone have any evidence that qualifies or contradicts Bob's statement that men are generally superior to women in mathematical and computational skills?"

Protect Minority Opinion. There is nothing inherently sacred about majority opinion. In a group, minority opinion often proves to be more sound, valuable, and correct than the majority opinion. The chairper-

PROMOTE EVALUATION OF ALL GENERALIZATIONS

son (and other participants as well) must accept the maxim: "I disapprove of what you say, but I will defend to the death your right to say it" (attributed to Voltaire). This maxim relates directly to the point made earlier on the importance of negative or critical information to management decision making. Protecting minority opinion is easy when one sees four group members assailing the statements of another member whom you know to be right; it is far more difficult when you, the chairperson, also thinks the dissenter to be misguided.

PROTECT MINORITY OPINION

It is in exactly these situations that the chairperson must work harder than ever to make sure that the minority viewpoint has a fair hearing.

Minimize Extrinsic Conflict. *Extrinsic conflict* refers to conflict between members over issues that have nothing to do with the subject at hand. Some members will use any meeting to relive a debate with another member which took place five years ago. Part of the motivation to attend certain meetings is "to keep that other guy honest." As a result, all sorts of extraneous information and red herrings get thrown into the information process. People get involved emotionally, and the productivity of the group declines sharply. Leaders must immediately step in and separate combatants who are taking up the group's time by speaking on irrelevant issues or personal agendas. On the other hand, genuine subject-related conflicts must clearly be encouraged if a group is to produce conclusions that are thoroughly weighed, debated, and examined by all group members. The conflict that emerges from this process is one that is healthy and desirable.

Perform Only Necessary Functions. This last point is a reminder that the best leaders are often the ones who function effectively without calling attention to their role. There is an inevitable tendency for chairpersons to dominate the discussion through substantive contributions and a defense of their views. A chairperson has enough to do in monitoring and controlling the information flow of a meeting to obtain the best decision without overpowering the group by taking on additional unnecessary functions.

PERFORM ONLY NECESSARY FUNCTIONS

Bringing the Group to Consensus

Consensus, the unanimous agreement of all members, is both a process and an outcome of group interaction which is widely assumed to be one of the highest goals. It is so highly desired because it is thought to result in better decisions and more participant satisfaction, as well as greater group unity and member commitment. It is a technique that has received greater emphasis recently as the corporate decision-making processes of the United States and Japan are compared, and as employee participation becomes an increasingly important element of those decision processes.

Although deemed universally important, this technique has its disadvantages: it is time consuming and often difficult to achieve in practice. The fact that consensus is often an elusive goal to groups should come as no surprise when one considers the many little facets of potential disagreement on different issues which various individuals bring to a conference table. When one speaks of consensus, in fact, one really means an agreement on the major elements of a decision, not the many specifics. Moreover, there is a necessary distinction that should be made between *apparent* consensus and *real* consensus. All of us have at one time or another been party to decisions that were labeled by the chairperson as being a "consensus of the group," but which were anything but that. The continuum of consensus ranges from the fully committed individual who takes real job risks on a position, from which there is no turning back, to individuals who are only marginally interested and have no real stake in the decision. There are managers who parade themselves as consensus builders but who revert to dictatorial form when the really difficult issues arise. Developing consensus on complex, intractable issues, however, requires special skills and patience. On some issues, consensus may not be an appropriate group goal:

◆

The major drawback of seeking consensus is that it tends to consume a lot of time. For important policy issues central to the group's work, time spent seeking consensus may be a sound investment. On minor issues, consensus may consume more time than appropriate, and when there are emergencies the group may have to act so quickly that seeking consensus is not possible. A second potential weakness of consensus is that it can result in uninspired decisions because they have been so watered down by the compromises necessary to secure unanimous agreement (Wood, Phillips & Pedersen 1986, 47).

Clearly, the strategy of gaining consensus is not a strategy for all seasons. Managers should not necessarily equate their managerial leadership abilities with the number of consensus decisions they have facilitated in their work groups each month. On certain decisions, however, there should be an attempt to gain real consensus on the issue. There are many advantages for doing so. Participants who feel they have personally contributed to the decision are likely to have a greater ownership in the outcome or implementation. They are more likely to have greater feelings of group unity and may be more committed to carrying out the decision.

The consensus process does not always result in a better quality decision, however. Hirokawa states that "clearly, it is a fallacy to assume that consensus decision making always results in better decisions." He cites two studies which demonstrate that groups can *unanimously agree on a completely incorrect solution to a problem*. His own experimental study of this process showed that groups which did not employ some systematic and rational method of decision making did not produce high-quality decisions. Only groups which used a decision-making strategy that allowed them to approach their task systematically and rationally showed a high correlation between the extent of their agreement (consensus) and the quality of the decision.

In addition, Hirokawa did not find any systematic relationship between consensus decision making and decision satisfaction. He reasoned that individual decision satisfaction may depend on the member's "perception of the correctness of the decision or upon the member's perception of the extent of his/her influence on the group's decision" (Hirokawa 1982, 413).

Despite the questions raised by controlled research, group consensus remains a highly desired goal for important discussions. Yet, specific guidelines for getting there are another matter. Specific instructions to help groups arrive at consensus take various forms, such as "Avoid arguing for your own individual judgments" or "Avoid changing your mind only to reach an agreement and avoid conflict." While these instructions are undoubtedly useful, the primary need is for a rational, systematic method that forces a group to explore the issues thoroughly before coming to a decision. There are several analytical methods listed in Appendix A which will suffice. They are step-by-step methods which call for fair, rational group judgments on subpoints or alternative solutions and which systematically inspect the pros and cons of each option. Hirokawa's method, which he terms "vigilant" decision making, is a four-step method used by a group in choosing among fifteen decision options:

1 Before ranking any of the fifteen items under consideration, participants are asked to discuss the value of each item carefully and thoroughly in terms of the overall goal of the group.

2 Participants are then asked to rank the five most and the five least important items.

3 Participants are then asked to go back and discuss the value of the five remaining items and rank them.

4 Finally, before submitting the group's ranking of the fifteen items, participants were asked to go back and systematically reconsider the rank assigned to each of the fifteen items with admonitions to not hesitate to change the rank after that final discussion, if warranted (Hirokawa 1982, 411).

The use of virtually any systematic and logical method goes far in developing real, broadly felt consensus. It should be said, finally, that consensus building should not be rushed. For example, in typical situations such as hiring new employees, some of the worst consensus decisions we have encountered stem from imposing unreasonable time limits on discussing the comparative potential and abilities of applicants. True consensus building takes time. This the Japanese know as a cultural instinct. To do otherwise is to develop a paper consensus and to confuse a process for a quality solution.

When and How to Conclude

Many business meetings drag on seemingly forever and only end informally, after several individuals have already excused themselves. Other meetings end on time, or seem to run out of time, as a decision — without consensus — is quickly made and seemingly forced upon the group. Both of these meeting scenarios can be avoided if you use the following guidelines.

Leave Enough Time to Conclude. Leave enough time to briefly review what has been accomplished, to answer questions, and to outline what expectations remain. In a one-hour meeting this can usually be done in five to seven minutes.

Repeat Items of Consensus. A good meeting is wasted if everyone leaves with different opinions as to what was decided and who is to do what by when. Specifically number the actions to be taken, have them written down by the recorder, and distribute copies of the assignments to all participants as a follow-up to the meeting.

Conclude on Time. It is to your credit as an efficient chairperson, and it is respectful of other group members, to conclude on time. If you don't, participants may be forced to leave awkwardly and may come to dread or even to avoid attending future meetings that you hold. If you make it a habit of ending on time, you'll find that your efficiency will increase and all agenda items will tend to get completed by the time the meeting is scheduled to end. Scheduling meetings just prior to lunch or at the end of the day forces *all* participants to make a stronger effort to finish on time.

Feedback Mechanisms and Evaluation

Any activity needs feedback to ensure proper functioning. As new behaviors are tried, specific feedback about the meeting activity should be sought. Group members should be told that ways to improve meeting procedures are being tried; then at the end of the meeting they should be asked for specific comments and suggestions. Since people are often suspicious when they encounter new behavior from those with whom they've already worked, be patient. Allow the new techniques time to take hold and have an impact. It takes an extended period to get the most out of new techniques and develop positive habits in the process.

Formal feedback can be obtained by distributing a survey at the end of the meeting, if appropriate. You can also specifically ask another person, such as your manager, to attend one or more of your meetings strictly as an observer. Later, have the individual relate his or her observations, as well as suggestions for potential improvements you could make.

You may wish to use a feedback method similar to the one used by the office administrative system of 3M Company. They were concerned with raising the general consciousness of all meeting groups about the cost of quality of meetings, so they devised a concise two-minute evaluation form to be used after each meeting (see form in Appendix B). This form allowed all groups and departments to systematically monitor both the procedural efficiency as well as the general task quality of their small-group meetings. These forms were used for several purposes: to locate or identify weaker meeting groups; to diagnose persistent meeting problems, which all types of groups seem to share; and to chart improvement of groups over time. The immediate feedback enabled some chairpersons to make immediate changes in leadership behavior. The quantification of broader data from several groups allowed management to prescribe more appropriate remedial training or other actions. According to Artie Lewis, a quality manager of this project, the selective use of these forms by different groups significantly improved the use of time, which improved the perceived quality of problem analysis and decision making. At the very least, all groups became very cost conscious of the high price of the time spent together. One additional unexpected benefit emerged from this feedback system. Participants became less dependent on the chairperson for making the meeting successful. They came to recognize their own responsibilities in this process and initiated more actions to make that happen.

Summary

In this chapter, we defined the purpose of most business meetings and examined some of the myths and realities of the leadership role. We found that certain attitudes about leader knowledge, such as not sharing leadership and not allowing dissent, could seriously jeopardize the effectiveness of the meeting. We saw that the best leader/manager is one who holds and practices three beliefs: that his expertise is but one part of the decision puzzle; that sharing leadership acts facilitates a more open, productive meeting; and that dissent or negative information should be positively encouraged, not discouraged.

We next discussed the importance for both meeting managers and participants to embrace contemporary attitudes toward the place of individual effort, competition, and group cooperation. We also discussed ways in which managers could manage the transitional period as organizations shifted from hierarchical to horizontal work environments. We explored the needs of individuals to participate in decisions that affect their lives and concluded that the business meeting was an ideal forum and opportunity to practice participative management. We found it was most important for the leader/manager to be absolutely clear about the limits of power sharing with his or her subordinates. Even though managers may be solely responsible for decisions, there are numerous ways by which subordinates can be given actual or psychological participation in the decision.

We next reviewed the concept of the chairperson's *orientation speech*, its general objectives and specific subpoints expressly designed to meet the major informational and motivational questions of group participants. This concept was highlighted as the single most important act of the typical business meeting. This leadership act was felt to be the most important process by which meeting time could be cut in half and still increase the probability of a much better decision.

Finally, the eight major responsibilities which are traditionally felt to be specific leadership functions were examined. We found that leadership of business meetings is most effective when it builds a permissive climate, follows a plan, obtains accurate summaries, clarifies vague statements and evaluates all generalizations, protects minority opinion, and minimizes extrinsic conflict but encourages dissent — all while performing only necessary functions. We concluded by discussing the special problems of bringing a group to a consensus, and by reviewing some of the very necessary mechanics of concluding.

Throughout this chapter we have emphasized that leadership acts are not restricted to leaders; they are acts contributed by anyone which facilitate the success of the group. We also feel, however, that meeting success is best guaranteed by a strong, well-prepared chairperson. Effective manager/leaders are those individuals who recognize the central importance of their position and go the extra mile to prepare for and manage meetings effectively. Such managers have taken the time to do it right the first time.

Everyone Plays a Part
The Participant's Role
in Business Meetings

Business meetings today have come to rely increasingly upon a wide range of skills of group members. In this chapter, we will discuss the leadership functions that group members need to perform, appropriate attitudes for collaborative team work, the preparation that participants need for business meetings, and additional meeting responsibilities every attendee should fulfill. In addition, we will discuss how participants can influence the group effectively and how they can manage conflict as it arises.

Each Member as Leader

As we mentioned in Chapter 6, in the most effective business meetings the leadership responsibilities are dispersed. This is only possible if participants take the initiative to assert leadership acts when those acts are needed. Given the chaotic informational dynamics of the meeting, it is everyone's responsibility to resist topic jumping and insist upon clear conclusions for each subpoint before proceeding. Group members need to follow the agenda and either supply or ask for internal summaries. In addition, group members need to share the critical thinking responsibility in the meeting. They should know how evidence is weighed and measured, how causal analysis may be tested, and how statistics and percentages can be distorted. Participants who take the initiative will not only improve the effectiveness of the meeting, they will also gain personal status, influence, and credibility with the group as they learn to practice leadership behaviors.

Participant Preparation

To make the most of their involvement in a meeting, participants need to prepare adequately. At the very least, they need to know what is expected of them for the specific topics being discussed. If you, as a participant, have not received an advance agenda when notified of a meeting, call the chairperson to obtain a better idea about what the meeting issues are and what will be expected of you. Participants should go even further in their preparation by conducting additional research into problems that will be discussed so that they come to the meeting prepared to offer stimulating, well-grounded views. In addition, participants may attempt to presell their ideas to other group members or to those individuals who will be involved in the final outcome of the group's efforts.

As a participant, avoid the passive role of one who attends meetings primarily to observe and to listen and not to actively participate. Typically, no advance preparation is done by passive participants unless they have a formal presentation to deliver at the meeting. The passive individual goes to listen and, occasionally, to add a comment or two, having no real commitment to the process or the final outcome of the meeting. If you don't play an active role in the group's discussion, you will most likely be perceived as being ineffective by other group members.

Participant Responsibilities

Participant Attitudes — Synchronic and Diachronic.[1] Committing to playing an active vs. a passive role in group deliberations is an essential first step. However, how you play that role is crucial since it often reflects fundamental attitudes about how you view yourself and your relationship with the group. Just as leaders must reexamine their myths and attitudes about leadership, participants must also uncover the deep structured attitudes they may have about these issues. Here we are saying something more than "be less aggressive and competitive, be more democratic, and be complementary in sharing talk time within the meeting." Until these fundamental attitudes are unpacked, each participant will have difficulty engaging in authentic cooperative interaction.

---

[1] These ideas are an elaboration of concepts first suggested by Lee Thayer.

At risk of some oversimplification, much of the talk that takes place in meetings of all kinds can be categorized as either synchronic or diachronic communication. *Synchronic* communication refers to communication that reflects an underlying attitude that is primarily self-focused, based on the general assumption of the general superiority of one's own point of view on a subject. The attitude is captured in the following statement from an engineer in a large American defense industry.

> I recognize that I must listen courteously to the contributions of others, give all parties roughly equal time, even credit a good idea on occasion. However, to be honest, in most meetings, my basic personal goal is to synchronize their imperfect, incomplete view of the problem, with my more logical, comprehensive realistic version of the issue. Am I saying that my view is 100% perfect? No, but it is usually far superior to that of anyone else's in our group. In the process, I must necessarily instruct, modify, and correct their mistaken perceptions, information, analysis, and general confusion. This is the best way I can help this group be successful.

Sounds like a group of pretty arrogant assumptions, doesn't it? Unfortunately this is probably a fair reading of the real beliefs of over 60% of participants in business meetings. Countless individuals who do not consider themselves elitist and who strive to use democratic methods, nonetheless, may find this basic attitude informing much of their behavior in groups. Much of it stems from the individualistic, competitive drives discussed earlier. These "synchronizers" have a compulsion to win the argument "and do it my way" because they know, without reservation, that their way is the best way for the group. And of course, this attitude is particularly true of very bright high achievers. Much of their interpretation of their success has been "always being right" — every day on every issue. They do not see themselves as ego-driven authoritarians; rather they think of themselves as leaders, teachers, guides, and mentors to the group. One of their favorite expressions is, "Let me help you with that." Our experience is that these "synchronizers" do not represent just a small percentage of meeting participants. This same mental set tends to operate with many of us who may have conveniently forgotten our "few" imperfect analyses of the past.

Conversely, there is a world of difference between the attitude of the participant with a synchronic view and that of the one with a diachronic view. *"Diachronic"* derives from the word "dialogue," which is suggestive of the way this person views any meeting exchange: as a genuine transaction of ideas that will mutually influence a group, not an individual, outcome. Going into the meeting, he or she assumes an attitude typified by this statement from a human resource manager in a large health organization.

> *I know I bring a lot of well-researched information and several years of management experience to this meeting, but I also know that my knowledge is incomplete, perhaps incorrect in some aspects, and above all but one part of the total information and analysis we will need to solve the problem. I intend to listen closely to others and resist overidentifying with my own interpretations. I know that the final decision will be some kind of a shared outcome reflecting many voices. Hopefully, the final decision might reflect some portion of my thinking, but that is hardly as important as the goal that it embody the best thinking of the whole group from whatever source.*

Sounds pretty idealistic, doesn't it? Especially in the rough and tumble of real business discussions. Perhaps, but the essential point is this: given the way teamwork is accomplished via the integration of specialized information of each team member, isn't this the most logical attitude to adopt going into the meeting? Excepting that small percentage who have credentials of god-like omniscience on all issues, isn't it bizarre for most of us to hold any other attitude than a diachronic view?

In simplest terms if I really believe, "I know it all," that my analysis really is superior to that of anyone else's in the group, I will tend to enact that role: by talking excessively as would any teacher who must explain and correct misguided pupils, by listening superficially and being less open to views of ideas, and sometimes by being unwittingly patronizing or dismissive of others. If I view the group discussion as just another competitive game or as a forum solely reserved for demonstrating individual influence, I can never develop a real understanding of the underlying dynamics or power of collaborative group work. Group synergy, group growth, and group insight are meaningless concepts to such an individual.

This generic attitude is more insidious than, say, acting in a stubborn or undemocratic manner. It goes to the heart of interpersonal respect. If, going into a discussion, I have no respect for the potential of the ideas of others to effect a change in my current position, I disrespect the most essential aspect of others — their thinking and ideas. Consequently, I limit the ability of the rest of the group to grow into a cohesive, productive unit. As importantly, I personally can never know the reward of genuine integrating, collaborative group work. For some of us, it may be time for an attitude check.

7 BASIC PARTICIPANT FUNCTIONS

Participants have certain responsibilities which contribute to the successful outcome of group interaction. Many of these duties are directed at helping participants clarify the ongoing information processing "mess" that occurs within meetings. Any participant can bring a good discussion to a dead halt through inadvertence or through deliberate sabotage (more on that later). The first three responsibilities relate to the need for clarity.

RESEARCH IS CONTINUING ON... OF COURSE, OUR MARGIN IS NOT WHAT IT WAS... BUT IN ALL DUE RESPECT... WELL, ANYWAY...

ORGANIZE YOUR CONTRIBUTIONS

Organize Your Contributions. Think before you speak. In an active discussion one needs to be mentally alert to keep up and add insightful contributions. The natural information chaos places a premium on clear thoughts stated crisply and unambiguously. In some cases, when you need to accurately present a complex proposal, you may wish to organize and actually rehearse the delivery of your statement some time before the meeting. Organize your thoughts by jotting notes or mentally structuring an extemporaneous contribution. (See impact formula later in this chapter.)

Speak When Your Contribution Is Relevant. This is more difficult than it sounds since contributions tend to queue up amidst much topic shifting. If you feel that you have a contribution that was passed over, interject it but with a signpost recognizing the interruption, e.g., "I know this may not be the right time to raise this topic, but sometime this hour, I hope we will discuss what many experts think is the real cause of the problem. . . ."

SPEAK WHEN YOUR CONTRIBUTION IS RELEVANT

Make One Point at a Time. Present one coherent thought at a time. Avoid giving multiple reactions to someone else's comment. Avoid making double- or triple-headed contributions, questions, or comments, which only serve to invite other group members to take off in as many different directions as you initiated. Both the unclear statement and the overloaded contribution function much like an information fragmentation grenade thrown on the meeting table. After the smoke of misinterpretation and alternative interpretations clear, you realize that you have been responsible for initiating ten minutes of needless discourse. When you do need to make several points, enumerate them for clarification and separation of thoughts.

Speak Clearly and Forcefully. Do not ramble or mumble, speak directly to the point. Your contribution should be easily heard and comprehended by others without straining. Sheer volume is an important element in getting one's ideas heard, though one should take pains that it is not overly loud and intimidating. Rightly or wrongly we tend to associate reliable information with assertive, confident voice work. Most participants are apt to command more attention in a group if they speak more loudly than they usually do.

Support Your Ideas with Valid Evidence. Beware of making vague statements or alluding to evidence which does not clearly apply to the topic under consideration. Make assertions with specific facts or research data. In some cases, it may be necessary to reference the credibility of the authorities you quote or to justify the relative superiority of one piece of evidence over another. The goal is not to become a logical nitpicker, but to know how to answer the question, "What is the best evidence to support this position?" Far too many discussions founder when a critical point is accepted based upon a nonrepresentative example or upon the testimony of a so-called expert whose credentials should have been challenged.

SUPPORT IDEAS WITH EVIDENCE

Listen Actively to All Aspects of the Discussion. Studies indicate that poor listeners tend to "tune out" on points of a discussion that do not interest them, as well as on extraneous signals that reinforce or discredit what is said. Keep alert to the entire discussion and reactions from other participants even if they do not initially appear to be pertinent. Active listening is hard work, but the listeners who stay in touch with the whole discussion tend to have a more complete and accurate grasp of what happened in the meeting.

Monitor Your Own Nonverbal Signals. Recognize that one negative facial expression can speak volumes to other group members about your distaste for, or dispute of, another person's remarks. Attempt to project a generally positive facial response and body position as much as possible. Lean forward and focus your eye contact on the speaker, avoiding signals that you are not interested in the conversation, such as yawning or doodling.

LISTEN TO WHOLE DISCUSSION

Don't Tune In and Tune Out

THAT'S NOT HIS AREA!

MONITOR YOUR NONVERBAL SIGNALS

THAT'S A VERY INTERESTING SUGGESTION

Especially *MIXED* messages

How to Influence Groups Effectively

Although there are some individuals who are content to play a listener-follower role in business meetings, they tend to be the exception. Most of us wish to be influential in a group's deliberations. As we have discussed in Chapters 1 and 2, we want to have impact on group decisions for many reasons. For instance, an individual may be sincerely committed to a specific idea or plan because he or she believes it to be the best solution to a problem. Often, managers seek to influence the course of a decision because they want the best decision for the company. They will argue their point zealously, but then defer to others when they recognize a better decision emerging. Many participants see influence in the meeting as a step toward receiving wider recognition by top management and thus advancement in the organization. Some individuals wish to get their ideas accepted at any cost simply as an ego-boost. Whatever the motivation, obtaining influence is an important skill in the group decision-making process.

Influence in groups is compounded by several situational factors. The status an individual possesses, the degree of trust or distrust between group members, and the amount of information or expertise available in the group may all take precedence in influencing the outcome of a business meeting. However, there are several critical variables in influencing a group that are under the direct control of every participant. These variables include the timing, frequency, and length of contributions; the speed, fluency, and forcefulness of the speaker; and the structure, relation, and support of contributions.

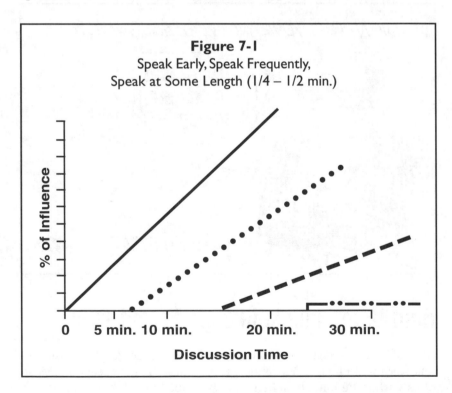

Figure 7-1
Speak Early, Speak Frequently,
Speak at Some Length (1/4 – 1/2 min.)

Contribute Early, Frequently, and at Length. It is important that group members contribute their ideas early and often in the discussion. Our research indicates that when an individual gets into the discussion in the first five minutes, that person is more likely to have greater influence throughout the discussion. When group members wait for fifteen or twenty minutes before making their first contribution, they have much less influence (approximately half as much as the early speaker). If members wait to speak until the middle of the meeting, their contributions are usually ignored and they have virtually no influence on the group's decision. Make an effort to contribute early in the discussion — even if it is only to ask a question or clarify a comment — to show that you are an active part of what is being said.

Participants must speak frequently in order to have continued influence in the group. The influence of participants in a group is determined chiefly by the number of times they speak. This statement seemingly fails to recognize the part that quality of contributions play. The sheer quantity of contributions does have an impact when one analyzes how ideas are accepted by groups. It is our experience that the range of abilities of meeting participants does not usually vary greatly. Most of the companies and government agencies with which we have been associated hire some of the best minds available. It is assumed that all individuals who are invited to a meeting have something worth while to contribute — or they wouldn't be asked to attend the meeting in the first place. Since there is a relative scarcity of available speaking time in any meeting, and all contributions have potential merit, the competitiveness of the situation makes the number of contributions a disproportionately influential factor in the business meeting.

The influence of contribution frequency was analyzed years ago, and a simple formula to measure and compare an individual's influence upon a group was developed.

$$\text{Individual Index of Influence} = \frac{\text{Number of recommendations accepted by the groups}}{\text{Number of recommendations attempted by the individual}}$$

If a person makes ten recommendations, five of which are accepted by the group, that person would have Index of Influence of 0.5 (Goldhamer and Shils 1939, 171–182).

Besides speaking more often, group members should attempt to make relatively lengthy contributions (thirty seconds or more) when they do speak. Brief comments such as "good idea" or "yes, an important point" or "I don't know" do relatively little when one seeks to establish influence — and can even diminish a person's influence in the group.

It is important that you contribute pertinent ideas whenever possible. Do not feel obligated, however, to respond to every point made or to constantly control the discussion. Although one needs to participate to have influence in the group, too much participation will preclude the contributions of other members and thus hinder the group's effectiveness. Assist the leader by allowing and encouraging each participant to contribute.

Speak Fast, Fluently, and Forcefully. As mentioned earlier, every participant must speak clearly and loudly to be heard and understood. To be influential, group members should also speak fairly rapidly, with a sense of urgency; fluently, with smooth articulation; and forcefully, with appropriate conviction. You can incorporate these characteristics into your speaking style largely by becoming more familiar with the material you wish to convey. Consider the half-minute contribution as a "minispeech," If the presentation of certain materials is critical to gaining group acceptance, these minispeeches should be *rehearsed* in whole or part before the discussion.

The speed of one's speech conveys a sense of urgency and reflects the enthusiasm one has for what is being said. Generally, one is able to speak faster simply by practicing to speak faster. Remember, research indicates that individuals can assimilate information four to five times faster than the average conversational rate of speech. Speaking too slowly and deliberately simply invites wool gathering. A former division director at Unisys stated it this way, "Speak faster, I can't follow you." Speaking faster not only helps to hold the attention of the group, but it makes communication in the meeting more efficient as well.

It is important to develop fluent speaking skills as well. Becoming tongue-tied when presenting a key idea is damaging to a person's image and impact. Most managers and technical professionals have adequate one-to-one speaking skills, but they are untrained in the give-and-take of group discussion. Perhaps the major error is cognitive, not verbal. Some individuals lack command of the entire thought-sequence they wish to convey; they introduce an idea in a haphazard fashion and then get tangled up in words attempting to explain what they meant.

Speakers should be as forceful in their speaking style as is appropriate. Most of us perceive a connection between forceful delivery and the urgency and importance of an idea. When a person feels strongly about a subject, forceful speaking tends to occur naturally, since volume usually correlates with the speaker's degree of conviction in the idea being expressed. Conversely, we tend to dismiss ideas that are presented in a half-hearted, slow, and unenthusiastic manner. Presenting ideas in a low-key, pause-filled casual delivery, which trails off into ambiguities, simply invites another participant to intervene with a more coherent comment. Individuals whose typical delivery is marred by hesitancy of a stop-and-start pattern of delivery should enlist special training to overcome those problems.

State, Relate, Support, and Integrate Your Contributions. Speakers with low influence seldom structure their contributions, relate them to the on-going group conversation, or support their points very well. The influential discussant uses some means of systematically structuring and relating comments in a discussion to protect the coherence of her contribution. She wishes that the complete thought survives intact and knows that there is a high probability that her utterance will be interrupted and diffused by well-meaning but unpredictable extensions from others. A four-point technique, widely used by debaters, is effective in forcing a group to pay attention to one's contributions. The technique involves the steps of stating, relating, supporting, and integrating.

The Impact Formula

1 *State* the idea you wish the group to consider. "I'm not sure we should adopt that conclusion so quickly."

2 *Relate* the significance of the idea to the previous statement. "A recent *Fortune* survey seems to directly contradict what was just said about the values of American businessmen. . . ."

3 *Support* the idea with adequate evidence. "There are three key findings which stand out in this poll of top American business executives. . . ." (Cite the three pieces of evidence and the conclusion inferred from this evidence.)

4 *Integrate* the comment into the discussion by asking the group to respond to the statement.

"Those conclusions seem based upon an excellent piece of research, and they tend to directly contradict some of the other research we have discussed. At the very least it seems to qualify our previous conclusions a good deal. Do you all agree with that statement?"

This simple system for presenting the significance and consequences of ideas to the group makes it easy for the group to efficiently assimilate your contributions. After making a related, coherent, well-supported statement, do not allow it to be ignored. In this integration phase, be proactive: ask the group what they think of this statement; how it supports or changes the previous analysis; or whether all of them agree with it. If you are not proactive, the full impact of your point will be diminished as the group quickly turns to someone else's idea.

How to Manage Conflict

Effective meetings have participants who know how to deal with conflict. When feasible, they deal with conflict openly, avoiding polarization of positions. They make sure goals are clearly defined and understood, and they have a fallback plan in case the conflict is not resolved. Some issues are selectively handled one-on-one to avoid conflict in the group setting.

Conflict Is Natural and Healthy

Conflict is usually a natural, normal aspect of group decision making. Therefore, group members should not attempt to "sweep conflicts under the rug" by pretending conflict doesn't exist or hoping it will disappear if ignored. Conflict avoidance is an unhealthy strategy and usually makes group members dissatisfied. Their rational, critical thinking abilities diminish because of increased anger or frustration with other people and ideas. Overall satisfaction and decision quality are likely to decrease as well.

Do not retreat from a tension-filled situation. When your ideas are challenged or criticized, do not withdraw under pressure. Reasonable amounts of conflict are a sign of a healthy group whose members may simply have different interpretations of the same information. View conflict more positively, and it will be easier to deal with openly.

Avoid Polarization

Try to avoid early polarization in group meetings. It is very easy for group members to state incompatible positions and then be inflexible in changing those positions. Instead, attempt to establish the criteria for a decision *before* getting into areas of potential conflict. Keeping the criteria foremost helps to minimize conflict over positions and thus makes final decision making easier to obtain.

Clarify Goals

Conflict involves two or more people who perceive their goals to be incompatible. They may, for example, be competing for limited resources and see each other as obstacles in reaching their goals. These perceptions may not be accurate, and, when clarified, the degree of conflict will diminish, if not completely disappear. Hence, a first step in conflict management is to understand the goals others have, as well as to clarify your own goals and how strongly you feel about them. For example, one manager might like to have three additional staff members but realizes one will suffice; that may be a better goal than incurring the comptroller's wrath and objections concerning three additional salaries.

To avoid such complications, follow these guidelines in clarifying goals:

1 Phrase goals clearly and simply, giving a brief rationale and statement of importance for each.

2 Look for commonalities in goals which may at first seem incompatible.

3 Phrase group goals in "do-able" terms; you can then later check to see if they're being achieved.

4 Identify goals which actually are incompatible.

Sometimes, clarifying goals indicates that individuals or groups are simply pursuing outdated goals out of habit. They may be pursuing goals they feel they should have pursued, but which are no longer important to group participants or relevant to the current situation.

There are several other advantages of goal clarity, which are presented below:

1 If goals are clear, there's a better chance of attaining them.

2 Clearly stated goals can be changed more easily and responded to more productively. (For example, it may be hard for an employee to respond to the boss who says, "Your work isn't quite up to par." The boss who states, "I want you to put in overtime the weeks the quarterly reports are due," provides a much clearer expectation for the subordinate.)

3 We can better note changing attitudes and positions throughout the discussion if people periodically articulate their goals. This may help the group leader and members to recognize moves toward consensus (Wilmot and Wilmot 1978, 90–92).

Goal-related conflict most often occurs when a group is attempting to solve a policy-related problem. At times, the conflict may simply revolve around disputed facts. In this case, the group should gather additional information and assess the root of the conflict.

Seek Increased Communication

When attempting to resolve a conflict, use accepted, effective communication skills for increased clarity. Paraphrase each other's positions and be willing to talk about the conflict and the communication that is occurring. Be willing to request additional feedback — even though it may be critical of you or your proposal. For example, "I'd like more information, Sam, about why you think this is a poor plan." Such a request enhances your credibility, reduces the tension level, and gives you more data to work with during the discussion.

Focus on Ideas, Not Personalities

Avoid assuming that a conflict is caused by problem personalities of one or two members. Rather, determine what environmental factors — the task, the organization, the leadership, the other participants, or even the weather — may have prompted the difficulty in the situation. Try to remain emotionally removed from the conflict. Occasionally, in all groups, interpersonal conflict will emerge which cannot be ignored and which calls for sensitive mediation on the part of the chairperson. However, a good number of these angry confrontations are often stimulated by inefficient processing of ideas. Similarly, many of these interpersonal conflicts can be averted by conscientious attention to good listening and information processing practices.

Offer Alternative Choices

Try to make many choices available to those with whom you have a dispute. One useful alternative, for example, is to divide a large conflict into several smaller areas of disagreement on which compromise may be more easily achieved.

Promoting Teamwork with the Two-Item Agenda*

"Don't eleimate company conflict — harness it"

Dear One Minute Manager:

It seems as though everyone in my department is at everyone else's throat, especially at our regular departmental meetings. We can't get through a meeting without conflict. Can you suggest a technique to help us function more harmoniously?

— A Minneapolis Fan

Dear Fan:

First, keep in mind that conflict isn't all bad. In fact, it's healthy in a dynamic organization. For instance, salespeople are naturally going to bump up against the folks in production and vice versa.

The issue is how to manage conflict to maximize results from its energy rather than to have it serve as a negative force. You can't or shouldn't eliminate it; otherwise you'll end up with a wimpy organization or department.

Take a page from Carl Rogers the father of nondirective counseling. At your next meeting, before getting into your agenda, introduce this system. Tell everyone they cannot speak until they are able to tell the last person who spoke what he or she said. That person must agree with what the listener thought was shared with the group.

I think everyone will be surprised when they are forced to repeat what they've heard. The eager contributor must digest the previous speaker's words before making his or her presentation. This won't eliminate conflict, but it should build some empathy among your folks.

Another idea is the two-item agenda. At your next meeting, announce that only two items will be included on the agenda. The first item involves a report from each person telling the group what he or she has accomplished since the last meeting. The achievement noted should be observable and measurable. In addition, each person should share with others the names of those who helped them over the past week. This builds teamwork and cooperation.

The second agenda item consists of going around the table and asking people to report on what they anticipate accomplishing before the next meeting.

In addition, they are asked to note which members of the group, or department, potentially can help them achieve their goals.

While the two-item agenda emphasizes performance and achievement, it also can build team spirit and eliminate needless conflict.

I believe the implementation of these two techniques will put a fence around the unchecked conflict you're experiencing in your department.

---

*Dr. Kenneth Blanchard, *Minneapolis Star and Tribune*, February 11, 1986.

Dr. Kenneth Blanchard is the coauthor of *The One Minute Manager*, an international best-seller since 1982. In addition, he is the coauthor of several other best-selling books, including: *Putting The One Minute Manager to Work*, *Leadership and The One Minute Manager*, and *The One Minute Manager Gets Fit*. He is chairman of the board of Blanchard Training and Development, Inc., of Escondido, California.

Have a Fallback Plan

If the meeting becomes bogged down by conflict, be prepared to take another approach. Repeat points of agreement, including participant goals for the group as a whole. Take a brief break, or suggest outside assistance when necessary (a third party to help mediate). Avoid jumping to a premature vote to avoid the problem.

Handle Some Issues One-on-One

Conflict can often be avoided by not bringing up a particularly sensitive topic in the group context. Do this when you are sure that others in the group seem so committed to their perspective that the possibility of changing their minds in a group setting is remote. In these cases, attempt to resolve the disagreement outside the meeting on a one-on-one basis, preferably before the meeting. If unsuccessful in changing the other person's opinion, you can at least agree to disagree with each other, making the conflict seem less of a personal affront during the actual meeting.

The Meeting Saboteur

Finally, we will conclude this chapter with a worst-case scenario of the wiles of the meeting saboteur. Yes, there are nasty folk out there who do not play by the book. Some, like the true Machiavellian that we discussed in Chapter 4, use these techniques routinely. Many of these ploys are simply the reverse of preferred small group techniques; others are a bit more devious. Usually these stratagems are blessedly infrequent, but vigilance is needed because when they do occur, they can be ruinous to groups. Remember to be forewarned is to be fore-armed.

How to Sabotage a Meeting

The following techniques are presented here, obviously not as a prescription for meeting behavior, but as an attempt to make everyone aware of the devastating influence of the deliberate saboteur. If individuals wish to disrupt a meeting or divert a group's progress, they will often use some of these techniques. They will . . .

1 Usually *begin interaction with compliant behavior* in the first 5–10 minutes to establish a good cooperative image to confuse cohorts when more contentious behavior later arises. They compliment and agree on definitions and information, help with summaries, compromise differences, and generally *positively reinforce* everyone.

2 Soon saboteurs deliberately begin to take *topic jumps, solutions jumps,* and *jumps in levels of abstraction.* Simple topic jumps relate (however incorrectly) the new to the old topic; solution jumps immediately propose solutions to the problem while ignoring the necessary problem analysis. They often lead others to suggest other solutions. Jumps "up" to some general principle or maxim or "down" to a specific example, however unrepresentative, easily mislead a group.

3 Saboteurs know the value of *constant interruptions* and soon interrupt as often as possible (finish people's sentences or abruptly interrupt with a feigned compliment, e.g., "that's a really sharp idea and ...") then take the discussion off in a *completely different direction.* By interrupting everyone and talking about their topics, they completely dominate the total talk time of the meeting.

4 Saboteurs talk *long and loudly* when they gain the floor. Rather than make brief 10- to 20-second comments, they speak for 1–2 minutes on a particular topic (having mastered the art of the filibuster). They also squash anyone who attempts interruption by using louder volume or by demanding "to be allowed to finish my point."

5 Good saboteurs use the ploy of *mixed messages.* They *always wear a smile* (except in periods of self-righteous indignation). They are pleasant and smiling even when they are being mildly insulting. Most people interpret the smile as a powerful symbol of peace and goodwill and are hopelessly confused when it is coupled with verbal criticism.

6   Saboteurs consistently use the powerful *claim of insufficient information;* the strategy of "not enough information" to understand or solve this problem will stop a discussion dead in its track. There is seldom, if ever, "enough" information *to resolve any question,* so members are always most open to a call for more studies, more information to . . . leading them to postpone the final decision. *(An able saboteur can tie up simple decisions for weeks with this strategy.)*

7   Saboteurs also *misuse critical thinking* by mounting persistent criticisms of the findings, the reasoning, or the conclusions of *the key* speaker. All sources are either questionable or dated. The saboteur's strategy is to *discredit* the *key ideas* of the *main spokesperson* either to stop any progress on the topic or to gain acceptance of the saboteur's.

8   Good saboteurs use *inconsistent techniques* to keep cohorts *off balance,* occasionally reverting to complimentary techniques after a period of criticism (to totally confuse colleagues), by *summarizing discussions* in a helpful fashion (but using only the*ir own points) and by trying to start needless feuds* between individuals.

9   When challenged or attacked, saboteurs use the *strategy of feigned indignation.* ("I have tried my best to supply arguments on the other side in hopes of coming up with a better solution, and now you tell me that I have been uncooperative and picky. . . .") By feigning anger, frustration, and hurt, the saboteur quickly gains the sympathy of the rest of the group and deflects the opponent's criticism, actually gaining *greater freedom* to state his or her views as the group attempts to "make up" with the "hurt" saboteur.

10   Saboteurs use *disruptive nonverbal techniques* with malicious intent: pencil tapping, turning one's back on the speaker, doodling visibly and obtrusively, yawning or sighing in bored fashion, looking at other people or the wall . . . all in the middle of another speaker's important statements.

These are but a few of the many techniques used by experienced saboteurs to manipulate meetings decisions to their own ends. Undoubtedly you have recognized a number of techniques to which you have fallen victim or that you have inadvertently used yourself. However, it is often far more difficult to react appropriately to these behaviors than we might expect. Why are we all taken in so effectively? Because we are generally not expecting such Machiavellian behavior. We expect that all parties to a discussion will act in good faith, attempt to cooperate, not lie, or use others solely as a means to their ends. We are easy pickings for the dedicated manipulator.

Summary

In summary, we have seen the role of the participant dramatically expanded in importance in recent years. We advise participants to take an active role in meetings, both in preparation and participation. We discussed the need for participant "attitude adjustment" to fit the new team-centered forms of organizational work. We suggested the need to be more dedicated to shared group outcomes rather than to "synchronizing" the views of others to our own goals and interpretations. We also noted that participants have a responsibility to organize their contributions; speak when their contribution is relevant; make one point at a time; speak clearly and forcefully; support their ideas with valid evidence; actively listen; and monitor their nonverbal signals. For greater influence in the group, participants should contribute early, frequently, and at length; speak fast, fluently, and forcefully; and structure their substantive contributions in a way which allows the group to process and assimilate these ideas efficiently.

Conflict can be managed primarily through goal clarification, but other techniques can be used, such as offering alternative choices; focusing on ideas, not personalities; and through the use of Rogerian playback technique and the two-item agenda, as Dr. Blanchard points out. Finally, we included a discussion of the deliberate meeting saboteur's tactics to sharpen our awareness of these practices. In business meetings, the role of the participant has become virtually as important as the chairperson in recent years. Today's group members can find significant opportunities in the meeting process if they take an active role and follow these recommended techniques.

Changing the Rules of the Game

The Changing Meeting Environment

Jack, the HRD consultant, eavesdropped on a late afternoon telephone call to Matt, the manufacturing manager, who was speaking to one of his plant supervisors in Detroit, some 500 miles away. Matt was speaking:

Hello, Jim. Thanks for returning the call ...You've got to be feeling a little bad about the Lion's game on Sunday.... Oh, you did ... good. ...Well I was wondering if you'd turn to page 20 of the latest printout.... Can you check line 14 (pause) ...yes ... yes ... oh.... Fine Jim, that's fine. I knew there was a good, logical explanation for that item. Those inventories look so out of whack. Yes, that's plenty clear. And of course that was exactly the right thing to do.... If everyone was as alert as you are our division would have no problems at all. Listen, thanks for straightening it all out. I've got to go, I've got Jack in my office, but I'll be looking forward to seeing you and Betty a week from Tuesday when I swing by. Good-bye.

As Matt hung up the phone, Jack commented:

That was a nice exchange. I guess I just heard a Theory "Y" guy in action.

Matt leaned back and chuckled out loud.

You apparently haven't been around long enough to have heard the stories about me, eh, Jack? Just four years ago I was known as the meanest, maddest manufacturing director in this company. The minute I hit those plants in Detroit or Texas they literally ran to get out of the way. Every group meeting was like a verbal dartboard, with me throwing the darts and others yelling! I knew that was no way to manage, but the plain truth was that I could never get my arms around all of the details I needed to know in the manufacturing operation. So I did the only thing I knew how to do: I yelled a lot, I chewed out anybody anytime I found an error, I kept them off balance with a lot of off-the-wall questions. In general, I scared them in the hopes of getting them to do a decent job.

Now, every morning, I get a complete printout of yesterday's activities at each plant. There are four pages of paper that contain every important operation detail I need to know. Not only do I know these details instantly, but my plant supervisors know I know them. They also know they better have a pretty good answer for every exceptional item I find in that report.

And in our operations meeting with top managers, we all have access to the same data. Everyone comes to those meetings much better prepared because they know that they have to defend themselves, not only from my questions, but from those of their colleagues as well.

So, for the first time in my life, I know what's going on and I can afford to be the nicest guy you ever saw. Five years ago, I wouldn't have believed a computer system could turn an old firebreather like me into a Theory "Y" guy but, like you said … Look at me — it really feels good!

Today, this example seems simply quaint and commonplace to many of us, so fast have been the technological shifts in our work life. However, it is a reminder of the incredible potential of each new electronic tool for affecting even the most intimate part of our managerial style. For many these changes are occurring with such rapidity that virtually everyone occasionally experiences some anxiety at being out of the loop. That anxiety is part of the price we pay for gains in convenience and information power that were unimaginable but a few years ago. Experts increasingly agree that this relatively brief window from 1990–2010 will represent a major paradigm shift in the way work is accomplished, comparable to the shift that took place during the industrial revolution. There is little question that information technology is today the main driver of virtually all aspects of organizational life. Digital technology is also steadily shaping and radically changing the rules of the game in meeting management.

In this chapter we will discuss a group of related technologies that are enhancing the meeting environment today: information search systems, group decision support systems (GDSS), computer-mediated communication systems, and other electronic conference methods including video conferences.

We've Got to Start Meeting Like This

Information Search Systems

Throughout this book we have emphasized the many chaotic influences on the way information is processed in business meetings of all kinds. Although small group researchers have long recognized the critical relationship between complete, accurate group data and sound decisions, comparatively little has been said about it because there has been little to add to conventional information gathering techniques. However, the virtual explosion of electronic information devices has forced a reexamination of the importance of this quantum leap in information gathering power. For Example, George Gilder, economist and media expert (1994), compares the creative power of the newly empowered individual at a computer workstation with that of a factory tycoon of the industrial age.

Is this simply more media hype? Hardly. If anything, with computer power roughly doubling every 18 months, today's hype is usually understated. Consider for one moment the powerful array of information antennae added in the last 10 years that have resulted in a 100-fold growth in the amount, accuracy, and speed of information acquisition. Currently, most major organizations have the capability of employing all of the following:

- Thousands of Bulletin Board systems that allow real-time access to thousands of libraries and subject communities

- Commercial on-line research services that can provide reams of specialized information in 24 hours or less

- Cable networks, satellite and broadcast media that allow dedicated company systems, networked or isolated individual workstations, and two-way interactive video conferences

- The Internet megalink of more than 46,000 interconnected computer networks that can provide the most arcane expert advice from an estimated 7 trillion e-mail messages sent in 1995

- The newest growth area of digital cellular systems that provide the mobility of the cellular phone and portable fax machines for convenient instant business transactions.

Gilder's one computer user sitting at home or in her office can instantly retrieve historical project data from the company network; get project advice from her professional counterpart in the U.S., Europe, or Australia; get a quick answer on policy via e-mail from the CEO, while she is downloading an expert project search from an on-line commercial research company, all in a matter of minutes. That is real information power barely conceived of a decade ago.

However, while most managers would agree that the potential for information power is here and now, they would point out that even if the information is now more current, accurate, and massive, the problems of what we do with it in groups is as challenging as ever, perhaps even more so.

Decision Support Systems for Small-Group Conferences

We know that time — whether group or individual — remains an ever critical factor in all decision-making processes. To Norman Maier's classic formula of quality plus acceptance of a decision we must somehow factor in the variable of time and timing. Any reader can supply countless examples of otherwise excellent decisions which were a day late and a dollar short. Most business decisions must be anticipated, configured, and accomplished in a relatively short period of time. The total amount of time a decision will take and the proper timing of a decision are critical components of all modern decision making.

There are many ways in which new powerfully networked management information systems assist the increasingly harried decision maker. Not all of them involve interrogating experts in exotic places a continent away. Most uses simply automate or refine traditional methods of information processing and interpretation, but in ways that powerfully augment small group decision making.

Advantages of Using Decision Support Systems

MIS and DSS computer-aided decision support systems can be used in a number of ways to assist the increasingly harried decision maker.

Standardized Data and Programmed Decisions. Standardizing routine data facilitates several common business practices. The better computer packages provide easily understandable forms of routine data, categorized in ways which are relevant to business, user friendly, and current. This allows the user to anticipate problems faster by timely recognition of changing patterns. In addition, management by exception can be used more effectively in troubleshooting minor deviations in operations or in faster delegation of task forces for special projects. The more decisions which can be programmed by standardizing information, the less decision-making time will be required and the more accurate one's timing will be. We know that the more reasonably digestible information (not too much, not too little, and the right kind) that can be assembled, the greater the probability of arriving at the best possible decision.

Decision Modeling and Simulation. One can be wise before the fact by modeling the impact of various possible decisions on various financial or personal criteria. Today many mangers routinely exploit this advantage by experimenting with various options and simulating decisions without forcing themselves to live with the consequences of a bad decision. This process teaches managers how to become better decision makers by exposing them to all the elements that go into an effective decision.

Business Insight and Forecasting. Even the most basic management information system provides managers and professionals with much greater insight into the total interactive business operation. By cataloging relevant business details, a realistic history of operations is assembled from which standards can be drawn and predictions or forecasts made. This is particularly helpful during the strategic planning process when one needs to see the interaction of various business elements in the future. Depending on the sophistication of the system, one can portray the interaction of a large number of marketing, financial, and human resource factors. This enables one to develop a far more realistic and potentially valid five-year plan. Because of the constant updating of information, the process of forecasting has become considerably easier and increasingly a semiautomated function.

Operations Evaluation. These systems permit much better evaluation of the effectiveness of much greater areas of organizational operations. They can facilitate the administration of total organization analysis in ways never before imagined. Representative groups or total organization populations can be routinely surveyed on a variety of topics, ranging from compensation to morale to career path planning, which can in turn be quickly compared with independently generated hard data of other aspects of business performance. Previously suspected problems and their causes can be more readily uncovered, investigated, and resolved. Results of these surveys can serve as barometers of an organization's health, and specific versus general profiles can be fed back to different groups at every level in the organization to help them chart, monitor, and correct their efforts.

These and many other functions will be provided to future decision makers. Potentially, the management information system and the decision support systems offer each manager and technical professional a survival vehicle for the next 20 years.

But what firm results are there from the computer revolution at present? Clearly, all companies with even basic information technology already have better data in the sense that it is far more complete than the information that informed past decisions. For many, part of the improvement in group decision making lies in the fact that companies now have current, constantly updated historical patterns and records at their fingertips, for the purposes of comparison. They have better categorized and more accurate printouts of their current operation to bring to the conference table. But as we all know, computer printouts do not a decision make. Managers, in general, still need more experience in selecting the right information at the right time to inform their decision. Few authorities in this field fear that the art of decision making will be immediately superseded by the science of the digital revolution. Undoubtedly, both the blessing and the curse of these communication and computational extensions of the human brain will be with us for a good while.

The trend of both the tools and methodologies of the knowledge industry is toward information specialization. We suspect that the use of these electronic extensions of decision making will be placed in the hands of a growing group of information specialists, whose work will most directly affect the quality of the group decision. Specialized information scientists, working alone, will significantly upgrade the information people bring to the average business meeting. However, as McLuhan (1964) has powerfully demonstrated in his study of behavior change brought about with the introduction of each new medium from print to television, we can surely expect computer-aided decision making to change small-group conference behavior.

What are some of the changes that can and should be expected as a result of these new tools? Before we examine some current and future changes, let us turn to some of the manager's immediate concerns. Managers must ask themselves how computers can assist them in resolving the most frequently reported problems they confront in daily business meetings. We see that a number of the 20 most frequently reported problems uncovered in our surveys (1995) can be directly or indirectly affected by new computerized techniques (see Table 8-1).

The Scheduling and Recording of Meetings

In follow-up interviews with managers in four of the companies surveyed, a significant number of managers dwelt upon lack of prepa-

TABLE 8-1   Frequently Reported Meeting Problems Affected by Computerized Techniques

Directly Affected	Indirectly Affected
Poor/inadequate preparation	Canceled/postponed meetings
Poor/no premeeting orientation	Meetings too lengthy
No goals or agenda	No follow-up of meetings

Source: Data compiled from Mosvick surveys, 1982, 1986, and 1995.

ration, lack of written agendas, and poor premeeting orientation of participants. One upper-middle manager in a Washington, D.C., firm summed up the sense of the group as follows:

◆

None of the textbooks talk about this but the timing of calling meetings is critically important. It is one of the biggest time wasters and ulcer producers in this company. It seems that the most important meetings are called late Friday afternoon and set for the following Monday when other meetings are already scheduled. Senior executives make arbitrary decisions on a meeting time which throws the whole operation into a frenzy. Other meetings have to be canceled and rescheduled and the whole business of systematic planning which we have been preaching up and down the line goes right out the window. There is relatively little time to prepare over the weekend and when the meetings roll around two bad things happen: (1) you don't have the right people there because some of them either could not or would not break other commitments made to customers or government officials, and (2) the right people who are there are not prepared for the meeting because they didn't know what information to bring or because their decision role was unclear. As a consequence, the meetings are very long, disjointed, and inconclusive. People must make calls for needed information and this itself is disruptive. Meetings go too long and some people have to leave for an equally important meeting and an important decision cog is out of the decision wheel. You simply cannot make sound decisions without the right people or information. We all know that but we still carry on in this medieval, chaotic fashion. This is the fourth company I have worked for and they are very much alike regarding this matter. This is the reason I say that most decisions are made by default.

As one steps back and looks at this entire cycle of frustration and misdirection, it is clear that much of this problem goes back to the arbitrary scheduling of meetings by upper management. However, as one senior executive said, "You must face it, current events force arbitrary scheduling and you have to have some priorities which say this is the more important meeting." This is unquestionably true, but it is the extent of the practice that many managers questioned in follow-up interviews. Arbitrary scheduling too easily becomes a part of the organizational culture too often.

Other managers, while admitting their frustration with the arbitrary scheduling issue, pointed to a related problem: that of the time-consuming efforts necessary to schedule any meeting, even those which are not hastily called by a superior. Some respondents reported making five phone calls back and forth in scheduling meetings, an enormous waste of time which could be better spent on other managerial tasks.

One answer to scheduling problems that many companies are turning to is computer-assisted scheduling. Networks of personal and minicomputers have become so prominent in some organizations that schedules can be coordinated with increased efficiency. Each person updates his or her individual and group meeting schedule on the computer at the beginning of each week and as necessary during the week. A general meeting coordinator can access numerous schedules without having to contact and discuss availability with each meeting participant. If tied into a facilities planning schedule, the meeting coordinator can match the group size to rooms which are available and lock in a meeting place. All participants can be easily notified of meeting times and places with minimal double-checking or cancellations.

Lack of premeeting orientation and proper briefings are continual meeting management headaches that can also be obviated by linking the scheduling with a standard company-wide computerized agenda format (see Appendix B). Once a convenient meeting time and place have been agreed to, the chairperson or convener can place all necessary premeeting orientation items on the local computer network. These items include the general purpose and goals of the meeting; all personnel invited; the time, place, and duration of the meeting; the key agenda items; plus short notes concerning individual responsibilities, such as reports expected from certain individuals. Depending on the sophistication of the system, this information can be stored for easy retrieval and distributed regionally or nationwide via electronic mail. It can also be easily converted to hard copy. In general, we feel that all participants should have a hard copy of this information in hand when they walk into the conference room so that everyone is working from the same agenda.

We have already discussed the appropriate recording of meeting agreements and action during the actual meeting. The final recording and disposition of these statements in some form of meeting minutes is indispensable to a high-quality meeting. This is part of the organizational memory. Without a clear, accurate record of group consensus and individual action items, misunderstandings and further information chaos are likely to ensue.

A recommended solution is to adopt a company standardized form and put all meeting minutes routinely on this form. When possible, information that is not unduly proprietary or controversial should be posted on company computer networks for the perusal of any member of the organization, as a step toward organizational awareness and openness. However, in many industries given the threat of commercial espionage and the relative ease of access to company networks, many meeting minutes will have to remain hard copies routed via closely monitored distribution lists. Yet most operations need not be this covert. Company network reports of team and project progress help keep everyone informed.

Meeting Management Tip: *When possible put everything on one page: the agenda for the next meeting on one side and the meeting minutes for the last meeting on the other side.* This one-page summary of past action plus directions for structuring current issues save much needless review and explanations.

A scheduling-recording system is doubly appealing both to work groups and the organization as a whole. First, such a system dispenses with the time-consuming chores of meeting arrangements. More important, it helps to inculcate a disciplined approach to all major meeting preparations. A computerized scheduling system brings participants to the conference table with more available information and thus a better frame of reference. Participants arrive with clear awareness of the goals, the main agenda items, and the part they are expected to play in the meeting. All of this makes for more efficient information processing and tends to shorten the meeting time considerably. In time, this process becomes a routine preparation for all chairpersons, in part, because of the relative ease of total planning and also because it becomes expected by all participants as an aspect of the organization's culture.

Computer-Assisted Decision Making

In 1995 it is possible that the great majority of meetings are still supported only by the overhead projector, but that scene is fast changing. Entrepreneurs and corporations alike are experimenting with a variety of electronic designs in an attempt to improve the quality of group problem solving during the actual meeting. Many complaints about meetings center on their chaotic nature: getting off the subject, talking about other topics, shifting topics, and jumping to solutions. Much of this chaos is created because of the inability of group members to focus on the same information at the same time — that is, to stay on track as a group. Additional confusion results from the conflicting priorities of individual members for different elements or causes of a problem and thus different preferences for solution alternatives.

During the last few years, a number of commercially available computer-assisted packages have emerged. Some systems (e.g., Visionquest, Groupsystems, Sage, and Samm) require a fairly high level of technology support including a workstation for each member and for a facilitator. Other mid-level technology systems (e.g., Innovator, Multisurvey, Optionfinder, and Quicktally) require only a keypad for each member and a workstation for a facilitator. Later we will describe three of these designs.

Initially, companies also attempted to restructure the physical meeting environment itself in an effort to facilitate collective decision making. These attempts have largely given way to simpler, more portable concepts such as a portable microcomputer with or without keypads linked to a projector, a viewing screen, or a white screen. While each of these new designs introduce some changes in the climate of the face-to-face meeting environment, they do tap some highly desirable meeting management features. Groups constantly need to know the current facts on project status, critical decision issues, policy constraints, etc., yet organizational memory is too often dependent upon quite fallible memories of individual conference participants. Computer systems are currently available that allow instant retrieval of information from a corporate data base, or from several information sources outside the organization. This will allow the group to check facts or trends as needed during the meeting with minimal delay and disruption.

Instant Information Retrieval. Several recurring meeting problems relate to the surprisingly difficult task of keeping the group focused with everyone "on the same page." Agendas, flip charts, and overhead projection of common data are all attempts to abet this process. Today computer meeting software systems permit attractive text or graphic displays of pertinent data that greatly enhance this focusing effect.

Multivariable Interaction. One of the more exciting features of current software systems is that they permit the multivariable interaction analysis within the meeting. For example, the interaction of specific marketing strategies with different competitive moves are projected on the outcome of a project. Use of standard software with minor company customizing provides pertinent data and models for decisions under consideration to be called up. This allows the group to experiment with different scenarios and calculate projections for instant comparisons. As is often the case, the potential of these systems is limited primarily by the technical sophistication and experience of the user group. These systems are most typically used for rapid assessment of group preferences by polling individual's priorities from a list of decision options and for displaying group data and changing consensus statements as the group works through a problem.

One of the earliest group decision support systems was Mindsight. This system employed a facilitator to help simulate real-life business decisions. The group was seated at a U-shaped table with built-in screens at each position which were programmed with simple touch commands for voting on selection options. After brief discussions, the group engaged a series of electronic ballots to determine their preferences (the balloting consisted of straight voting, numerical rating of issues according to some criteria, and ranking of options). After each poll, the system statistically analyzed the group's vote and graphically displayed the outcome on a large screen in the front of the room, as well as on the individual CRTs.

Executives who have used this system were generally pleased with it, citing several advantages related to status inhibitors: the rapid, anonymous group prioritizing of issues; the focus on the group displays rather than individual votes; the way the process facilitated depersonalizing criticism of positions and encouraged different frames of reference while making the prejudices of group members concrete and visible (Kull 1982, 82).

A similar system requiring mid-level technology is Optionfinder, a keypad-based group decision support system. This system was fairly thoroughly evaluated by a research group sponsored by the 3M meeting management institute who described Optionfinder as

◆

... a portable system consisting of general purpose vote collection and analysis software, a keypad for each group member, and IBM compatible personal computer and a public screen. ... The LCD screen is placed on an overhead projector and used to display to the group the information on the computer's screen. At appropriate stages in the meeting, the facilitator asks the group to vote on issues generated in a prior stage. Voting prompts are displayed on the public screen and group members enter responses through a keypad. ... Voting may be forced-choice paired comparisons or rating using either a Likert, discrete or nominal scale. When voting is complete the results can be displayed as a single axis bar chart, showing the results of one vote, or a two axis X–Y grid that compares the outcomes of two votes. (Watson et al. 1991, 2)

Computer-assisted packages such as these must be seen as but one aspect of the total group decision-making process. They do not eliminate the spontaneity or creativity of face-to-face exchanges. Instead they supplement and enrich them by providing visual displays; a more structured framework of interaction; and another language of graphs, distributions, and percentages to understand the diversity of options in the group.

The researchers did an in-depth case study of Optionfinder used in a fortune 500 company, conducted interviews with 20 facilitators who used this device, and analyzed questionnaire responses from 54 users in 19 countries. Among other things, they found that:

- OF meetings take about the same amount of time in planning and duration as non-OF meetings.

- OF changes the conduct of a meeting because it enhances evaluation and feedback by way of the new communication channels of the keypad and the public screen.

- OF contributes to the success of meetings because it requires careful planning. As a result, OF meetings have a clearer agenda and more clearly formatted questions, and they are both more productive and more efficient.

- OF is mainly used for planning/designing and opinion gathering meetings, and its usefulness for and effects on these meeting types are relatively uniform.

- All the features of OF contribute to its success, with fast feedback of voting considered the most important (Watson et al. 1991, 4).

It will not be long before the streamlined versions of these units find their way into most conference rooms. Clearly, if any computer-assisted device is to change the long-standing habits of business conferences, it must be very simple and user friendly. The best bet to replace the workstations or keypads will eventually be small hand-held personal computer/communicators that can be used for electronic voting and weighing of group alternatives.

At an even lower level of technology, the "Tecretary" developed by Bernard De Koven provided perhaps a simpler yet more robust approach to the marriage of computers and meetings by combining a simple interactive display device with commonly available PCs and software programs. Whereas in the previous decision support systems each participant was provided with a CRT for display and voting, this latest invention allows for the manipulation of data by only one person — perhaps a new kind of specialist who is half secretary, half listener/recorder whose main function is to analyze and structure the ongoing discussion.

> Basically, what De Koven does is load up his PC with an "outline processor" such as ThinkTank, a simple graphics program, and a spreadsheet. He uses a special overhead projector to display what's on the screen to individuals gathered at a meeting. Then, people just talk. De Koven plays the role of "tecretary" (his neologistic twist on "secretary") and dutifully types into the computer key points made by various speakers.

> Something very subtle and extremely important soon happens. People watching this flow of comments on the screen begin to say things like "Hey, this point relates to something earlier," or, "Wait a second, that contradicts what you said 10 minutes ago." Meeting participants add to or alter what is on-screen. They create links and connections and priorities about what's been discussed. They use the outline processor to begin structuring freeform discussion. The digressions become more obvious. The subtle, but important, points soon assume their rightful position on the discussion map that is being instantaneously edited on-screen (Schrage 1985).

Any excellent secretary can make a good "tecretary" given appropriate training, according to De Koven. Our experiences in observing similar computer processing of ideas during meetings generally confirm this point. Increasingly many meeting participants, like court reporters, bring their computers to meetings and record the idea flow during the meeting. It should be clear that the "tecretary" represents an evolutionary new step in meeting management: the introduction of a technical specialist into the business meeting. Although participating far less vocally than other participants, this individual can become more important than the chairperson in focusing, monitoring, and directing the flow of ideas.

The fact that this system is available now, with minor modifications for specific companies or work groups, is the single most attractive feature of this system. There are other aspects, however, which have impressive potential for changing and improving how we work together.

First of all, the notion of observing and using something like a group cognitive mind in action is a truly novel feature. As the developers point out, "You simply can't do this with a piece of chalk or felt-tip pen on a transparency: that's too slow and cumbersome. The computer as 'intelligent chalkboard' is an incredibly effective device that really can change the texture of a meeting" (Schrage 1985).

In addition, participants tend to focus more on the information being displayed than on the person making the point. This tends to filter out some of the "dueling egos" mentality which often surfaces in meetings.

Another aspect that should not be overlooked is actually a secondary benefit: that all key information for meeting minutes is immediately available for printing and hard copy distribution to all participants at the conclusion of the meeting. One can only speculate on the time and money lost in countless meetings because the chairperson, recorder, or secretary could not recall an important agreement from the group's earlier discussion. The immediate retrieval feature of this system should prevent many important points from slipping by unnoticed. More important, it should facilitate the clear-headed commencement of the next meeting and clarify the important action steps of the much neglected implementation phase.

Computers can also be used to double-check decision making. For example, respondents are asked to give a numerical rating of perceived desirability to various alternatives. The respondents, as is often the case in many decision-making situations, are probably not consciously aware of how they are weighing the various criteria used to arrive at their decisions. However, a computer program, performing calculations much like a multiple regression analysis, is able to identify the criteria that the participants are using and rank the criteria in order of the respondents' preferences. The use of the computerized rankings helps the respondents to better understand how they make decisions. With such understanding, they are better able to communicate their positions to others during a face-to-face discussion.

Using computer-assisted decision making will not guarantee acceptable compromises in decision making, but it may well make conflict more manageable by helping individuals identify and articulate the *sources* of their disagreements. Such a resource will obviously not supplant the need for face-to-face discussions, which are essential to effective decision making.

Typically, early adopters of various group decision support systems just plunge in and experiment, using what works. Many other managers and professionals tend to be wary that "computerizing a meeting" will interfere with established meeting routines and outcomes. Some fear that these devices and formats will disrupt group dynamics, diffuse decision responsibility, and limit power or leadership capacity. Others may resent the supposed waste of time in arcane training and gadgetry involved in learning how to use the new methods.

Today a typical Group Decision Support System (GDSS) now combines communication, computer, and decision technologies to support decision making and related activities. It utilizes a number of features familiar to many users. Among other features, they typically include e-mail and teleconferencing, multiuser operating systems, decision modeling methods such as decision tree or risk analysis, structured group methods such as nominal group technique, and rules for directing group discussion procedures.

There is clearly much that we do not know about how these new computer-supported formats affect group dynamics and group decision processes. Although some research has gone on for about a decade, findings are mixed, and few firm generalizations are available. For example, one typical study comparing decision making in computer-supported groups and nonsupported groups found that in general nonsupported groups performed better than computer-supported groups on a majority of key criteria such as task focus, equality of participation, critical examination of ideas, etc. (Poole et al. 1993). We suspect that most of these negative findings simply indicate that we are on the early stages of the learning curve.

In fairness, both formats and appropriate research methodologies are in their infancy. We know more about what should work than we do about the causes, "the why" of different formats of interaction. Then, too, many academic research programs have broader research agendas than do managers who are concerned primarily with the effectiveness in the workplace. The final test as always will be the test of the market place. Despite many unanswered research questions, the burgeoning market for new groupware is telling us loud and clear that this is not a new management fad, or soon-to-be obsolescent technology. It is an ever-perfecting survival mode of the information worker of tomorrow.

Electronic Conference Tools for the Present and Future

In 1936 technical visionaries were predicting that telephones would be replaced by the direct sight/sound communication of the video-phone. It has been a long wait, but today the video-phone is commercially available. Some sixty years later, we are finally seeing the rapid growth of the electronic marvels of business communication, including the video conference. Like computer-assisted decision-making devices, some of these advances have immediate or near-future application to the business conference. We will discuss three of these new conference tools: the conference call, computer conferences and electronic mail, and the video conference.

It is clear that each of these conference tools will increasingly supplement, but not replace, the traditional business meeting. The major commercial motivation for the extension of these devices is to make dyadic and small-group communication more cost-effective. Each of these conference tools is seen as a substitute for the enormous expense in time, travel, and energy found in the traditional meeting. Some companies have documented significant cost savings; others have found other functions for these devices to justify their cost-effectiveness.

The Conference Call: A Cheap Low-Tech Tool

While many business organizations wait for the more futuristic devices to get debugged, they are exploiting the cheap low-tech potential of the reinvented telephone system. Along with the arguable advantages of call waiting and caller identification, advances in electronics have provided a much more versatile audio system that permits significantly better utilization of the old conference call. The latest devices are locally networked, with a clear, accurate sound. They are simple, easy to use, and as near as your telephone. They require no redesign of rooms or trips out of the office. Advances in electronics have made it much easier and cheaper to develop company-run systems with local, national, and international networks, which are simple to operate and efficient to use.

The organizational use of the conference call varies considerably. Typically, however, the main configuration of the conference call includes two or more groups of one to five persons, located at two or three sometimes widely dispersed sites, conversing together over a telephone hookup. For example, you may have a small group of executives in Philadelphia, a group of manufacturing personnel at a plant in Baltimore, and a group located in a research lab in England, all discussing a specific problem together.

In follow-up interviews with our survey respondents concerning their use of electronic aids, virtually all of them cited the time savings potential of this device as the key advantage of the method. One middle manager interviewed gave the following representative assessment:

◆

We've used conference calls for a number of years. Prior to this time there were probably 5 to 8 trips a year I had to take to three different plants, one about 100 miles away, the other two about 800 miles away. This was one whole day shot plus overnights to the longer destinations. There is no question we have all saved considerable time, energy, and stress by using the system. It used to have lots of problems (e.g., listening to "voices coming out of a barrel"), but electronic advances have resolved a lot of these problems. The main advantage over video conferencing is that I don't have to interrupt my work and get up to go to some special room across the plant. We can do it right here in this office with a minimum of hassle.

Anyone who has been involved in a three-way telephone hookup is well aware of the problems conference calls can have: roles are poorly defined, and leadership responsibility is difficult. The various nonverbal aspects that allow a person to manifest leadership behavior in a face-to-face meeting, such as personality, charisma, vocal patterns, eye contact, or body positioning, are lost in the conference call setting. In a conference call, whoever is speaking is the temporary leader. Leadership acts tend to get muddled, and the subordinate roles are similarly ill-defined. Without the contextual and nonverbal cues, the decoding of various nuances of status is difficult. Subordinates are often unclear as to whether their contributions are expected, desired, or discouraged.

The problems associated with conference call meetings, as discerned through our interviews with selected survey respondents (Mosvick 1982 and 1986), tended to fall into four main categories:

1 The meetings are loosely structured, with no agenda or little control of agenda.

Conference calls are best suited to routine group reports or to topical, short-term crisis meetings. Conference calls fulfill this function, precisely because they are a simple extension of our instincts to grab a phone and solve a problem directly. It is obviously not as simple as a one-to-one phone conversation, however, when as many as fifteen people are waiting to get "on-line."

Because of lack of preparation, many meetings start with no analytical consensus of how to go about discussing the problem (that is, an agenda). This tends to double the amount of topic jumping and recycling of issues, in addition to promoting general confusion. Consequently, to solve this problem, we suggest that chairpersons give even greater attention to agendas and opening procedures than one would in a face-to-face conference. Chairpersons should begin with a short, precise orientation speech, followed by a simple, clear agenda.

2 There are many interruptions and too much general confusion where many individuals are talking at once.

This problem clearly results from the lack of nonverbal signaling. The subtle interruption protocols, or regulators, that regulate the back-and-forth nature of normal conversation are absent in the conference call. The only regulators available in a conference call are voice signals. After an ambiguous moment of silence, three or more individuals start responding at once. Another problem with large-group conference calls is the mistaken attribution of statements. In large groups, we tend to forget who is participating or who put forth a previous idea. All of this contributes to mistakes, misunderstandings, and imprecise communication — as well as to longer meetings.

To help resolve these problems, we suggest that all individuals clearly identify themselves and their location. Individuals should know the full context of their communication so they do not say things that are inappropriate about persons they did not know were in attendance. If possible, questions should be directed to specific individuals; for example, "I think Jack should answer this first" or, "Ben, will you share your perspective on this issue first?" These are simple, effective devices for keeping the audio traffic in a manageable order.

3 **Oversized conference call groups cause information overload and tend to be dominated by a few persons.**

The more people you have on the party line, the greater potential for overload, which can occur via interruptions, mistaken attribution of statements, or responding inappropriately. Conversely, as the discussion continues, what happens in large face-to-face groups also happens in large conference calls: most of the speaking tends to be done by two to three people. This tends to defeat the general purpose of the conference call unless a participant's purpose for being at the meeting is simply to listen to the discussion.

Our major recommendation to meet this problem is a common sense one: to cut down on the number of people required to attend the meeting. More important, cut down the number of scheduled speakers to perhaps two individuals from each of the sites, but do invite contributions or comments from each of the designated "speakers" group.

4   The pace is very slow and individual speeches tend to be longer.

Because of the combination of interruptions and "doubletalk" (when several individuals are speaking at once), participants try to be very careful so that no one misses any aspect of their statements. Their prescription for doing this is to adopt a very slow rate of speech and to say more when they finally get the floor. The net effect is often a very tedious meeting. The average person is able to decode verbal information four to five times faster than the average speaking rate. The typical conference call, however, tends to be even slower than a normal conversation.

To resolve this problem the chairperson should set the tone of the telephone conference by speaking at a regular rate with good inflection and intensity. Other participants tend to follow the leader in style and rate. The chairperson should also ask participants to restrict their contributions to a reasonable length (for instance, to one and a half minutes, and to allow some questions for clarification).

Our research indicates that successful phone conferences lend themselves well to discussing questions involving quantification versus the more ambiguous qualitative questions of goals and values. They tend to be more effective when individuals in different sites are working with well-established displays of data — such as sales forecasts — where everyone can rank order, vote on priorities, or reorder the data for different outcomes. Similarly, if a group is dealing with a well-known set of issues or with routine procedures, the phone conference tends to be fairly effective.

The phone conference retains a place in the broad spectrum of management meeting formats, aided and abetted by faxes, e-mail, and other digital technology. Adopting some of these basic rules will greatly improve the effectiveness of information flow in "distanced" meetings. Eventually they will be supplanted by the video phone and video conference, but until that time they remain a low-cost conference substitute particularly for small companies.

Computer-Mediated Communication (CMC)

Computer-mediated communication has become the umbrella term to refer to any type of communication that is mediated in any way by a computer. It covers a wide range of electronic devices and methods that aid the small group decision process. They now include such devices as personal communicators and information organizers, notebook videos, and language translators, as well as the more conventional decision support systems of e-mail, computer conferences, groupware, and video conferences.

Electronic Mail and Computer Conferences

Clearly the fastest growing star of the new technologies in the mid-1990s is e-mail used in real time or delayed computer conferences. Although the explosive growth of business e-mail has evolved hand in hand with burgeoning recreational and personal usage, the sheer amount of business traffic is stunning. Leslie reports that since 1984 the number of business users alone has increased 16-fold and that North American e-mail users sent 5 to 6 billion e-mail messages in 1993 (Leslie 1994). In February 1994, the number of Internet users was estimated at perhaps as many as 20 million users in 146 countries (Rogers and Albritton 1995). Today, few managers can survive without becoming computer-literate e-mail users. They sense intuitively what researchers have found over the last 15 years — that CMC is a very user-friendly form that has transformed conventional notions of space, time, and environment of communicating.

Everett Rogers, one of our more experienced international media scholars, along with Marcel M. Albritton recently reviewed interactive communication technologies in business communication. They summarized a number of claims and characteristics also noted by other researchers:

- *E-mail is fast.* It is exponentially faster than the telephone or postal service and is rapidly displacing "snail mail." A user can send a message across the hall or across the world within a few minutes.

- *E-mail is cost-effective.* Communication costs, both personal and financial, are virtually a non factor. Apart from some on-line service charges users can send messages anywhere to one person or 300 persons without regard to limiting factors of cost, time, geographic space, or status levels.

- *E-mail enhances personal control.* The degree to which an individual can choose the timing, content, and sequence of a communication act is greatly improved. One can choose when to initiate or receive a message without the problems of users forced to use the same time simultaneously.

- *E-mail is flexible and convenient.* It obviates the problems of telephone tag, of incomplete or missed messages, and permits time for a more considered response. It allows the communication content to be stored in a complete form for later retrieval either as a hard copy printout to be disseminated widely or catalogued and filed as part of the organizational memory.

- *E-mail promotes ideational diversity.* Connecting individuals together worldwide who are relatively more diverse than would be found in the usual space limited personal networks ... brings a broader range of perspectives and information to group problem solving than is found in traditional methods.

- *E-mail is open and decentralizing.* Within the organization e-mail creates a kind of decentralized control in which there is a wide sharing of power and decision making (Rogers and Albritton 1995).

While today's managers applaud the exceptional gains in information search and decision analysis provided by these tools, they are also more aware of some of the trade-offs involved. Much has been written about various antisocial behaviors such as "flaming" (tactless inflammatory statements) associated with e-mail use. This disregard for social norms is usually attributed to the relative anonymity of the recreational user. While undoubtedly true of "stranger groups," business users are not faceless "virtual groups." In most business computer conferences, individual identities and status are well known along with the possibility of retribution for stepping out of line. Spears and Lea, who have examined a number of CMC studies, point out:

CMC may admittedly provide increased access to information, social networks, and organizational possibilities....The point here is that although knowledge is power, its use is bounded by roles and relations (Spears and Lea 1994).

Similarly, it is probable that some of the claims for this convenient flexible form (e.g., equalization of status, power sharing, etc.) are overstated. Obviously, the widespread sharing of information does not immediately equate to the sharing of managerial power. Sharing key information with a group of supervisors or colleagues simply gives a manager the potential to act in ways that enlarge his influence. It does not guarantee it. Then, too, more managers are increasingly aware of some negative aspects of CMC that make it easier to issue impersonal, unpleasant messages divorced from human consequences. Anyone who has ever been notified of a major corporate downsizing via e-mail message knows this power all too well. However, while these issues are the subject of vigorous debate by researchers, they are of less immediate concern to the average manager than are the related problems of information overload and heavy time requirements for processing electronic mail.

From a technical standpoint, one of the key concerns that has emerged from a growing number of studies on CMC is the fact that CMC communication is less efficient than face-to-face communication in conveying the same amount of information. Although CMC sessions last much longer, only a fraction of the comparable exchange takes place (Spears and Lea 1994). Because of these and other factors, managers are spending more time on this activity than they were 10 years ago. In interviews conducted by Mosvick in July 1995, both German and American managers were surprised by the average amount of time they spent each day (7–10 percent) reviewing and responding to e-mail messages. While most suggested that this was a faster substitute for more conventional mail review activities, over half of the respondents did indicate that it was more time than they had previously spent on this area. Most felt that this was due to the much wider accessibility, unfettered by hierarchical barriers, to everyone in the organization. Variously, they were referring to system-induced information overload. This results in greater quantities of information to process every day. When asked about the quality of the messages, most gave positive reactions. However, one American summarized a common concern of many managers interviewed:

---◆---

> After a while you can develop shortcuts messaging with work mates and colleagues, and your own written style becomes more concise and clearer, but this gain is often offset by the surprising number of half-baked ideas. Besides the usual rumors, I receive a lot of ideas which while provocative were often premature or not well thought through. ...A lot of these come from my boss, but many come from subordinates who are displeased if you do not

quickly respond to this new channel of upward communication. Some resent being asked to re-think the full consequences of their idea. Its a little bit like what happens in a live small group when someone puts an unclear, poorly thought through idea on the table. It usually results in about twenty minutes of needless explanation, repetition and further misunderstanding. All of this takes a lot of time.

Computer Conference Groupware

As electronic conferencing grows exponentially, the experts tell us to keep our eye on the new "Groupware" packages because they are the platform for real meeting innovation. It is here in the new facilitating software developments where we see the greatest impact upon decision making. New software concepts will merge all stages of information processing in information searches prior to meetings, in retrieval and manipulation of data within meetings, and in monitoring of results after meetings, as a hybrid substitute conference form or as an adjunct to traditional meetings.

Lotus Notes, which IBM recently purchased for $3.3 billion, is perhaps the best current example of a number of these new forms of "groupware." That price tag is clear recognition of the growing importance of group-oriented software to facilitate powerful information searches and sharing in computer-mediated communications of all kinds. Lotus Notes is a software tool that is an apparent answer to the single most persistent need in organizational communication. It is designed to allow users to easily navigate across their organization, fetching just the *right information* at just the *right time* to the *right person or group*.

Currently there are about 1.5 million Notes users worldwide, but this will likely accelerate with IBM's strong marketing support. Users tend to rave about Notes. The International Data Corporation (IDC), a technology consulting firm, called the product, "an agent of change" and predicted that "Notes may be the elusive holy grail of white collar productivity" (Oslund 1995). Lotus Notes is finding its way into businesses, professional groups, and governmental units of all sizes. John Lally, deputy commissioner of the Minnesota Department of Revenue, is a big convert. He values the different applications that allow users to do group editing and commenting on documents, which is possibly the biggest meeting saver of all. "That way you don't have to have a meeting to have a meeting," Lally said.

We have feedback databases where we take questions from taxpayers. We throw them up on Notes — the question is up there as well as the answer — so the next time the questions comes up, the person who answers doesn't have to conduct the original research. The answer is there." (Oslund 1995)

In 1996 Lotus Notes software will be available on IBM's global network that will allow customers who don't want to invest in their own network hardware to share documents and work together from far-flung offices (Williams 1995). No current groupware can handle all of the important functions that Notes can. The planned 1996 interface with AT& T's global network will significantly expand its footprint for global services and shared group work. The prospect of on-line negotiation, commenting, and coediting with company colleagues and customers on the other side of the world presents a powerful conference capability.

Currently, the biggest competitive threat to Notes is the Internet. This megasystem-system is quadrupling in size every year and allows organizations to share information in many of the same ways that Notes does, but for a fraction of the cost. The main appeal to users of Notes is that most electronic business conferences work with proprietary information and Notes provides a secure system. At this point, Internet does not.

How cost-effective is this kind of groupware? To answer this, IDC (the technology research firm) interviewed 50 users that range from manufacturing companies such as ASEA, Brown, and Boveri to service firms such as Hewitt Associates, to government agencies such as the Minnesota Department of Revenue and health care providers like the Yale New Haven Hospital. So, what's the payback?

Stunning, IDC says. The three-year return on investment (ROI) for Notes applications in its 50-company survey ranges from 16 percent to 1,666 percent on an average investment of $240,000. Average ROI was 179 percent! (Oslund 1995)

The Video Conference

"You will know that video conferences have truly arrived in American business when major corporations hire new recruits via video interviews and when major negotiation sessions are concluded via video conferences," remarked an experienced communication specialist in a high-technology company in the Midwest recently. This is a typical bottom-line business test of this medium, and one that is close to being met at this date. A number of countries are currently operating and studying teleconference systems, including Britain, Australia, Canada, Japan, and the United States. These systems are still far removed from use by the average middle manager, however. The kind of high-resolution, satellite-relay video conferencing used by Ted Koppel's "Nightline" at NBC represents the state-of-the-art to which a small percentage of executives at only a few of our top corporations have access. At this juncture, the video conference is still viewed as an experiment by most American businesses and is being studied cautiously for user acceptance more than for general effectiveness.

The combination of growing sophistication of information technology — particularly gains in digital video compression — with the fast decreasing costs of components, have driven costs down dramatically in the last decade. Video conferences are typically staged and delivered via phone lines and dedicated corporate networks or through systems provided by private service vendors using both cable and satellite transmission. The sample statistics below are cost effective today and will inevitably decline almost quarterly in the future.

◆

Buying a fully equipped conference room might cost $38,000....
Rental charges for video conferencing rooms (including phone
time) run from $200–$300 per hour for point-to-point calls....
According to TELESPAN, an Altadena, CA, industry news letter,
about 22,000 room systems will sell this year. (Parker 1995)

Computer-linked real-time video conferencing, though currently more expensive, will soon be more widely available. *Time* magazine, in a recent special edition assessment of the field, illustrates the powerful new features:

◆

Vice President James Zeigon is able with the click of his computer
mouse to dial his London and San Francisco branches and within
five seconds conduct a face-to-face meeting with two colleagues
thousands of miles apart. Using an advanced teleconferencing
system from Avistar, the Chase banker gets consistently sharp video
images in synch with clear sound and smooth movement. Their
system allows for the on-screen display of documents as well as
people from up to four locations at one time.The cost per seat for
such systems currently ranges from $2000 to $5000, but it could
decline, say analysts to $500 during the next two years (Jaroff
1995, 40).

Desktop Video

The commercial availability of the video simply adds another dimension to the new world of audio-video connectivity. Of course, making predictions about the future conferencing methods via videophone and related devices is hazardous primarily because of the exponential rate of changes occurring each year.

◆

> Most analog video conferencing products are collaborative work programs that have a video window on screen giving users video conferencing capabilities as well as providing file transfer capability, an electronic white board for discussions and ability to annotate a share document. Industry analysts point out that although the current market for desktop video-conferencing systems is small (only 30,000 shipped last year vs. 18 million PCs) they expect it to explode in the next two years, predicting one million DVC systems may be shipped by 1998 (Salamone 1995, 24–25).

The current debate is whether the video conference or the video phone will become the dominant managerial medium. With desktop PC kits soon to be available in the $200–$700 price range, including camera, some researchers call it a toss-up.

◆

> Desktop video presents an even more dynamic option with live, real-time video transmitted from PC to PC, typically in a quarter screen picture but potentially on full screens. It is too soon to predict which will be the dominant medium. Most researchers bet on a complementary usage with the desktop used like a video phone on predominantly one-to-one interaction ... and many migrating up to higher quality group conference facilities once they've gotten used to the low-end experience at their desk (Parker 1995).

The bottom line question of course is whether video conferences are cost-effective. Analysts have followed closely the experiences of early adopters such as 3M, U.S. West, Ashland Oil, and others. For all intents and purposes the question has been answered. Systems that cost $500,000 a decade ago can now be set up for about $15,000. 3M, arguably one of the most representative of corporations in America producing 60,000 different products, is a good test case. They now operate 90 video conference rooms in 54 locations around the world. According to Ken Destasia, 3M video services product manager:

Given these favorable costs, managers large and small simply
cannot afford to continue to ignore the video conference as an efficient, economical management tool. As importantly, the above figures
indicate that video conferencing is not simply another expensive toy
for the large corporation. The ability to communicate by video cheaply
and instantaneously, and to query huge libraries of data, tends to level
the playing field by giving smaller firms tools that were once available
only to large corporations. For the first time video conferencing is truly
accessible to everyone.

Futurecomm: Not So Wild a Dream

At the turn of the century and the beginning of a new millennium, we
must all be futurists. The pace of change is simply incredible. For a
quick reality test, simply recall when fax machines were thought of as
exotic. Envisioning the future world of group decision making is
inseparably linked to the fusing of all aspects of information processing. This presents us with groupwork configurations as yet barely
dreamed of.

Virtually every month new computer communication devices are
launched that have implications for both distanced and live group
meetings. They range from devices with immediate applicability to
design of great visionary potential. Ponder for a moment the implications of but a few of these future scenarios.

Portable computer video will support future meetings. Recently
Panasonic introduced TV-quality video to the portable computer
market with the first notebook video. . . . It uses the latest Pentium
processor and an integrated CD-ROM drive to provide the first full-
screen, full-motion standards of video playback with 2,562,000 colors.
Although the device is aimed at markets such as interactive training
meetings, sales presentation meetings, and research and data retrieval,
it could find its way into many kinds of meetings (Blodget and Ouellete
1995).

The development of hand-held computers will expand mobility and
accessibility. The reduction of personal computer/communicators to

pocket-size pager-like clipons which combine computer, phone, and faxing functions will affect individual and group interaction in unknown ways. Will it mean that we are always available "on call" to join an ongoing conference distanced or live? (Jaroff 1995)

Wireless computing will accelerate worldwide connectivity. Apple Computer recently requested that the FCC give computers with built-in radio receiver and transmitter that communicate via radio waves free access to a large slice of the unclaimed radio spectrum. . . . 300,000 computers already have wireless capacity. By 1998 3 million will. This may spur a wireless infrastructure that can bring low-cost, high-speed communications to everyone (Morris 1995).

Advances in simultaneous language translation will create instant global intelligibility. CompuServe, the popular commercial on-line service with access in 150 countries, has just opened a worldwide forum in which messages can be automatically translated between English, French, or German. . . . Over the next 25 years . . . it is conceivable that we'll be able to master the very tricky art of reliable translation of natural language in real-time . . . Once it's solved, what happens then? Anything you write could be read by anyone on the planet in his or her native tongue. You could pick up the telephone, or its successor, the video phone, and hold a real-time conversation with anyone in any country (Leyden 1995).

Summary

It is clear that we need to explore any and all changes in the meeting environment that will allow meetings to be as effective as possible. While in the short-run we had best not put our entire faith in technology to make major breakthroughs in the gridlock of meeting problems, neither should we adopt a technophobic approach to these changes at our doorstep. The world of real-time, interactive "distanced" group conferences is the growing reality for knowledge workers, in the next two decades and beyond. The computer conference, with growing elements of technical sophistication, is already a mainstay in organizations around the world. Use of the video conference via desktop video or office systems is here today, comparatively cheap and easily accessible. The video conference is still in its infancy and will likely make major gains in the next two decades. An open attitude is called for from the great majority of us. Instead of continually comparing these new media/formats to the dynamics of face-to-face conferences, we need to analyze them for what they are: new, potentially promising, and under some situations *preferred* modes of conferring. We should also implement them, wherever possible, as complementary methods to the traditional face-to-face meeting. While they will probably never totally replace person-to-person interaction, we are witnessing a quiet revolution in the man-machine interface of group information processing and decision making. All of us should be participants and guides rather than mere observers of that revolution.

PART 3

Appendixes

Special Meetings for Special Purposes

This book has focused on meetings as they are commonly conducted in business: interactive, small-group, problem-solving sessions. One of the main emphases of the general approach to small groups presented here is that managers lose a great deal of time and money and often frustrate all members of a group by using a roundtable discussion format to solve every group task. Part of the secret of efficient meetings is to **choose the right kind of format to fit the specific task.** Each year there is an increasing number of innovative formats being developed in business, academic, and government settings. We will discuss but a few of these formats to suggest the range of options available to every meeting manager.

Most of these formats are primarily designed to facilitate a problem-solving or decision-making process. There are, however, other occasions that call for meetings with specific purposes other than problem solving, such as information gathering or solution implementing. Whatever the specific purpose, one should take enough time to select the appropriate meeting format which can best serve the objective of the specific group and task with which you work. An appropriate meeting format selection, based upon a clear identification of the meeting's purpose and a careful consideration of the advantages and disadvantages of available formats, will help to achieve many benefits: attainment of meeting goals and better-quality decisions, satisfaction of meeting participants, and savings of time and money.

Leadership Styles

Along with choosing the right format for your meeting, it is also important to spend some time thinking about the choice of the right type of leadership style to fit the problem and the format. Over the years, research has uncovered a few basic styles usually based upon the degree of participation and decision influence allowed by the officially designated leader. Brief descriptions of the main choices follow.

The Directive Style

Note that this is not synonymous with the so-called authoritarian style, exemplified by the authoritarian personality discussed earlier. Although it is essentially characterized by the group leaders engaging deliberately and predominantly in giving directions, and guiding and directing other group members with relatively little participation or shared decision making, it need hardly be conducted in the dictatorial manner conjured up by the word "authoritarian."

The directive style is a perfectly legitimate leadership mode to use in briefings, staff meetings, and symposiums when your purpose is to disseminate information quickly and clearly. One can obviously dispense information in a brisk, friendly, and persuasive manner with a firm understanding that this is not the appropriate time to engage in a lot of discussion beyond a few questions of clarification.

The Consultative-Participative Style

We call this common leadership style consultative-participative style rather than democratic style because most organizational groups are not essentially democratically governed groups. As noted before, the decision ownership often cannot be shared, but resides in designated managers. However, this fact, given necessary clarification, should not prevent any manager from using the essential elements of a democratic style. The essence of this style is to consult with colleagues and subordinates in a clear, respectful, nonmanipulative manner in bringing about better decisions. This means that leaders must demonstrate reasonableness; openness to airing conflicting viewpoints; flexibility in changing positions when faced by certain facts; and a democratic concern for the view of the majority of the group despite their own feelings or position on an issue. This style is the one most often recommended for the great majority of formats discussed in this appendix.

However, we need to remind ourselves that in actual practice all leadership styles contain a mixture of styles. For example, to be effective, even this style must be introduced with a strong directive style in that phase of the discussion of the chairperson's orientation speech.

The Nondirective Style

The nondirective style, though seldom used in most business meetings, is quite appropriate to certain formats. The essence of the nondirective style is to refrain from all but the bare minimum of direction giving and step back to allow the group to do the leading or guiding in the discussion of an issue. Typically, a nondirective style is most appropriate in certain kinds of creative innovation sessions or in feedback sessions in which one wishes to bring out emotionally charged issues. In a brainstorming session, the leader should lay out the ground rules and then step aside to encourage the free flow of ideas. The leader's role should be restricted to only intervening to discourage judgmental comments or to encourage a more concise expression of ideas.

TABLE 1   Summary of Meeting Formats

1. Common Information-Sharing Meetings
    A.   Staff Meetings
    B.   Ad Hoc Meetings
    C.   Standing Committees
    D.   Symposiums
    E.   Instructional Groups
2. Decision-Making and Problem-Solving Formats
    A.   Reflective Thinking Format
    B.   Single-Question Format
    C.   Delphi Method
    D.   Nominal Group Technique
    E.   Ideal Solution Format
3. Creative Ideation Formats
    A.   Brainstorming
    B.   Synectics
    C.   Post-It Notes
4. Solution Implementation Formats
    A.   Maier's Posting
    B.   PERT Method
    C.   SAPS Method
5. Hybrid Meeting Formats
    A.   3M Post-It Format
    B.   Symposium-Reflective Thinking
    C.   Panel Discussion/Buzz Groups

These are the three main choices of leadership styles. The choice of style must obviously be governed by the same factors that lead one to choose one format over another format. It would make little sense to use a nondirective style in a briefing session, or a directive style in a creative ideation meeting. The choice of leadership style becomes clear once the best format has been chosen to fit the task at hand. Therefore, let us turn now to those format options (see Table 1). The following descriptions of various meeting formats are categorized by purpose and presented with advantages, disadvantages, and relevant comments.

Common Information-Sharing Meetings

As we discussed in Chapter 1, there is limited agreement among business organizations in categorizing types of meetings. Some meetings, such as the "ad hoc" meeting, are more accurately defined by an emergency time frame than by any special function. Other meeting formats often serve more than one function, e.g., information sharing and decision making. We will first discuss some common business meeting formats, and then we will discuss some of the advantages and disadvantages of various other formats that are best suited to serving different meeting functions.

Staff Meetings

We give special attention to the staff meeting since it is often the single greatest time consumer in many organizations. Studies report anywhere from 30 to 45 percent of total meeting time taken up by staff meetings. Staff meetings are not only the most used, they are usually the most abused since they have some special characteristics that are often not well understood.

Staff meetings are primarily supervisor-led administrative meetings of subordinates. Occasionally, other supervisors are involved. Though a staff meeting can be used for many purposes, it is the one meeting designated to carry out broad organizational communication functions: most often communication of information from management down to subordinates ("top down" information). The supervisor acts as an official organization spokesperson, transmitting organizational messages as well as briefing staff on the appropriate group tasks. As such, staff meetings are critical vehicles for organizational control. Staff meetings are a necessity in most organizations and they can be extremely useful.

The Five Main Functions of Staff Meetings

1 *Organizational Communication* — transmitting official organizational messages

2 *Task Assignment* — clarifying tasks, avoiding duplication of effort, and establishing supervisory control

3 *Progress Appraisal* — checking task and subtask status

4 *Task Information Exchange* — soliciting performance deviation and possible solutions; avoiding major surprises

5 *Motivation and Persuasion* — developing group and individual "buy-in"; team building, and stimulating high productivity

So why are these valuable meetings a problem? The 3M Meeting Management Institute reports that staff meetings are the single most resented meeting type. First, they can suffer from the same weaknesses any meeting can exhibit: poor preparation, unclear goals or agenda, late starts and finishes, disorganized leadership, unfocused subjects, inconclusiveness, and other infamous faults. Second, they suffer by their very nature as routine, predictable, and familiar events. The typical staff meeting has fewer surprises and even fewer opportunities for meaningful subordinate involvement. They often run to two extremes: the coldly efficient military briefing or the informal coffee klatch. Neither model properly exploits the opportunities afforded by this special type of meeting. As one hospital supervisor observed, "The staff meeting is the one meeting I can attend half awake. I know I will be lectured at for an hour on material I already know and my only required input is an occasional nod of agreement." Fortunately, most frequent criticisms of staff meetings can be resolved or greatly moderated.

Staff Meeting Problems and Solutions

1 *"There are too many staff meetings."* Meetings are scheduled by habit or outdated precedent. Though there are sound organizational reasons to have regular staff meetings, no meeting type better illustrates one of Parkinson's Laws: "Work will expand to fill the time allotted for its completion."

Solutions: Sound preparation should limit staff meetings to one per week. Make it a policy to occasionally cancel unnecessary staff meetings, perhaps up to 25 percent. This makes it clear that the group meets only when the work warrants.

2 *"Staff meetings are too long."* See Parkinson's Law above.

Solutions: Again, sound preparation should provide an accurate assessment of necessary meeting time, which should be communicated to staff. The supervisor or manager should vigilantly track time and dismiss the meeting as soon as the work is done.

3 *"The supervisor talks the whole time."* Because this is an administrative meeting "owned" by the boss and the organization, the leader will usually dominate staff meeting content in a way inappropriate to other meeting types, especially problem-solving and decision-making meetings. Staff members should not expect that the entire meeting will be an open sharing of viewpoints. However, most leaders abuse this opportunity and may take up to 80 percent of the time. Subordinate participation is jammed into the last few minutes and is often cut short by time pressure. This chokes off critical "bottom up" information, including important responses to organizational issues.

Solutions: Leaders should restrict their contributions to a maximum of 50 percent of the allotted time. (This figure should be *much* lower in most other meeting formats!) Leaders should ruthlessly edit their briefing material to keep the percentage of time spent on that material as low as possible. Stimulate subordinate contributions through assigned reports, inclusive agendas, and encouraging comments.

4 *"The boss runs meetings like a dictator."* This is too common and may be perceived to be the case even when the leader solicits participation. A recent survey of 275 upper-level personnel at *Fortune* 100 companies found that 33 percent characterized meetings they attended as "authoritarian"; another 19 percent reported responding to management's unwritten message, "Don't rock the boat." This environment is counterproductive and inefficient.

Solutions: As in solution 3, leaders must encourage participation and be wary of inhibiting projections. Interrupting, scowling, and poor eye contact are improper leader behavior. Videotaping staff meetings and reviewing these tapes is an invaluable step toward solving this problem.

5 *"Staff meetings are disorganized."* Most meetings naturally move toward chaos even when a strong chairperson is in charge. Though regular and predictable content should make staff meetings the most organized of all meeting types, their familiarity causes most supervisors to forgo the necessary preparation. They tend to use the same informal agenda every week and seldom follow items systematically. Participants need to know what to expect during a meeting, and the chairperson needs to meet those expectations.

Solutions: One more time — meeting leaders must prepare! Meeting leaders must prepare an agenda for each meeting and anticipate necessary subordinate reports. Do not use the same agenda for every meeting. Leaders must select only relevant topics. And leaders must open each meeting with rehearsed, rapidly paced briefing information.

6 *"Supervisors tell us what we already know."* Some of this just has to be lived with, as some important organizational information requires that it be communicated through "official" channels, regardless of the fact that many individuals are already clued in from the grapevine.

Solutions: Proper preparation, including good editing of agendas and agenda items, can minimize this problem. During meetings, frequent "reality checks" with subordinates can streamline the amount of duplication. Routinely ask, "Has this been covered adequately elsewhere?"

7 "*Staff meetings are always the same.*" Like problem 6, some of this is unavoidable. By their nature, staff meetings are regular, predictable events. But more and more, the accelerated pace of change in the work group requires that staff meetings reflect immediate circumstances, not last week's news.

Solutions: Vary meeting agendas based on the work at hand. Occasionally, meeting formats and techniques rarely associated with staff meetings, such as brainstorming or normal group techniques, should be employed. Meeting agendas may reflect hybrid formats, like staff-meeting decision making. Leaders must clearly delineate formats and expectations for participation and results, especially if the activity falls within the time frame of a regular staff meeting.

For additional variety, the wise manager should rotate meeting leadership. Along with giving issues new perspective, this is a useful management tool for developing your associates and team members.

8 "*Meeting documentation is poor.*" It is often incomplete, inaccurate, or unavailable. This makes a great contribution to problem 9. Each meeting must have a clear, concise recording of key assignments, decisions, and unresolved issues. This documentation is the progressive work diary of the group, guiding work and deliberations while correcting misunderstandings.

Solutions: One group member must assume the role of recorder at each meeting and devote the majority of his or her attention and energy to recording key decisions and assignments. Other discussion must be accurately summarized. (See the following solution for more suggestions.)

9 "*Staff meetings lack follow-up.*" This is the bottom line for any meeting. Without consideration of this issue, positive meeting activity is rendered useless. Follow-up is critical both for implementing major tasks and responding to employee questions, suggestions, and grievances. Too many issues get a nod of the leader's head followed by his or her immediate mental dismissal of them.

> *Solutions*: Meeting minutes must be utilized, not just recorded. Minutes must be checked as the meeting progresses to ensure they contain accurate summaries. Issues, especially grievances, must be verbally acknowledged by the leader and included in the minutes. All tasks and future assignments should be accompanied by due dates and the names of the responsible parties. This is the familiar and invaluable "action item" system. These items should be reviewed as a regular part of the staff meeting. *Distribute and post meeting minutes.*

Finally, if an issue demands it, separate it from regular staff business and deal with it in another meeting, a one-to-one, or a formal memo. This makes completion of that item and regular business easier.

Ad Hoc Meetings

Description: This type of meeting is called on short notice, usually to handle an emergency situation. It is held for as long as necessary to resolve the problem and is thus very focused in purpose.

Advantages: Timing is the main advantage of an ad hoc meeting. Decisions can be made in a timely manner and then immediately implemented. Such meetings usually have a sense of urgency which can help to produce effective meetings.

Disadvantages: A lack of preparation can limit the effectiveness of ad hoc meetings. Key individuals may not be available for the meeting, and those who are present may not have the authority or information needed to make quality contributions. The likelihood of the meeting being unstructured is high since no advance agenda is prepared and little prior planning has occurred.

Comments: Do not allow ad hoc meetings to become the *norm* of your organization's culture. Demand adequate preparation whenever possible and resist this form of meeting if it can reasonably be avoided. When trapped by circumstances into calling or attending an ad hoc meeting, focus first on giving the meeting some structure. It is important that even meetings called on short notice have an agenda and follow some plan. Quickly construct a simple three- or four-point agenda and make it visible to all at the meeting. Put it on a chalkboard or display it on a chart of some sort. As chairperson, give some kind of short orientation speech; get concurrence or changes on your agenda; then structure and track the discussion in an orderly fashion. Don't forget the one thing always missing from ad hoc meetings: meeting minutes — a short one-paragraph record of what was decided will suffice.

Standing Committee Meetings

Description: By committee meetings we are not referring to the usual task forces or project committees, which are typically one-time groups of variable duration. We refer to the various standing committees that all industrial, professional, and government organizations have. They are typically of longer duration, have member tenure of from one to two years, and are charged with overseeing some recurring problem area that requires attention throughout the year (e.g., employee benefits advisory board, technical professional councils, etc.). These meetings are established for a specific purpose, often having a cross-section of expertise from throughout the organization. These meetings also have a formal structure; minutes of the prior meeting are distributed and reviewed. Group members may send substitute delegates if they are unable to attend specific meetings.

Advantages: They provide the chance to collect information systematically and move ahead on the resolution of specific organizational problems. Standing committees allow one to appoint professional, organizationally committed members with specialist knowledge to key committee spots, thereby ensuring continuity of leadership on critical issues. They also allow one to introduce a broad measure of representation by appointing members who reflect various management or technical levels.

Disadvantages: As with staff meetings, committee meetings can become too routine, involved more with procedure than results. Some standing committees take on a life of their own and continue to meet long after their primary reason for being has ended.

Comments: The problem with standing committees is essentially that of any long-term group. The group meets over and over again with the same personnel addressing the same general subjects. Because you will need to function together for a fairly long period of time, more attention should be directed from the beginning at developing smooth, interpersonal relationships. Because the groups get to know one another fairly well, there may be a tendency to get diverted into irrelevant interpersonal interests. Special efforts are often required to stick to the committee business at hand. Focus on keeping meeting time active and producing decisions and results, not just discussing interesting but irrelevant issues.

Symposiums

Description: A limited number of people — three to five experts — share their opinions on a topic for five to ten minutes each without interruption. Communication is structured, formal, and controlled by a moderator or chairperson. This format usually becomes a symposium forum. Members of the audience ask questions either after each expert's presentation or after all experts have spoken. The moderator may direct the questions to the appropriate panel members.

Advantages: This is an efficient, organized way to get information to listeners, particularly if the audience is to meet later in a roundtable discussion to make a decision. Speakers are likely to be concise and organized because of the lack of interruptions. It is an effective way to provide listeners with background information and expert opinion on a topic.

Disadvantages: The weaknesses of symposiums are familiar to all of us who attend professional meetings. If the experts talk too long or aren't very effective public speakers, the listeners become bored. Presentations are often of uneven quality, containing duplication of information and ideas. We should keep in mind that symposiums are not "real" meetings in the sense of an interactive sharing of information — information is shared only in a one-way direction. For this reason, symposiums are best used in conjunction with some other interactive formats.

Comments: Clear communication with the panelists before the symposium is necessary to clarify the expectations. All experts may speak to the same questions, or each may address a separate subquestion. In the latter case, a clear indication of topic limits is needed so speakers don't overlap in content. The moderator can help control time by giving clear signals to panelists.

Instructional Groups

Description: A small group is assembled in an informal, interactive setting with a group leader who facilitates the group through learning and group activities.

Advantages: Ideal for applying learned skills to the work environment, this meeting format is well suited for adult learners. This format is particularly effective for appreciating concepts and applying complex material to concrete situations.

Disadvantages: This is not the most efficient method of learning factual information; instructional groups can be time-consuming.

Comments: Instructional groups assume that people learn better when they are actively involved and communicative during learning, as in small-group, freewheeling discussions and conferences. The group leader should be a facilitator — one who helps the "students" share their expertise, and who also learns from those students. This obviously requires a nonauthoritarian style on the part of the group leader.

Decision-Making and Problem-Solving Formats

This section discusses meeting formats that provide balanced attention to both the problem-solving phase and the solution-finding phase of a small-group meeting. They are better oriented to the whole decision process than some other formats.

Reflective Thinking Format (The Standard Agenda)

Description: This is the most traditional format used throughout business. It was developed by John Dewey, an American educator, and patterned after the scientific method. Groups apply the following steps to solve a problem:

1 Recognize the problem.

2 Locate and define the problem.

3 Establish criteria to evaluate solutions to the problem.

4 Analyze the causes of the problem.

5 Find solutions to the problem.

6 Select the best solution and test it.

This format, thoroughly discussed in Chapter 3, is the most frequently used problem-solution discussion format in modern organizations. Advocates of this method suggest that this rational, systematic method follows a natural pattern of thinking. Its wide acceptance among Western managers and technical professionals perhaps reflects more the acceptance of a kind of scientific method than a universal thinking process since it clearly does not reflect the pattern of many Arabic or Asian business discussion groups.

Advantages: The main advantage of the reflective thinking approach is that it forces a thorough analysis. Reflective thinking is useful in problem definition (note that half of the steps in the agenda focus on the problem) and in a complete decision-making situation (problem and solution).

Disadvantages: Efficiency is not a hallmark of the method; thus, if the problem is of relatively little consequence, it's not wise to invest time and energy sifting through the amount of information this format requires. The method also requires a fair degree of skill in order to be properly implemented.

Comments: First, ask yourself, "How much time is available to the group?" When used to analyze the problem and determine a solution, this method requires enough time to complete all steps. If there is a wide range of possible solutions, other solution-oriented formats may be more efficient.

The sequence of steps in reflective thinking should be used with some flexibility and a willingness to "back up" to previous steps when necessary. Remember, this was Dewey's proposal for how groups should deliberate; the natural tendency of groups is not to follow such a format in lockstep fashion.

Single Question Format (Larson 1969)

Description: Many discussion formats and discussion techniques flounder because groups have not developed the instincts or techniques to formulate the right kind of questions to give them the right answers. The logic of this method is essentially to determine the main questions first, which will provide the main answer or solution to a problem, and then to work backward in developing those subissues or questions that the group must first answer before dealing with the larger main question. This technique forces the group to get down to business quickly by prioritizing those questions and narrowing the discussion to the essential subproblems. The steps (Larson 1969, 453) of this format follow:

1 What is the single question, the answer to which is all the group needs to know to accomplish its purpose?

2 What subquestions must be answered before we can answer the single question we have formulated?

3 Do we have sufficient information to answer confidently the subquestions?

4 What are the most reasonable answers to the sub-questions?

5 Assuming that our answers to the subquestions are correct, what is the best solution to the problem?

An example of a single question appropriate under step 1 would be, "What short-term promotional strategy is most likely to create a 10-percent increase in fourth quarter sales?" Note that this approach quickly clarifies problem analysis by keeping the group's attention on the main question.

Advantages: The single-question format is a particularly good choice for the leader who is under time pressure and needs the group to make a quick decision. One-time groups, as opposed to ongoing groups, may prefer to use this approach. (Note that when operating under time pressure, such groups may make tentative decisions subject to later revision and confirmation.)

Disadvantages: This method should not be used with a conflict-ridden group or with a very complex issue. Note that the approach in steps 2, 3, and 4 requires the participants to reach agreement on preliminary issues before discussing the final solution. A conflict-prone group may become so bogged down in discussing preliminary issues that it never reaches the final step in the process. Consequently, use this method on easily defined problems and with groups you feel are capable of reaching agreement.

Comments: This is a "real life" format because it pushes a group to make a decision even though they may not have complete information — a common fact of life in business. People must make their best guesses about the answers to subquestions based on the information available.

Delphi Method (Dalkey 1967)

Description: The Delphi Method has rapidly become a favorite format of the 1990s because its generic method allowed ready adaptation to computer-assisted decision making. It does not require face-to-face meetings and allows participants to solve problems through anonymous responses to questions supplied by a separate administrative staff. The development and use of the Delphi technique typically entails the following steps:

1 A staff determines what information is desired to solve a problem and then formulates a question — for example, "What policies should a state legislature enact to improve the business climate?" Desired information could include subquestions such as: "What are current barriers to a sound business climate?" or "What are appropriate short-term solutions?"

2 The appropriate sample size and respondents are selected. (A typical sample size for a homogeneous group is about 30 respondents.)

3 Questionnaire items are developed, pretested, and sent to e-mail addresses.

4 Results are analyzed by sorting and grouping similar suggestions.

5 Questionnaire 2 is developed. This questionnaire summarizes responses; seeks written clarifications and statements of agreement or disagreement; and requests respondents to prioritize or vote the suggestions by either rating or ranking.

6 Questionnaire 2 is analyzed. The "votes" (rankings or ratings) are tallied and summarized.

7 A final report stating the original goals of the inquiry, the procedures employed, and the results received is published and sent to appropriate parties, usually via e-mail.

Variations on these steps may include developing, circulating, and analyzing responses to a third questionnaire, based on responses to questionnaire 2.

Advantages: (1) Anonymity of responses prevents interpersonal issues (such as high source credibility of one person and conformity pressures) from inhibiting the comments of others.

Disadvantages: Earlier disadvantages of this format focused on the clumsiness of the method and on the time delays between responses, which sometimes took five months to complete. All of this is obviated by e-mail which allows very rapid dissemination and compilation of expert reflection on an issue. The one remaining disadvantage is present in all accelerated computer-based communication formats; the urgency associated with faster response times may force less thoughtful, more superficial comments by respondents.

Comments: Before selecting the Delphi Method, ask yourself whether the issue of concern is significant enough to require the time and effort of the large structured process involved. Often the question can be answered sufficiently by a less formal series of e-mail dialogues with, say, three organizational experts.

The Nominal Group Technique (Delbecq, Van de Ven, & Gustafson 1975)

Description: The nominal group technique is probably the fastest growing format in use in contemporary business organizations for many reasons. It can be used in all phases of the discussion, from problem identification to solution generation and implementation. It gets everyone in the group immediately involved, working on the problem, and putting forth their own ideas. This sets a pattern for a more even distribution of contributions. It allows the group to quickly arrive at a basic consensus about the relative importance of several aspects of the problem or solution. Finally, the nominal group method is based on research that showed that people produced more and better ideas when they were working silently face-to-face than when they were working alone. This format is valued because it saves time, gets everyone involved, and heightens the probability of agreement on the important elements of a discussion. Of the six steps noted below, four of them — the silent generation of ideas, round-robin recording, serial discussion, and a preliminary vote — are usually the most important ones.

1   While together, group members write individual responses to a question posed by the chairperson. For example, "What obstacles do you expect in instituting a quality circle program in your department?"

2   Each participant orally states one idea at a time which the leader writes on a flip chart or computer display that is visible to all group members. Ideas should be listed using the participant's own words.

3   The leader reads each item from the list in order and asks for clarification or questions from the group. The purpose is to clarify, not to win, arguments. Duplicate items may be eliminated at this point.

4   Each respondent writes a specified number of top-priority items and then ranks his or her choices. (Note that at no time have criteria for solutions been explicitly discussed. If the group is quite heterogeneous, this can be an appropriate time for the leader or group members to suggest some criteria for prioritizing.) Respondents anonymously vote on preferred choices. The ballots are tabulated by hand or electronically. (It is reasonable to request that people select from five to nine top-priority items; research on human information processing indicates that sorting and ranking becomes more difficult above the nine-item limit.)

5   The group discusses the preliminary vote. If there are extreme discrepancies in ranking some items, the group should discuss the variance, especially to determine whether it is caused by misinformation about the item.

6   A final vote is taken using rankings or ratings.

Advantages: It is useful to achieve any of these three goals: (1) to identify elements of a problem, (2) to identify elements of a solution, or (3) to set priorities for a solution. Assuming you have the time and an appropriate problem, the technique minimizes conformity pressure and draws out shy, reticent members of the group. This individual work plus the controlled, round-robin sharing of ideas encourages honest input of each member's ideas.

Disadvantages: It is unnecessarily time-consuming for simple problems. It also focuses the group on only one question at a time. If several questions are to be answered in a limited time period, this method is not appropriate.

Comments: The nominal group technique should be applied when the problem or potential solution is complex. The nominal group technique should be used only with a skilled group leader. The leader must create a climate in which all ideas are encouraged, but the leader must also maintain firm control over the process.

During step 1 — individual idea generation — the leader should also model appropriate behavior. Leaders shouldn't provide substantive direction. If a member requests more direction on the topic, an appropriate response is, "Any idea that you think is appropriate or of value should be written down."

In step 2 — round-robin listing of ideas — the leader should make sure each person contributes only one idea at a time. If a member chooses not to contribute in one round, the leader should encourage the person to contribute in later rounds.

In step 3 — clarification — the leader's most important task is to pace the discussion. The group shouldn't spend too much time on one idea or get into arguments. Be careful not to spend so much time clarifying items listed first that there is not adequate time to consider the items listed later.

In steps 4, 5 , and 6, the leader should be clear and concise in explaining voting procedures, noting criteria (if any), and requesting further clarification.

Some meeting situations revolve primarily around the solution. The problem may be persistent or recurring or one that, though well defined, defies resolution. The "good" solution remains the vital but missing element. Some meeting formats focus heavily either on generating a large number of solutions from which to choose, or on obtaining solutions that are most acceptable to the group.

The Ideal Solution Format (Larson 1969)

Description: With this approach, the group seeks the best solution to a problem by looking at all of the ideal solutions. The format forces the group to answer each of the following questions:

1 Do we all agree on the nature of the problem?

2 What would be the ideal solution from the point of view of all parties involved in the problem?

3 What conditions within the problem could be changed so that the ideal solution might be achieved?

4 Of the solutions available to us, which one best approximates the ideal solution?

Advantages: This technique is particularly effective for selecting the best solution from among several possible choices. This approach is particularly useful when conducting a one-time meeting. The first question in the sequence pushes the group to formulate the problem (problem definition does not entail many steps on the agenda). The ongoing concern with the ideal solution keeps the group from generating a large number of alternative solutions. This also contributes to the method's efficiency.

This strategy is also effective when group members differ in their individual goals and interests. When one person is advocating cutting staff to solve the budget problem and another person wants to delay a new project to save money, focusing on the ideal solution can prevent the group from becoming polarized around only these two solutions. Emphasizing the ideal does encourage the group to examine both the problem and solutions from several different viewpoints. When there is clear conflict between two factions, each strongly supporting a different solution, this format remains a good choice. Try to delay the discussion of the competing solutions until the group reaches consensus on what is ideal. Then compare each advocated solution to the ideal. The comparisons can help the group evaluate the relative merits of the two solutions in conflict.

Comments: Note that in step 2 of this format the group implicitly suggests criteria for the final solutions as they discuss what the ideal solution would be. It is important to remember that these criteria are not binding. When the group reaches step 4, it is to select a solution which best approximates the ideal. This process attunes the group to solutions without rigidly binding them to inflexible or unrealistic criteria.

Creative Ideation Formats

The seminal work of the Creativity Institute at the University of Buffalo, under Dr. Sid Parnes, has influenced a variety of creative ideation formats used in quality groups and project teams in countless organizations. We will examine only the generic format, "Brainstorming" and a recent hybrid which we call the 3M Post-It method. Other proprietary methods such as Synectics are more complex but quite rewarding systems which have been widely and successfully used on many companies.

Creative Ideation Format (Brainstorming) (Osborn 1957)

Description: In the last three decades, researchers from creativity institutes have evolved elaborate formats that constitute full problem definition and solution-decision methods. The core of the creative ideation method, however, which proved to be a unique breakthrough in group processing of ideas, is built on the four basic steps of the brainstorming phase of idea finding.

1 Suspend all evaluation or criticism of ideas. Permit and encourage all ideas. The absence of criticism is vital in freeing up new perspectives and unrelated associations. Remember, that complimenting an idea is also an evaluation of it and thus should be initially avoided.

2 Freewheeling ideation is encouraged. Brainstormers say that the wilder and crazier the ideas the better, since it is a much easier ideation process to tear down critically than to build up creatively.

3 Quantity, not quality, of ideas is the group goal. By focusing on achieving a large number of ideas, the probability of stumbling into one unique solution is heightened. Remember, fixating on quality is being judicial and dries up the very creative juices the group is seeking to free up.

4 New combinations and improvement of ideas are encouraged. Participants, inspired by another person's contribution, are urged to "hitchhike" on that idea by continuing or embellishing that thought. These interruptive, spontaneous, and synergistic combinations are given immediate attention and recorded.

Advantages: If constraints are few and the goal is indeed a creative approach, this format is useful. It is a good sequence for stimulating participation when there are some quiet group members. The brainstorming phase in the creative ideation format can enliven a somewhat apathetic group. It stimulates the creative thinking process early in the meeting, thereby establishing a climate encouraging creative suggestions.

Disadvantages: Don't attempt to brainstorm unless the whole group plays exactly by the rules. Many groups try brainstorming and find it doesn't work precisely because they did not understand the rationale for suspending judgment or encouraging wild ideas. Instead, they will toss ideas around and engage in those insidious evaluations which the brainstorming process seeks to avoid. Experienced brainstormers know that they are taking a few minutes to escape from our judgmental lives and associate freely in a search for new perspectives. They deliberately separate the idea-generating phase from the idea-evaluation phase, leaving the latter process to another day and often another group.

Comments: The brainstorming method is not particularly useful when a group is dealing with complex, value-laden questions. It is more applicable to the kind of practical, solution-oriented problems often found in business. We feel that all problem-solving groups should develop skills in creative innovation and be provided with the opportunity to use this specific format option on occasion. Meetings should be held at the times when the group feels the most creative, and last from thirty minutes to one hour at the most.

Membership should be rotated so that all department members are exposed to this format. The brainstorming session should be preceded by a brief warm-up session with a different question so that participants can practice the skills and the process. This practice session is followed directly by a session where the extensive list of ideas generated gets culled for duplication. The last step of this process is spent clarifying, ordering, and evaluating the remaining ideas. Many groups assign this task to another specialized group.

Synectics (Prince 1972)

Synectics is a solution-oriented creativity approach developed by Prince (1972) which has been used successfully by many organizations for twenty-five years. It is a complex and proprietary design requiring training and certification of facilitators. The eclectic system synthesizes techniques and assumptions from operations research, creativity experiments, and management consulting practices to resolve intractable organizational problems.

Some of its basic assumptions suggest the novelty of this design. First, three specialized roles are involved: the trained facilitator who guides the process, the client who owns the problem, and the general participants who ideally have no special knowledge of or relation to the problem and whose main functions are to help generate ideas and suggest fresh ways of viewing the problem and/or solution. The developers assume that the solution to a problem often lies within the person (the client) who owns the problem and is closest to the problem, if it can be 'teased out' of that individual. For this reason, this individual is interrogated extensively about the nature of the problem to provide the fullest briefing possible on what is known. They also emphasize a generally positive frame in suggesting that no idea is a complete waste, that every idea has some potential good if it can be reframed creatively. To this end, various exercises are used to "make the strange, familiar and the familiar, strange."

Another basic assumption is that there is a fundamental need to reframe difficult problems by thinking metaphorically or analogically about the problem (e.g., "What is the problem similar to?"). This phase loosens up conventional ways of viewing the situation, and it pushes individuals to make unorthodox connections that might serve as building blocks for eventual solutions.

Although applications vary with organization and problems, the basic steps are these:

1 A Synectics team of between 5 and 10 people is drawn from the organization. Like a dedicated task force, they operate full time as a customized group to assist the entire organization in helping provide workable solutions to long-standing problems. Often the selection process includes screening for the more creative, intelligent individuals who also must know the organization well. They are then trained to understand the method and the general creativity process.

2 The facilitator, who has usually been thoroughly trained by the Synectics group, calls the group together, reviews the process, and plunges into the "problem as given." In this stage, the client has the major input defining the problem parameters but is required to first state it in the form of a "how to" question, e.g., "How to develop a vandal proof automobile?"

3 The client is then asked to describe organizational requirements or goals and what has been tried or thought of concerning the problem. While this exchange between facilitator and client is going on, the partici-

pants are listening silently, attempting to understand the stated and unstated problems, desires, and goals. They in turn jot down some of their own "how to" analogies and metaphors for later feedback.

4   The facilitator then lists selected "how-to" statements of the client and participants on a display board. He or she then asks the client to choose one idea upon which the group focuses by building and extending it metaphorically without changing the direction.

5   The client is then asked to respond to the idea proactively by first identifying those things she or he likes about the idea before turning to her concerns about the idea. Even in this phase the client is asked to frame concerns positively by indicating additional features that might overcome possible obstacles in the embryonic solution.

6   The same cycle takes place with each of a series of ideas. After each idea is presented, the client is asked to review the steps for implementing the idea. This elaborates on and teases out more problematic elements of the solution that might arise during the implementation of the idea.

7   After a number of these cycles, the client has an array of well-elaborated possible solutions from which to choose using appropriate criteria. Many of the criteria have been discussed in the process, but the client is responsible for the final evaluation and choice.

Advantages: This method is a highly systematic way of forcing full analysis of the issues involved in the problem and its potential solution. As important, it taps intuitive knowledge of the problem and teases out critical criteria and hidden reservations that will come into play in making the final decision. Client evaluation of participant ideas is nonthreatening since the client is asked to list some things he or she likes about the suggestions and to frame reservations about the suggestions positively by stating them in the form of "additional features I would like to see." Allowing participants to join in the synthesis of ideas further develops team-centered collaborative work attitudes.

Disadvantages: This method requires an extensive selection process and a good amount of training for both the facilitator and the group. Like brainstorming, it works best in dealing with tangible products rather than with major value questions. The process is highly structured, and the metaphorical excursions can be problematic to some linear-thinking managers and participants.

Comment: This technique has been used successfully with a number of large companies such as Ford, General Electric, and IBM. It appeals to many managers because it is structured to focus on and build upon the intuitions and knowledge of the manager who owns the problem.

Methods for Implementing Solutions

There are several methods of focusing upon the implementation of solutions that have been generated by group meetings. In this section we will discuss: Maier's posting, PERT, and SAPS.

Maier's Posting Format (Maier 1963)

Description: This form of posting is a method of comparing two or more competing ideas — usually proposed solutions. For example, compare the hypothetical solutions proposed to solve a budget problem: cutting staff (Solution A) or delaying new product development (Solution B). In posting, you would list the two solutions on a flip chart with columns headed "advantages" and "disadvantages" under each solution:

A. Cut Staff		B. Delay Product	
Advantages	Disadvantages	Advantages	Disadvantages
1. _____	1. _____	1. _____	1. _____
2. _____	2. _____	2. _____	2. _____
3. _____	3. _____	3. _____	3. _____

etc.

Group members suggest advantages and disadvantages of cutting staff. Proponents of Solution A must state some disadvantages of their idea; opponents of Solution A must state some advantages. After completing the Solution A list, the group considers Solution B. Again, its opponents must note some advantages; its advocates must indicate some disadvantages. At the conclusion of the listing, the group returns to open discussion of the solutions.

Advantages: This is a fine technique for reducing polarization. It forces individuals to see both sides of an issue. Often, simply by publicly declaring good points of an opponent's solution, an advocate will become more willing to compromise. Furthermore, it serves to cool down intense discussions. While the technique is not a sure-fire cure for eliminating conflict, it does help the leader and the group to manage competing ideas in a rational manner.

PERT (Program Evaluation and Review Technique) (Phillips 1966)

Description: The program evaluation and review technique, as originally used, is an elaborate statistic-based method for systematically organizing and coordinating highly complex and interrelated group decisions. It was first introduced by the U.S. Navy in the late 1950s and has been used extensively by government and military contractors since that time. Most business groups can best profit from understanding the logic of the system and devising a modified version of this elaborate schema to fit their own department or company needs. This method attempts to account for all critical steps in the implementation of a solution by starting with the finished product and working back through the assumptions and processes required to make that final event happen. PERT is helpful in specifying how a solution is to be implemented and in double-checking all of the assumed or hidden decisions which must be made before the solution can be fully in force. The steps in PERT are these:

1 Specify the final event or goal to be accomplished.

2 List all events that must occur before the final event can be accomplished. (Generate as comprehensive a series of events as possible. Do not worry about getting events in chronological order at this point.)

3 Chronologically order these events and make a diagram that connects these events in that order. Determine which events must occur simultaneously, as well as all serial events. This takes time, but it is well worth it since this will be your basic road map for the project.

4 List the specific activities which must occur between each pair of events. Here each group develops an action plan to proceed from one item to another.

5 Make time estimates for each activity. Estimate the best, the worst, and the most likely times required to complete each subactivity.

6 Calculate expected completion times, including subactivities. Combine all serial and simultaneous time estimates into a time estimate for the whole project.

7 Determine the feasibility of deadlines. The group must have estimates with expected deadlines. If there is slack time at any point, the group members must determine where they can cut time further. If there are problematic events, they need to determine how to plan more time to surmount these problems.

8 Specify and support the critical path. The last step is a matter of determining a critical path, or master plan. The more critical steps within the whole process must be determined for all contingencies by allocating supplies, equipment, and personnel to those critical points. Time periods for accomplishing crucial areas of the total plan need to be adequately buffered to allow for an overall schedule that will have a high degree of probable success.

Advantages: An advantage of PERT, in addition to systematizing implementation, is that it forces a group to anticipate the most efficient route as well as the major and minor roadblocks to its goal. It also encourages the group to come to consensus on often forgotten intermediate steps. The group comes to understand the whole process and can plan to use resources efficiently in resolving bottlenecks in the critical path of implementation.

Disadvantages: Few organizations have the time or resources to employ this technique in its entirety. Some operations, even large, complex ones such as those involved in the building of a major rocket system, involve massive amounts of time and effort in constantly changing, revising, and updating changes to maintain an accurate master schedule.

Comments: Any large-scale, complex, and interdependent community or organizational project requires some kind of master plan or organized approach. A modified version of PERT, custom-designed to fit those requirements, is still an excellent exercise in planning and implementing key projects.

SAPS (Standard Agenda Performance System)

Description: A variation of the PERT system, the standard agenda performance system, combines the reflective thinking approach with five steps that guide solution implementation:

1 Recognize and define the problem.

2 Establish criteria to evaluate solutions.

3 Analyze the causes of the problem.

4 Find solutions to the problem.

5 Select the best solution and test it.

6 Determine final objective and completion date.

7 List necessary tasks in time sequence.

8 Prepare diagram.

9 Complete each event.

10 Evaluate each event as completed.

This method, like the PERT system, forces the group to consider the entire process before moving ahead. Evaluation and review are structured into the process at three points: (1) when the events are first listed, (2) when the events are placed in sequence, and (3) when the final diagram is prepared.

Advantages: A key advantage of this format is that this approach combines a well-known system, the reflective thinking method, with a proven solution-implementation technique. It is appropriate when the group needs to clearly determine the allocation of personnel and time in seeing the problem through from beginning to end. For simpler problems it retains the logic of the PERT system without the elaborate methodology. It is also one of the few systems to include an evaluation of each event.

Disadvantages: Group members need to be familiar with all dimensions of a problem from problem definition to solution finding and solution implementing. There is no room for the person who cannot go beyond conception or analysis to the state of practical enactment. In addition, the entire method can be somewhat lengthy; energy and commitment may become exhausted. Therefore, there is some logic in devoting different periods and specialized groups to these three phases.

Hybrid Meeting Formats

There are a number of current decision-making and comparative evaluation formats that have evolved from Operations Research study, and the quality movement in Japan and America. Managers should investigate such approaches as the Ishikawa Fish Bone diagrams, force field analysis diagrams, fault tree analysis, risk analysis diagrams, among others. Many of these methods have been adapted for computer manipulation and display, making them even more efficient tools for group use.

The 3M Post-It Format

In the early 1990s, an innovative team at 3M Company developed an interesting hybrid creativity method that combined some of the strengths of brainstorming and nominal group technique with the convenience of their widely popular Post-It notes. The method has been used quite successfully within 3M and in other organizations and universities. Although it can be used in all stages of deliberations, e.g., solution criteria and problem analysis, it seems to be most successful when used to assemble alternative solutions, and the basic steps are the following:

1 An appropriate group, usually a multidisciplinary team, is briefed on the basic question and possible subquestion a few days before the group meeting to enhance the incubation stage of creativity.

2 The group then meets together and is asked to individually engage in creative ideation by writing as many discrete interpretations of the problem or solution as they can within a fifteen-minute period. They must write one idea per Post-It note.

3 The facilitator presents a board or display which may contain from three to seven broad dimensions (including a miscellaneous category) of the problem or solution. In sequence, each individual is asked to state and explain briefly each of the Post-It ideas. After explaining, they are asked to post their ideas under the appropriate board category. This process continues until all ideas have been posted.

4 The group is then asked to study the various ideas and their placement briefly in order to remove duplicate ideas and to further group or combine ideas. (Some facilitators follow this phase by another brief round in which participants are asked to submit more creative "hitchhike ideas" stimulated by the preliminary pool of ideas.)

5 The entire group or subteams are asked to prioritize the ideas from the "best" idea to the least valuable ideas and then to explain the ordering. The entire group is then asked to vote upon the five best ideas, and, in some groups, the five worst ideas.

6 This process quickly identifies the group consensus of the more creative ideas and consequent direction for the group's focus in later meetings. Depending on the phase of product development, project teams may then consider each prioritized criterion, problem, solution, or implementation suggestion in roundtable format until all requisite dimensions leading to the next phase of the program are explored.

Advantages: This technique taps the research regarding nominal groups that shows individuals are more creative when working silently in the presence of others. It also borrows one of the strengths of brainstorming in allowing others to submit hitchhikes or combinations or improvements of ideas given by others, and in separating the nonjudicial presentation of ideas from the judicial evaluation of ideas. Like other round-robin information processes, it involves everyone, including the more reticent. A particular strength of the method is its emphasis upon the sheer physical placing of ideas on the master board and upon the attendant informal, simultaneous discussion of ideas. Some of the best analysis and discussion take place during the milling-around process.

Disadvantages: The method is subject to the same general qualifications stated about brainstorming and similar methods. Then, too, the technique is new; and like other elaborations of creative ideation, it is often called a marketing solution in search of a method. Although there will be need for more systematic evaluation of validity, the preliminary information suggests that the technical and marketing teams who have used it have found it a success.

Symposium-Reflective Thinking Hybrid

This meeting format combines the symposium with an open roundtable discussion to identify the best solution to the problem being discussed.

1 Chairperson presents an overview with problem or solution parameters to group participants several days prior to meeting and requests analysis.

2 At the meeting, each participant presents a five- to ten-minute uninterrupted analysis of the problem or solution (25 to 50 minutes total).

3 Symposium changes to open roundtable discussion with the chairperson using standard reflective thinking method to explore problem definition and causes and/or determine solution options and one ideal solution.

Advantages: This hybrid method allows the group to use the first part of its meeting as an intensive information dump, to get most of their biases, preconceptions, and personal perspectives — their most important information and interpretation — out on the table as coherently as possible. It borrows the strength of all symposium formats: the brief speeches reflect the time and effort devoted to composing a well-considered, well-supported position. The discussion following can then proceed in a much more informed manner. Participants know the rationale behind the position of each participant, thus allowing the discussion to proceed in a more comprehensive and timely manner.

Disadvantages: The main disadvantage of this method is that it encourages, if not forces, people to establish positions prior to a discussion. Unfortunately, most of us are susceptible to the human tendency to "live up to our word" and justify our previous analysis. Consequently, compromise or revision of positions becomes more difficult. A debate rather than a discussion often ensues.

Comments: With sufficient attention by the chairperson to the need for all participants to shift roles from advocate to cooperative synthesizer, this hybrid format can work most effectively.

Panel Discussion-Buzz Group Hybrid

All large group meetings, particularly comprising representatives of various groups with little previous history of interaction, share a common problem: how to get everyone in this large group involved in the group's deliberations. Most conventions and professional meetings feature one speaker after another, with predictably unfortunate results. Two of the most popular answers to this problem that are combined in this hybrid format designed for public discussion are the panel discussion and the buzz group.

The Panel Discussion

The panel discussion is essentially a roundtable discussion performed before an interested audience. The word "performed" is used advisedly since these formats are often found in radio or television settings. The essence of this meeting is to publicly present various positions on an issue without resorting to a formal debate before a viewing and/or listening public. Participants may be from certain regions or represent various disciplines, expertise, or positions on an issue. Experienced discussants who are accustomed to the "fish bowl" environment often do an exceptional job of discussing and interacting while seeming to be oblivious of the public audience. Leadership and participant functions are identical with those found in the common roundtable discussion, but also include necessary explanations of "inside information" which may not be known to the viewing or listening public. Most panel discussions last from 30 to 50 minutes and are usually followed by questions from the audience directed at various panelists or to the group as a whole.

Advantages: The advantages of the panel discussion rest squarely on the expertise of the participants. If they are well versed on the issues under discussion and comfortable in a public platform or broadcast setting, they can, as a group, render a most enlightening, entertaining, and informative session for any audience. Conversely, unexperienced public discussants will cause the audience to leave or tune out en masse.

Buzz Groups (Phillips 1948)

Buzz groups, also called Phillips 66 Groups, have proven to be one of the most effective methods for getting every member of a large audience involved in key issues of an organization. Originally, larger audiences were broken down into groups of six members each and asked to "buzz" for six minutes on a specific topic such as, "What questions do we want the CEO to address tomorrow?" Buzz groups have evolved over time into more serious-minded groups that meet for longer periods of time. In our hybrid, buzz groups would be used immediately following a 30- to 50-minute panel discussion that would define certain key issues for later discussion. Groups of six members each would be assigned a period ranging from 30 to 50 minutes in which to discuss one specific topic and to make recommendations on those topics to the larger group. The topics need to be clearly defined, relevant questions or issues for participants to become sufficiently involved in this progress. Some preplanning by the previous panel group is usually necessary to arrive at the key questions the larger group must deal with to ensure that buzz groups will deal with serious, not trivial, questions. To save time, leaders of each group should be chosen ahead of time and informed of their duties, which consist largely of informing the group of its mission, guiding the discussion, and assembling a list of suggestions with which the group concurs. At the conclusion of these meetings, if the main group is small enough, each leader may be called on to stand and state the group's key recommendations. If the main group is a large one, it is probable that as many as five to six different groups have been assigned the same topic. This will require that group leaders meet and assemble their combined recommendations, minus duplicate ideas, for later presentation to the main group.

Disadvantages: The format is often used primarily as an icebreaker and not as a serious attempt to elicit the suggestions or concerns of all members of the group. Groups quickly perceive this and become only marginally involved in the task, thus wasting group time and energy. Moreover, in meetings of representatives of groups, key ideas are not represented or get lost, and resentment of wasted effort increases.

Comments: With sufficient preplanning, selection and briefing of leaders, and careful collating of ideas, this hybrid format can produce a very successful meeting which involves everyone, occasionally producing valuable ideas and information for an organization. Symbolic value is also created when an organization takes the time to seriously solicit the ideas of all of its members.

B

Meeting Planners' Packet

The meeting planners' packet is designed for use by both the experienced, as well as the inexperienced, meeting managers. It contains a number of useful checklists and evaluation forms that can be used in the planning phase before the meeting, the processing phase during the meeting, and in the follow-up phase after the meeting.

Planning Phase — Before the Meeting

This section contains a number of forms for use by meeting planners prior to the meeting. Form 1 is a twelve-item checklist designed for all chairpersons and meeting managers who are preparing for typical small-group business meetings. It is suggested that copies of this form be duplicated and distributed to all chairpersons for reference each time they prepare for any meeting of consequence. Like all checklists, some items are optional, and some are simply quick reminders, while others require the planner to invest time formulating statements and writing them down. This planning phase is facilitated by Forms 2 and 3, both sample meeting notification forms, designed to be used with the twelve-item checklist. Form 4 is a detailed example of how the meeting notice might be filled out for a major meeting when you want everyone to be as fully briefed as possible. Whenever possible, some items should be delegated to a trusted assistant or secretary (e.g., for coordinating individual schedules), but others can only be accomplished by the chairperson.

Processing Phase – During the Meeting

This section contains two types of forms: (1) A description of the Recorder's role and the Devil's Advocate role as well as two forms, one to assist the chairperson in preparing the orientation speech and another—the impact formula—to assist all participants in increasing their personal effectiveness. We have also included a tip sheet on "meeting seating" to consider prior to the meeting. (2) An explanation of evaluation methods by which the process of group interaction and individual influence can be evaluated during the course of the meeting (followed by several forms to facilitate this evaluation). The recorder checklist and duties should be required reading for all recorders. The meeting analysis forms are optional. Because of the usual time pressures, few business meetings are systematically evaluated in this fashion. However, in the long run, with problem groups it often proves most efficient to take the small amount of time required to carry out this type of analysis. Nonparticipant observers can record the group interaction using one or more of these forms, analyze the results, and feed them back to the group. These forms are educational tools designed to develop pictures of meeting activity and an individual's meeting roles. Often this information can help explain meeting success or failure and help individuals get a more objective look at the pattern of their meeting behavior. Form 7 is a more elaborate form designed to capture the individual's profile concerning several procedural and structural group activities: discussion regulation, information processing, critical thinking, climate building, and processing errors. Forms 8 through 13 are elaborations of this form that are useful in isolating specific difficulties of problematic groups: for example, poor critical thinking or use of evidence, ineffective information processing or procedural skills, or weak group relations.

All of these forms are group forms used to assess all participants' profiles, except Forms 8 and 13. These forms allow an evaluator to monitor the performance of one individual's leadership skills (Form 8) or other participants' skills (Form 13). Form 14 is an important one, in which an observer concentrates on recording the total talk time of each individual during the course of the discussion. The observer ignores content and records the frequency and length of each person's talk time in seconds. This allows a precise analysis of the frequency and total talk time of each individual. It also allows a computation of each individual's MLU (mean length of utterance) — that is, how long each individual talks, on average — which is useful in analyzing individual influence.

Follow-Up Phase — After the Meeting

This section includes three forms designed to tap three different types of follow-up activities. Form 13 — the meeting action plan — is a form similar to that used by several corporations to record the results of a meeting. This form (used here with the permission of the 3M Company) notes key issues discussed and action to be taken by specific persons with specific due dates. These forms, properly completed, can serve as meeting minutes to be distributed to all attendees after the meeting. Form 16 is a special form developed by the office administration division of 3M and used here with their permission. It is used to estimate the cost of quality for each meeting. This form can provide immediate feedback to the chairperson of a quantified estimate of effectiveness (cost of quality) of the meeting, as well as suggestions for improvement. The last form, Form 17 — the Individual-Group Productivity Ballot — seeks a general impression from a knowledgeable observer about the overall effectiveness of one meeting or a series of meetings. This form can be duplicated and distributed to participants or observers to poll the group's perception of the most influential and/ or compatible team member. The observer is asked to make general comments about how well the group functioned in dealing with procedural problems, group dynamic problems, and problem-solving problems.

Simple Methods for Critiquing Small-Group Conferences

Although researchers in small-group communication have produced numerous methods and scales for studying small-group interaction, virtually all of them are too complex to meet the needs of the typical business meeting participant. We encourage meeting participants to use simple but efficient evaluation methods such as those evaluation forms which follow the brief description below.

Meeting Evaluation Activities

Good managers realize how important effective meeting leadership and participation are to the overall effectiveness of their units and companies. Consequently, they realize the need to do in-service training of all their important work teams, to build appreciation for the need for these occasional evaluations as part of their week-to-week meeting activities. Taking a few minutes to familiarize participants and observers with some of these forms and how to use them is time well spent. Most of these forms follow the general pattern of the "simple participation code."

Critics simply list each participant's name and keep track of the comments each individual makes. A participant's name followed by ℍⅡ ℍⅡ ℍⅡ = 15 contributions. This simple method is used to assess comparable gross participation among participants as a rough indication of the domination of total task time and an even cruder indicator of probable influence of each individual. The total number of contributions also provides some indication of the activity and intensity of the group at work. For example, in a one-hour simulated business discussion, total participant contributions may range from 80 to as many as 250 or 300 contributions. The lesser number may indicate that the group is slow, apathetic, confused, or uninvolved, or conversely, that there have been several long contributions typical of a seriously committed, reflective group. This is easily determined by noting (or timing) the number of lengthy contributions and by watching the talk-to-pause ratio. The apathetic group always has many lengthy periods of silence. The high number of contributions can signal an intensely interested and dynamic group but can also indicate that it is too competitive and frenetic for good progress on the topic.

Similarly, the Structure-Functions Form focuses primarily upon discussion regulation, information processing, and critical thinking with some space provided for noting harmonious and disruptive comments. Names of participants are listed at the top. Each statement from each participant is noted by a simple check, e.g., ℍⅡ (five statements of one kind), and placed in the proper category box. The form allows one to check each individual's profile to see if it is broadly distributed as recommended or related to one type of role, such as critical thinker or information giver. It also indicates much about where the group spends most of their time by giving group totals on each area or phase of the discussion.

Form 1
Meeting Planners' Checklist
Before the Meeting

Copy this checklist and post it for reference each time you plan a meeting.

____ 1. State the general purpose of the meeting. State specific (or unique) objectives of the meeting. Assign clear reasonable due dates to each task.

____ 2. Determine degree of decision sharing and group autonomy. Is this an ad hoc consultation group, a recommendation group, or a delegated decision-making group?

____ 3. Choose the type of meeting format and leadership style to fit task and purpose: e.g., roundtable, symposium, brainstorming formats; directive, consultative, or nondirective leadership style.

____ 4. Choose who will (and will not) participate. Note those required to attend and those invited, but not required, who care to attend.

____ 5. Select who should serve as chairperson and recorder, distributing these tasks whenever possible among those who need meeting leadership development.*

____ 6. Schedule the time, place, and duration of the meeting as appropriate to the task and purpose. Delegate coordination of meeting schedules to an assistant.

____ 7. Determine how and when participants will be briefed as to their individual meeting responsibilities — by telephone, meeting notice, etc., — with adequate lead time.

____ 8. Determine necessary audiovisual meeting aids, possible refreshments, other physical details of meeting. Order these or delegate this task to an assistant.

____ 9. Structure the tentative agenda to coverall major foreseeable elements of the problem. Fill this out with the rest of the meeting notice and distribute.

____ 10. Determine in advance how agreements and results will be recorded. Determine the follow-up mechanism by which implementation steps or action items will be monitored.

____ 11. Determine in advance if the meeting process itself should be evaluated, and by what method during or after the meeting. If so, appoint someone to do this.

____ 12. Complete a comprehensive chairperson's orientation speech and rehearse it. If someone else is the designated chairperson, check to see that this person has completed this vital assignment.

* Normally the manager in charge of a business unit or someone else formally designated to head up a committee will act both as the meeting planner and the chairperson of that group. This is the best practice since it centralizes the responsibility for the two essential functions of meeting planning and leadership in one person.

Form 2

To: _____

From: _____ Phone: _____

Date: _____

Meeting Notification

Date: _____

Time: Start: _____ End: _____

Location: _____

Agenda

_____
_____
_____
_____
_____
_____
_____
_____

Meeting objective: _____
_____
_____
_____

Premeeting preparation: _____
_____
_____
_____
_____
_____
_____
_____
_____
_____

Form 3
Meeting Notice

MEETING DATE	DAY	TIME	PLACE	INVITATION LIST	
				ESSENTIAL ATTENDEES	OPTIONAL ATTENDEES:
SUBJECT					
SCHEDULED BY		TELEPHONE NUMBER			
MEETING OBJECTIVE					
PREPARATION MATERIALS REQUIRED					

Notes (Agenda):

_____
_____
_____
_____
_____
_____
_____
_____
_____
_____
_____
_____
_____
_____
_____
_____
_____
_____
_____

The Recorder: Function and Duties

All business meetings can profit from using a recorder in addition to a chairperson. From a procedural standpoint, the recorder can be looked upon as being second in command. It is his or her special task to serve as a monitor in maintaining orderly, clear progression of the group's deliberations. The presence of a good recorder can significantly improve the productivity of any meeting; an inept recorder is worse than having no recorder at all since much of the group's precious time is spent untangling confusion and misinterpretation introduced by this person.

Not everyone in a group makes a good recorder. The skills required to be a good recorder are not immediately apparent. Being exceptionally fluent or a sound critical thinker will not solely guarantee that a person will perform well in the recorder's role. Perhaps the most obvious requirement is that the person be a good listener and that he or she be able to restate the positions of others accurately and completely. (This may indeed be a good one-minute test for prospective recorders of a group.) Secondly, a good recorder should be able to process information on several levels simultaneously. Being designated as a recorder does not divest persons of their usual responsibilities as participants. They are also expected to continue to contribute their special insights, information, and critical assessment of ideas. A good candidate for this position is one who can operate on two wavelengths — as a typical participant who listens, interacts, and contributes to the substantive discussion and, at the same time, processes this input with a recorder's "organizing" perspectives. Third, good recorders tend to be excellent organizers, integrators, and synthesizers of the ideas of others. They pay attention to the relationship and structure of ideas, their subordination and sequence, their commonalities and differences, and help the group organize this perspective. They respect the importance of orderly progression and consistently ask directive questions such as "Where are we in the agenda now?" or "Have we concluded anything at this point? If so, would somebody state it?" Finally, this organizing, integrative mindset is usually accompanied by another personality trait rarely found in business meetings: they are usually selfless individuals who are far more dedicated to ensuring that individual statements are clear and that group progress is systematic and orderly than they are to seeing that their personal position on an issue be adopted.

Although a number of people have natural skills to be good recorders, recorders — like leaders — are made, not born. While it is wise to avoid appointing individuals who do not listen well or who are poor integrators of others' ideas, it is also important to circulate this duty among colleagues or subordinates in a group. Few duties invoke such a quick appreciation for the need for timely summaries and orderly procedures in meetings. The habits of a good recorder are very close to those of a good chairperson and one of the reasons good recorders often become equally competent chairpersons. Distributing this function routinely among all meeting participants can be one of the best methods of management development toward making everyone aware of the importance of efficient group processes, and also in training future leaders in meeting management.

The Devils Advocate Role

The group chooses one person who will serve, for a specified period of time, as a major critic of the group's analysis, thereby building in a self-correcting mechanism. The role is assigned to different group members for each new task force or major issue.

These are the main duties of the devil's advocate:

1 Research evidence and arguments contrary to current group thinking.

2 Present this contrary information and make sure it gets a fair hearing.

3 Require that all decision consensus procedures are observed: for example, "Can we please take a few minutes to see how many of us still have strong reservations?"

4 Challenge and test all major assumptions, evidence, and arguments in support of various propositions through sound critical thinking techniques and common sense questions. Following are some examples:

- What real evidence do we have that this is a significant problem?

- Is it possible that a change like this will bring about more problems than the current program?

- Do we have any precedents to give us insight about this new procedure?

- Are the conditions of that study similar enough to our organization so that it is applicable?

- Does anyone have evidence or experience that contradicts this conclusion?
- Is it possible this is just a symptom and not an underlying cause?
- Do we have enough evidence and planning to adopt this decision?
- Are we sure that the cost/benefit analysis is complete and correct?

The need for the role of devil's advocate is premised on two well-researched group tendencies:

1   *The Counterproductive Dominance of Strong Leaders.*
Research shows that subordinates seldom challenge the assumptions, reasoning, or proposals of dominant and successful managers. In fact, they often withhold negative findings out of fear, thereby contributing to "executive isolation" and uninformed decisions.

2   *The "Group Think" Complacency of Cohesive, Successful Groups.* Research indicates that the very groups we think are least likely to err—proven, cohesive, successful groups—often fall victim to their own success. They ignore contrary evidence, rationalize away problems, negatively stereotype critics, and uncritically accept typical group proposals.

The Devil's Advocate Is Not Negative

The devil's advocate is a *positive role* designed to help the group come to the best possible decision. The group concludes that a forthcoming decision is so critical they simply cannot rely on the usual individual or group processes to surface necessary vital criticism. Members recognize that any major decision arrived at without sufficient criticism, objection, and debate is uninformed and likely disastrous. They therefore empower one member to supply this criticism, and so guarantee that the decision will be a fully inspected and reasonably valid one.

The proper devil's advocate recognizes that he or she is there to help the group more fully analyze the implications and test the strength of their deliberations. The role does not give license to raise every niggling criticism or to be obstructive or confrontational. Only major evidence, arguments, and proposals are to be addressed. Timing is important. Comments are usually made when the group is leaning toward confirming a major, but unchallenged, conclusion or summary.

When an individual elects to play this role without the group's assent, needless competition and emotionality often result. Tempers flare and opponents verbally lash out at one another, since they assume others are trying to cut them down through criticism of their proposals.

When the group assigns the role and duties to one individual, the group dynamics significantly improve. Individuals can more easily separate criticism from the person and forego wasteful ego hassles, because they know that the individual is simply "doing her job" for the benefit of the group.

Useful Tips for Playing Devil's Advocate

Devil's advocates often find it useful to signal their role by speaking directly to their duties (as positive, constructive, helpful, assigned by the group, not their own choice, etc.).

"As you all know, it's my job to raise important questions and criticisms when they are relevant, as I think they are here. I honestly think a reasonable critic would say that we do not have enough evidence to support Bob's conclusion. Does anyone agree with this?"

"Although I think I'm also in favor of the group's proposal, we simply cannot ignore the findings of one of the most prestigious commissions in the United States, which are directly contrary to our thinking."

One of the most effective techniques a devil's advocate can use is to place the criticism in the mouth of an authoritative figure who will judge the group's decision.

"Jim, I know you and the rest of the group are ready to approve this project today, and, for the most part, I am with you. But I also know that our time and effort are not going to be effective unless we can get the project past Carl. And I know Carl is going to have three questions he has to ask about projects like this. Unless we have good answers to those questions, he is not going to think well of our group or the project. What kind of answers can we give him when he asks these three questions?

- "What problems are we likely to encounter in the implementation phase?
- "Why haven't we done a human resources impact statement on this program?
- "How sure are we that our competitive position in the next five years won't change in Europe or Japan?

"Now, what kind of answers do we have to the first question?"

The good devil's advocate uses "we" language, which symbolizes his or her involvement in and ownership of the group's objective to select, sharpen, and justify their decision. He or she seldom says "I," but more often uses "we" and "our."

Suggestions for Note Taking in Conference

1 Certain highly important meetings should be recorded. Tapes should be transmitted to word processing for rough copy, later editing, and reduction to minutes.

2 Most routine meetings should not use a tape recorder. This sometimes inhibits discussion and results in lengthy notes and inordinate amounts of transcribing time.

3 All meetings should have a designated individual as the recorder. The chairperson is usually the worst person to do this job. The recording function should be rotated.

4 Each recorder should practice the taking of full, comprehensive flow notes (at some other meeting) to develop the ability to organize and synthesize main ideas.

5 During the meeting, the recorder has chief responsibility for the following:
- Seeking clarification of vague, disorganized, ambiguous statements
- Seeking transitions, internal summaries, and major conclusions
- Seeking rank-order consensus of facts, reasons, rationale

6 During the meeting, the recorder should record only:

- The major conclusions of each subpoint or major point of conference. (Get this right by asking for precise rephrasing acceptable to all)
- The general rationale for the decision (if controversial), including key supporting arguments, facts in support of the decision, refutation of NOAS, etc.
- The specific action items taken. Individual responsibility should be designated with all due dates specified.

7 After the meeting, the recorder should organize his/her report on one page, if possible, with the reverse side used if necessary, keeping the report as brief as possible.

8 After the meeting, the recorder should organize the meeting report as follows:

- Standard format headings: meeting subject, when called, chairperson, members present or absent, etc.
- Major conclusions, either numbered for discreteness or in one concise paragraph
- Action-responsibility items with due dates designated, as appropriate
- Rationale for decision (if necessary)

9 After the meeting, the recorder should check the meeting report with the chairperson (or supervisor) for corrections and additions.

10 After the meeting, the recorder should publish and distribute the report according to the distribution list: Those in attendance and "For Your Information," (using distribution list banked in word processing).

Remember . . . "The person of power without limits is the one who writes the minutes!"

Form 4
Meeting Notice

MEETING DATE	DAY	TIME-TO-TIME	FORMAT	PLACE
12/10/90	MONDAY	9:00–10:30	ROUND TABLE	L-11 CONFERENCE ROOM

SUBJECT		
PHASE I DEVELOPMENT — TECTRILL/COLLAGEN PRODUCT		

	REQUIRED ATTENDEES	INVITED ATTENDEES
SCHEDULED BY BENNET SMITH (CHAIR) **TELEPHONE NO.** 696-0079	V. JENSON B. HAMMEL C. MARZITELLI D. FINESTEIN G. JEFFERSON S. MACARTHUR D. OLSON F. PETERSON S. MALKOVICH	J. WESTIN B. CALDERSON S. PHILLIPS E. WU

MEETING OBJECTIVE

ANALYZE THE MAIN POTENTIAL PROBLEMS AND THEIR CAUSES IN THE PILOT PROJECT PHASE. SUBMIT FINAL LIST TO MANUFACTURING MANAGER WEDNESDAY, 9:00 A.M.

ASSIGNMENTS/MATERIALS REQUIRED

READ: CONSULTANT REPORT — BRING 2@ D PROPOSAL
RECORDER JEFFERSON D.A. MACARTHUR

TENTATIVE AGENDA	ASSIGNMENTS/NOTES
ORIENTATION (CHAIR)	(BRIEF REPORTS)
1) INITIAL MARKET ANALYSIS & RESEARCH (10–15 MINS)	
CONSULTANT ANALYSIS — KEY POINTS	MARZITELLI — 2 MIN REVIEW
F.D.A. GUIDELINES AND CONSTRAINTS	OLSON — 3 MIN REPORT
FINESTEIN'S INITIAL FORMULATION	FINESTEIN — 3 MIN REPORT
DENNEX'S THEORETICAL APPROACH VS. OURS	
2) PILOT PROJECT PROBLEMS (20–25 MINS)	
PREDICTIVE VS. ACTUAL VALUES (TESTS 6–15-90)	PETERSON (VISUAL PRES. 5 MINS)
KEY TOXICITY PROBLEM	MALKOVICH/JENSON COMMENT
OTHER MAJOR/MINOR PROBLEMS (LIST)	5 MINS
3) ANALYSIS OF MAIN AND CONTRIBUTORY CAUSATION (20–25 MINS)	
VARIATION IN PREDICTED VS. ACTUAL VALUES	HAMMEL DESIGN ANALYSIS 5 MINS
TOXICITY RESULTS	
CAUSES OF OTHER PROBLEMS LISTED	
4) RANKING OF PROBLEMS/CAUSES — SUGGESTED APPROACH (15-20 MINS)	
(SYSTEMATIC REVIEW OF EACH PROBLEM WITH BEST	
ON KEY CAUSES AND RECOMMENDED INVESTIGATIVE APPROACH	
FOR MANUFACTURING MANAGER — WEDNESDAY, 9:00 A.M.)	

Meeting Seating

Nonverbal Dimensions of Influence

King Arthur was right: The round table solves all sorts of problems and invites equal participation. There are not many large round tables to be found in corporate America, except in the cafeteria. But if you've got them, use them!

According to Professor Donald C. Stone, the Dean of "Chair Administration," the *best configuration for moderately large groups (9 to 20 people)* is a *square or U-shaped block* of tables with peripheral seating only, which provides face-to-face communication.

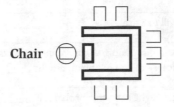

For those of us who must live with the rectangular tables in most meeting rooms or the larger oval tables in executive board rooms, research confirms the following:

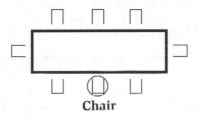

The chairperson usually sits on the end, but probably *should sit* in the *middle seat on either side.* This gives the chair direct eye contact with more people at the table. It is a more centralized communication spot.

People who sit directly across from you probably are individuals who *oppose* or wish to *confront proposals* they expect from you. (Please don't label them "the enemy.")

People who choose to sit on either side of you probably are your *allies* — those who, consciously or unconsciously, wish to align themselves with you or your ideas.

Whenever possible, *people who talk a great deal* should be seated on *either side of the chairperson,* out of the chair's direct line of visibility. This allows the chair to recognize others more and the over-talker less.

People who tend to sit at the corners of the table often symbolically reflect their marginal attitude about the topic or the group (with "one foot in and one foot out" of the group).

Form 5
The Chairperson's Orientation Speech
(3-5 minutes)

Instructions: You are the chairperson for this group. Either use the topic that has been assigned to the group or choose a typical real-life problem-solving or task force meeting and briefly outline your orientation speech.

1. *State problems, objectives, and procedures: How shall we proceed?*
   The basic problem before us today is _____

   _____

   The general *objectives* and *due dates* of the group are _____

   _____

   The *procedures* or *formats* we will use are _____

   _____

2. *Provide the information base* for the discussion: *What are the key facts?*
   Most of you are aware of the *history* of the problem. Briefly, _____

   _____

   The *present status* is fairly critical. Right now this problem is _____

   _____

   I think most of us would agree that there are three or four *basic causes* of the problem. They are:
   A. _____ B. _____
   C. _____ D. _____
   We need to note *the consequences* if we do nothing about the problem. _____

   _____

3. *Note boundaries* and *constraints* of the discussion: *What are the limits of the discussion?*
   Let us focus mainly on _____

   _____

   Let's agree we will *not* talk about_____
   because_____
   Another constraint on our discussion will be the criteria for a *good solution.* For our problem, a good solution is one that
   A. _____
   B. _____
   C. _____

4. *Announce the recorder duties: How will agreement be monitored?*
   (Name) _____ has agreed to be recorder for this session. We definitely want his/her ideas, but the recorder's main function is to state and record the group's consensus on each of our main agenda items. Please number each subpoint for clarity.

5. *Review agenda for possible revisions: How shall we structure our deliberations?*
   You all have the tentative agenda before you. Let's take all the time we need now to make *any changes* or *revisions.* What do you suggest? (Make changes on the agenda that meet consensus with brief discussion.) Let's begin with the *first* agenda item.

We've Got to Start Meeting Like This

Form 6
The Impact Formula

Instructions: The impact formula is a "mini-speech," a prepackaged key idea in which you state the point clearly; show how it relates to the issue at hand; support the claim with logical, clearly documented evidence and testimony; and, finally, ask members to respond or react to your basic conclusion:

1. Think about the three most important ideas you want to express about either the problem analysis or possible solutions.

2. Outline each of the key ideas on one of the forms below. Each "statement" should take only 30 to 60 seconds.

3. Rehearse each of these statements *out loud,* then state each idea to your paired colleague, alternating ideas.

1. *State* the idea you want the group to consider.
   _____
   _____
   _____

2. *Relate* the *significance* of the idea to the previous discussion or overall topic. ("This proposal is important because ...")
   _____
   _____
   _____

3. *Support* the idea with adequate *evidence*. ("There are three key findings that stand out in support of this proposal ...")
   A. _____
   B. _____
   C. _____

   "So, on the basis of this kind of evidence, I can only conclude ..."
   _____
   _____
   _____

4. *Integrate* the comment into the previous discussion, and ask the group to respond to the statement. ("I think this is sound, authoritative evidence that seems to conflict with or support some of our analysis thus far. Now I'd like to know what you think of this. Jim, what is your reaction?")

Structure-Functions Code

1. Discussion Regulation	Name A	Name B	Name C	Name D	Name E	Name F
1.1 Introductions						
1.2 Defines Terms						
1.3 Proposes Procedure						
1.4 Mediates Conflict						
1.5 Summarizes						
1.6 Expedites Discussion						

2. Information Processing

2.1 Presents Information						
2.2 Presents Opinion						
2.3 Seeks Information						
2.4 Clarifies Information						
2.5 Seeks Clarification						

3. Critical Thinking

3.1 Interprets Reasoning						
3.2 Uses Causal Analysis						
3.3 Generalizes from Data						
3.4 Criticizes Other's Reasoning						
3.5 Faulty Reasoning or Generalization						

4. Climate Building

	Name A	Name B	Name C	Name D	Name E	Name F
4.1 Approving Comments						
4.2 Humor/Tension Relaxing						
4.3 Personal Hostility						
4.4 Self-Aggrandizing						

4. Process Errors

5.1 Topic Jump						
5.2 Solution Jump						
5.3 Abstract Analysis						
5.4 Interrupts Others						
5.5 Irrelevant Comments						

Individual Totals

Discussion Procedures & Summaries

FOCUS ON GROUP A B C D   OBSERVER_____

DIRECTIONS: Listen only for statements which regulate, organize and expedite the discussion, especially for procedural and summary statements. (Place participants the top.) Simply classify and check every procedural statement in the appropriate box (𝖳𝖧𝖭 = 5 comments).

Participants' Names →					Group Totals
Orients Group on General Procedures					
Reviews, Revises Agenda Items					
Defines Terms					
Requests Procedures					
Requests Summary					
Proposes Summary					
Expedites Discussion					
Requests Response					
Mediates Conflict of Ideas					
Mediates Talk Turns					
Proposes Criteria (for Best Solutions)					

Final Grade. Please assign a grade to the entire group on their procedural abilities.

1	2	3	4	5	6	7	8	9	10
No/Low Procedural Skills				Average Procedural Skills				Excellent Procedural Skills	

Form 9
Evidence Quality/Reasoning Skills

FOCUS ON GROUP A B C D   OBSERVER_____

> **DIRECTIONS:** Place the names of the participants across the top of the form. Then listen only for the *quality of evidence and the reasoning skills of the group*, not the specific content. Categorize each statement in terms of the way individuals present and reason with different levels of support for their ideas. Place mark in appropriate box (⊤⊤⊣ = 5 comments).

Participants' Names →					Group Totals
Cites Personal Opinion					
Cites Personal Example					
Cites General/Hypothetical Example					
Cites Expert Testimony					
Cites Research Study Statistics					
Clarifies, Supports Arguments					
Criticizes Evidence or Reasoning					
Defends Evidence or Reasoning					
Presents Contrary Evidence/Argument					
Presents False Information					
Presents Fallacious Reasoning					

> **Final Evaluation.** Please make a summary judgment of the *overall quality and quantity of evidence* and *reasoning skills of this group* as a general score on the scale below.

1	2	3	4	5	6	7	8	9	10
No/Low Evidence/Reasoning				Average Evidence/Reasoning				Excellent Evidence/Reasoning	

Form 10
Information Processing Skills

FOCUS ON GROUP A B C D   OBSERVER_____

Participants' Names →					Group Totals
Presents New Information & Ideas					
Requests New Information & Ideas					
Requests Clarification of Ideas & Information					
Presents Clarification of Ideas & Information					
Double-Headed Contribution					
Comments Unclear, Disorganized					
Repeats Old Ideas, Information					
Interrupts Others					
Yields to Interruption					
Analysis Too Abstract					
Jumps to Another Topic					
Jumps to a Solution					
Comments Untimely, Irrelevant, Unrelated					

Final Evaluation. Please make a summary judgment of the overall information processing skills of this group as a general score on the scale below.

1	2	3	4	5	6	7	8	9	10
No/Low Information Processing Skills				Average Information Processing Skills				Excellent Information Processing Skills	

Form 11
Group Relations/Compatibility Skills

FOCUS ON GROUP A B C D   OBSERVER _____

DIRECTIONS: Place the names of the participants across the top of the form. Then listen only for the statements related to *group relations, cooperativeness and compatibility,* not specific content. Categorize each relevant statement in terms of its positive or negative impact on harmonious group relations by placing a mark in the appropriate box (ʰʰ⅃ = 5 comments).

Participants' Names →					Group Totals
Agrees with Others' Comments					
Compliments Others' Reasoning/Evidence					
Encourages Others to Speak					
Defends Others From Interruption					
Uses Humor, Climate-Building Comments					
Harmonizes, Mediates Personal Conflicts					
Positive Nonverbals (Smiles, Nods, Etc.)					
Negative Nonverbals (Frowns, Withdraws)					
Ignores Comments of Others					
Abruptly Interrupts Others' Comments					
Yields to Interruption by Others					
Uses Sarcasm, Personal Hostility					
Uses Self-aggrandizing Statements					

Final Evaluation. Please make a summary judgment of the *overall group relations and compatibility skills of this group* as a general score on the scale below.

1	2	3	4	5	6	7	8	9	10

No/Low Cooperativeness/   Average   Excellent Cooperativeness/
Compatibility   Cooperativeness/Compatibility   Compatibility

Form 12
Discussion Procedures & Summaries

FOCUS ON GROUP A B C D   OBSERVER_____

> **DIRECTIONS:** Listen only for the statements which regulate, organize and expedite the discussion, especially for procedural and summary statements. (Place participant names along the top.) Simply classify and check every procedural statement in the appropriate box.

Participants' Names →					Group Totals
Orients Group on General Procedures					
Reviews, Revises Agenda Items					
Defines Terms					
Requests Procedures					
Requests Summary					
Proposes Summary					
Expedites Discussion					
Requests Response					
Mediates Conflict of Ideas					
Mediates Talk Turns					
Proposes Criteria (for Best Solutions)					

> **Final Grade.** Please assign a grade to the entire group on their procedural abilities.

1	2	3	4	5	6	7	8	9	10
No/Low Procedural Skills				Average Procedural Skills				Excellent Procedural Skills	

Mosvick Personal Meeting Participant Assessment

Date_____   For Participant _____

                             From Critic/Observer _____

1. Frequency of contributions (frequent, timely, evenly distributed, etc.)

1	2	3	4	5
too few		average amount		too many

2. Length of contributions (long enough to have good impact, influence group thinking)

1	2	3	4	5
too short, no impact		right length, good impact		too long, overload

3. Information evidence quality and quantity (well researched, relevant information and evidence)

1	2	3	4	5
too little, opinion		good quality & quantity		excellent quality & quantity

4. Idea clarity (introduces and develops ideas clearly and coherently)

1	2	3	4	5
vague, confusing		average clarity		excellent clarity

5. Criticism of ideas (constructive, critical analysis of ideas)

1	2	3	4	5
no critical evaluation		appropriate criticism		overly critical

6. Speaking dynamics (dynamic, enthusiastic, clearly articulated, loud, fast enough, etc.)

1	2	3	4	5
too soft, unenthusiastic		clear, dynamic		too loud

7. Positive reinforcement (encourages, supports and compliments ideas of others)

1	2	3	4	5
no positive comment		adequate positive comment		solely positive, overdone

8. Group relations (cooperative democratic, open minded, tactful, etc.)

1	2	3	4	5
hostile, rigid, uncooperative		average cooperativeness		highly cooperative harmonious tactful

9. Reasoning skills (reasons logically, tests evidence, notes fallacies, etc.)

1	2	3	4	5
no critical thinking, illogical		average critical thinking		excellent critical thinking

10. Procedure commentary (proposes procedures, summarizes appropriately, etc.)

1	2	3	4	5
no procedural contributions		some procedural comments		many procedural contributions

11. Assertiveness (balance of protecting own rights and respect for rights of others)

1	2	3	4	5
non-assertive, always yields to interruptions		assertive proper balance		dominating, interrupts, cuts off others

Personal Commentary

Please add any other additional comments which you feel to be warranted concerning the behavior of your colleague in these meetings. You may wish to provide a rationale or expand on any of the above ratings. Note anything you especially like about his or her meeting behavior. Note any other behavior not covered above which you feel especially important in the improving of his or her meeting behavior. Be honest but positive and reasonable in recognizing the limitations of this learning setting. Please do this on the back of this form.

Form 14
Small Group Communication

Mosvick and Associates

Total Talk Time Segment Analysis Form

FOCUS ON GROUP A B C D

DIRECTIONS: Simply time each participant's contribution irrespective of content and place a check in the proper time length segment (ΙΝΙ = 5 marks). At the conclusion total the number of individual contributions and compute the total minutes talked. Then, total the group contributions by time segment and add the total talk times and total minutes for the group as a whole. Last, look for patterns of talk time for each participant and on the BACK of this form write one instructive comment for each participant concerning the frequency and/or length of contributions, individual patterns (e.g., mostly short utterances vs. overly long and verbose), relations to influentiality in group, and impact on getting agreement on key decisions.

Participants	5 sec.	10 sec.	15 sec.	20 sec.	25 sec.	35 sec.	45 sec.	55 sec.	1 min.	1.25 min.	1.5 min.	1.75 min.	Frequency Individual Time	Individual Total Minutes
1.														
2.														
3.														
4.														
5.														
6.														
7.														
Group Totals														

Final Evaluation. Please make a summary judgment of the overall talk time skills of this group as a general score on the scale below.

1	2	3	4	5	6	7	8	9	10
No/Low Talk Time Skills				Average Talk Time Skills					Excellent Talk Time Skills

Meeting Action, Plan

_____ Meeting

Meeting Date: _____ Recorder: _____

Chair: _____

Action to Be Taken	Person Responsible	Deadline	Completed

Key Issues or Discussion

_____
_____
_____
_____
_____
_____
_____
_____
_____
_____
_____
_____

Time: End: _____

List of Attendees Attached   Start: _____

Next Meeting _____   Length: _____

Form 16
Effective Meeting Appraisal

This form, reprinted here at 70% of actual size, comes with two sheets attached to the form. It is designed to be used immediately after the meeting to provide a collective assessment on the general efficiency of the meeting and to estimate the total cost of quality for that meeting. Each participant marks the form appropriately, gives one to the chairperson, and sends the carbon copy to an individual designated to collect data on all groups for a period of time. These forms can be quickly modified to meet the needs of any organization by simply changing the cost of quality (or burden rate) and substituting that organization's cost of quality or burden rate estimates.

Form 25869 - B - PWO

Meeting Date	Chairperson	Group (Dept.; QIST; Vendor; Seminar; etc.)	Length (In Hours)	No. Of Attendees

Good Meeting Criteria
- Provide Agenda
- State Objective
- Start/End on Time
- Appoint Recorder
- Stick to Agenda
- Keep Meeting on Track
- Summarize – Review – Decisions & Assignments

What could the Chairperson have done to improve the meeting?

Participant Responsibilities
- Be On time
- Be Prepared
- Participate More/Less
- Limit Discussions to Agenda Items

What might you have done to help the meeting?

Was this meeting necessary/appropriate? ▲ ☐ Yes ☐ No   Was my presence needed/required? ▲ ☐ Yes ☐ No

% Success

How successful was this meeting for You? Did it meet the stated objective?

☐ 0% ☐ 25% ☐ 50% ☐ 75% ☐ 80% ☐ 90% ☐ 100%

Cost of Quality

Circle Cost of Quality below as appropriate based on job level and % Success above.

Manager	$46	$35	$23	$12	$9	$5	0
Supervisor	32	24	16	8	6	3	0
Professional	23	17	12	6	5	2	0
Non-exempt	14	1	7	4	3	1	0

$ _____ x [Length (in Hours)] = $ _____ = $ _____ COQ

Multiply circled $ figure by length of meeting if other than 1 hour.

Your Name (Optional)

Complete at end of meeting and give to Chairperson   Chairperson: Send Canary to: Artie Lewis-Office Administration-225-IS-01

Form 17
Individual-Group Productivity Ballot

Check whether you are   Participant _____

Focus on which group? A B C D

                                         Observer _____

1. Who was the *one* person you felt was *most influential* in guiding and shaping the actions and conclusions of this task group?

                    (name of most influential)_____

2. Who was the *one person* in this group *with whom you would most like to work* in completing any important management task?

                    (name of most compatible co-worker)_____

3. Please evaluate the *group productivity* or *accomplishments*. Compared to other typical management groups, and considering the short time allotted to them: How efficient were they in the use of their time? How thorough were they in their problem or solution analysis? How much work did they get done? Please give a combined judgment of both the quantity and quality of this group's final product or conclusions. (Circle one number that approximates your judgment.)

1	2	3	4	5	6	7	8	9	10

No/Low   Average   Very High
Productivity   Productivity   Productivity

References

Preface

Bower, Joseph, and Thomas Hout. 1988. Fast-cycle capability for competitive power. *Harvard Business Review* (November–December):101.

Drucker, Peter. 1992. The new society of organizations. *Harvard Business Review* (September–October):101.

Lee, William G. 1994. Manager's journal: The new corporate republic. *The Wall Street Journal* (26 September):A14.

Schellhardt, Timothy. 1994. Managing your career. *The Wall Street Journal* (20 April):B1.

Stewart, Thomas. 1992. The search for the organization of tomorrow. *Fortune* (18 May):93.

Chapter 1

Boone, Louis E., and David L. Kurtz. 1993. *Contemporary business.* Ft. Worth, Texas: The Dryden Press, 247.

Hoover's handbook of American business, 1995. eds. Gary Hoover, Alta Campbell, and Patrick J. Spain. Austin, Texas: The Reference Press.

Hosansky, Mel. 1989. The rise of the third party. *Successful Meetings* (April):6.

Hsu, Spencer. 1990. *International Herald Tribune* (1 July).

Josephs, Earl. 1985. Future trends in organizational work. Lecture presented at Macalester College, St. Paul, Minnesota.

Lawler, Edward E., III, and Susan A. Morhman. 1985. Quality circles after the fad. *Harvard Business Review* (January–February).

Leyden, Peter. 1995. The changing workscape. *Star-Tribune* (18 June).

Mosvick, Roger K. 1982. Communication practices of managers and technical professionals in four large scale high technology industries. Paper presented at national convention, Speech Communication Association, Louisville, Kentucky.

Mosvick, Roger K. 1986. Communication practices of managers and technical professionals in high technology industries: An update. Macalester College, St. Paul, Minnesota. Manuscript.

Mosvick, Roger K. 1995. Communication practices of managers and technical professionals in high technology industries: An update. Macalester College, St. Paul, Minnesota. Unpublished manuscript.

Reich, Robert B. 1987. Entrepreneurship reconsidered: The team as hero. *Harvard Business Review* (May–June):82.

Rice, Paul L. 1973. Making minutes count. *Business Horizons* (December).

Rogers, Everett M., and Marcel M. Albritton. 1995. Interactive communication technologies in business organizations. *The Journal of Business Communication* (1 April):32.

Schellhardt, Timothy D., 1994. Managing your career. *The Wall Street Journal* (20 April):B1.

Sigband, Norman. 1985. Meetings with success. *Personnel Journal* (May).

Stewart, Thomas. 1992. Welcome to the revolution. *Fortune* (13 December).

Tillman, Rollie. 1960. Problems in review: committees on trial. *Harvard Business Review* (May–June):162–172.

Toffler, Alvin. 1970. *Future shock.* New York: Random House.

Tubbs, Stewart L. 1984. *A systems approach to small group interaction.* Reading, Massachusetts: Addison-Wesley, 6.

Van de Ven, A. H. 1973. *An applied experimental text of alternative decision making process.* Kent, Ohio: Center for Business and Economic Research Press (Kent State University).

Chapter 2

Goss, Blaine. 1989. *The psychology of human communication.* Prospect Heights, Illinois: Waveland Press, Inc., 125–131.

Harms, L. S. 1974. *Human communication: The new fundamentals.* New York: Harper and Row, 98–99.

MacKenzie, R. Alec. 1972. *The time trap.* New York: McGraw-Hill, 98.

Chapter 3

Algie, J., and W. Foster. 1985. How to pick priorities. *Management* (March):60.

Buckley, William F. 1985. How to sway decisions. *Self* (May):88.

Cline, Rebecca J. Welch. 1990. Detecting groupthink: Methods for observing the illusion of unanimity. *Communication Quarterly* 38:112–126.

Dewey, J. 1910. *How we think.* Boston: D.C. Heath & Co.

Drucker, Peter F. 1966. *The effective executive.* New York: Harper and Row, 143.

Drucker, Peter F. 1974. *Management: Tasks, responsibilities, practices.* New York: Harper and Row.

Gouran, Dennis S., Randy Y. Hirokawa, and Army E. Martz. 1986. A critical analysis of factors related to decisional processes involved in the Challenger disaster. *The Central States Speech Journal* (Fall):37/3, 199–135.

Hirokawa, Randy. 1985. Discussion procedures and decision making performance: A test of a functional perspective. *Human Communication Research,* 203–224.

Hirokawa, Randy. 1992. Communication and group decision making efficacy. eds. Robert S. Cathcart and L. Samovar. In *Small group communication: A reader.* 6th ed. Dubuque, Iowa: William C. Brown.

Janis, Irving L. 1982. *Groupthink: Psychological studies of policy decisions and fiascoes.* Boston: Houghton Mifflin, 245.

Koehler, Jerry W., Karl W. E. Anatol, and Ronald Applebaum. 1981. *Organizational communication.* 2d ed. New York: Holt, Rinehart and Winston, 277–278.

Kotter, John P. 1982. What effective managers really do. *Harvard Business Review* (November–December):156.

Larson, Carl. 1969. Forms of analysis and small group problem solving. *Speech Monographs* 36:452–455.

Maier, Norman R. F. 1963. *Problem solving discussions and conferences.* New York: McGraw-Hill, 5.

Mintzberg, Henry. 1975. The manager's job: Folklore and fact. *Harvard Business Review* (July–August):49–61.

Redding, Charles. 1985. *The corporate manager's guide to better communication.* Glenview, Illinois: Scott, Foresman and Company, 29.

Rothwell, Jan D. 1995. *In mixed company.* 2d ed. New York: Holt, Rinehart and Winston, 207–208.

Tversky, Amos, and Daniel Kahneman. 1980. The framing of decisions and the psychology of choice. *Science* (January):211.

Chapter 4

Adler, Nancy J. 1992. *International dimensions of organizational behavior.* 2nd ed. Belmont, California: Wadsorth Publishing Company, 44.

Allen, Thomas J. 1977. *Managing the flow of technology.* Cambridge, Massachusetts: MIT Press, 39.

Anderson, Peter A. 1992. Nonverbal communication in the small group. eds. Robert S. Cathcart and Larry A. Samovar. In *Small group communication: A reader.* 6th ed. Dubuque, Iowa: William C. Brown, 274.

Barron, Robert A. 1985. *Understanding human relations.* New York: Allyn and Bacon, 154, 157–158.

Berscheid, Ellen, and Elaine Hatfield Walster. 1969. *Interpersonal attraction.* Reading, Massachusetts: Addison-Wesley.

Borisoff, D., and Merrill L. 1992. *The power to communicate: Gender differences as barriers.* Prospect Heights, Illinois: Waveland Press.

Bradac, James J., and Anthony Mulac. 1984. Powerful and powerless speech styles. *Communication Monographs* 5, 1:307.

Brilhart, John K., and Gloria J. Galanes. 1995. *Effective group discussion.* 8th ed. Carmel, Indiana: Brown and Benchmark, 89.

Burrel, Nancy A., William A. Donohue, and Mike Allen. 1988. Gender-based perceptual biases in mediating. *Communication Research* 15:447–469.

Butler, D., and F. L. Geis. 1990. Nonverbal affect responses to male and female leaders: Implications for leadership evaluations. *Journal of Personality and Social Psychology* 58:48–59.

Dearborn, D. C., and H. A. Simon. 1958. Selective perception. *Sociometry* 2, 1:140–144.

Eakins, Barbara W., and R. Gene Eakins. 1978. *Sex differences in human communication.* Boston: Houghton Mifflin, 156, 170.

Hall, Edward T. 1976. *Beyond culture.* Garden City, New York: Anchor Press.

Hofstede, Geerte. 1980. *Culture's consequences: International differences in work related values.* Beverly Hills, California: Sage Publications.

Hofstede, G., and M. H. Bond. 1988. Confucius and economic growth: New trends in culture's consequences. *Organizational Dynamics* 16, 4:4-21.

James, S. P., I. M. Campbell, and S. A. Lovegrove. 1984. Personality differentiation in police-selection interviews. *Journal of Applied Psychology* 69:129–134.

Karlins, M., T. L. Coffman, and G. Walters. 1969. On the fading of social stereotypes. *Journal of Personality and Social Psychology* 13:1–16.

Korda, Michael. 1975. *Power! How to get it, how to use it.* New York: Random House.

Laurent, Andre. 1983. The cultural diversity of western conception of management. *International Studies of Management and Organization* 13, 1–2 (Spring–Summer):75–96.

Leo, John. 1985. Is smiling dangerous to women? *Time* (January):82.

Lustig, Morton W., and Laura L. Cassota. 1992. Comparing group communications across culture: Leadership, conformity and discussion procedures. In *Small group communication: A reader.* 6th ed. Dubuque, Iowa: William C. Brown.

Maybry, E. 1989. Some theoretical implications of female and male interaction in unstructured small groups. *Small Group Research* 20: 536–550.

Mosvick, Roger K. 1966. An experimental evaluation of two modes of motive analysis instruction in an industrial setting. Ph.D. diss. Department of Speech, Communication, and Theatre Arts, University of Minnesota, Minneapolis.

Mulac, A., et al. 1988. Male/female language differences and effects in same-sex and mixed sex dyads: The gender-linked language effect. *Communication Monographs* 55:315–335.

Mulac, Anthony, Pamela Gibbons, and Stuart Fujiyama. 1990. Male/female language differences viewed from an intercultural perspective: Gender as culture. Paper presented at the Speech Communication Association Annual Convention, November, Chicago.

Parlee, Mary Brown. 1979. Women smile less for success. *Psychology Today* (March):16.

Rosenthal, Robert. 1979. *Skill in nonverbal communication.* Cambridge, Massachusetts: Oelgeschlager, Gunn, and Hain.

Rothwell, J. Dan. 1995. *In mixed company.* 2d ed. Ft. Worth, Texas: Harcourt Brace College Publishers, 72–73.

Scheflen, A. E. 1972. *Body language and social order: Communication as behavioral control.* Englewood Cliffs, New Jersey: Prentice-Hall, 54–72.

Scott, Niki. 1985. Words, ways keys for women. *St. Paul Dispatch and Pioneer Press* (May):8c.

Seifert, C., and C. E. Millhem. 1988. Subordinates' perception of leaders in task-performing dyads: Effect of sex of leaders and subordinate, method of leader selection and performance feedback. *Sex Rules* 19:13–28.

Stewart, L., et al. 1990. *Communication between the sexes: Sex differences and sex-role stereotypes.* Scottsdale, Arizona: Gorsuch Scarisbrick Publishers.

Tannen, Deborah. 1990. *You just don't understand: Women and men in conversation.* New York: Ballentine Books, 16, 21, 77.

Chapter 5

Bales, Robert F. 1950. *Interaction process analysis.* Reading, Massachusetts: Addison-Wesley.

Fischer, B. Aubrey. 1974. *Small group decision making: Communication and group process.* New York: McGraw-Hill.

Hackman, J. 1987. The design of work teams. In *Handbook of organizational behavior.* ed. J. Lorsch. Englewood Cliffs, New Jersey: Prentice-Hall, 315–342.

Hosansky, M. 1989. The rise of the third party. *Successful Meetings* (April):6

Mosvick, Roger K. 1995. Communication practices of managers and technical professionals in high technology industries: An update. Macalester College, St. Paul, Minnesota. Unpublished manuscript.

Sundstrom, E., et al. 1990. Work teams: Application and effectiveness. *American Psychologist* (February):120–133.

Rothwell, J. Dan. 1995. *In mixed company.* 2d ed. Ft. Worth, Texas: Harcourt Brace College Publishers, 39, 72–73.

Chapter 6

Drucker, Peter F. 1974. *Management: Tasks, responsibilities, practices.* New York: Harper and Row, 473.

Hirokawa, Randy Y. 1982. Consensus group decision making, quality of decision, and group satisfaction. *Central States Speech Journal* 33:411, 413.

Howell, William S., and Donald K. Smith. 1956. *Discussion.* New York: Macmillan

Johnson, D., and F. Johnson. 1987. *Learning together and alone: Cooperative, competitive, and individualistic learning.* Englewood Cliffs, New Jersey: Prentice-Hall.

Johnson, D., and F. Johnson. 1991. *Joining together: Group theory and group skills.* Englewood Cliffs, New Jersey: Prentice-Hall.

Forsythe, D. 1990. *Group dynamics.* Pacific Grove, California: Brook/Cole Publishing.

Michaelson, J., et al. 1989. A realistic test of individual versus group consensus decision making. *Journal of Applied Psychology* 74:834–839.

Rothwell, J. Dan. 1995. *In mixed company.* 2d ed. Ft. Worth, Texas: Harcourt Brace College Publishers, 72–73.

Wood, Julia T., Gerald M. Phillips, and Douglas J. Pedersen. 1986. *Group discussion: A practical guide to participation and leadership.* 2d ed. New York: Harper and Row, 47.

Chapter 7

Goldhamer, E., and E. Shils. 1939. Types of power and status. *American Journal of Sociology* 45:171–182.

Wilmot, Joyce Hocker, and William W. Wilmot. 1978. *Interpersonal conflict.* Dubuque, Iowa: William C. Brown, 90–92.

Chapter 8

Blodget, Mindy, and Tim Ouellette. 1995. TV quality video comes to the portable market. *Computerworld* (7 August): 12.

Gilder, George. 1994. *Life after television: The coming transformation of media and American life.* New York: W.W. Norton.

Jaroff, Leon. 1995. Age of the road warrior. *Time* (Spring):40

Kull, David J. 1982. Group decisions: Can computers help? *Computer Decisions* (May):82.

Leslie, J. 1994. Mail bonding: E-mail is creating a new oral culture. *Wired* (March):42–48.

Leyden, Peter. 1995. Dawn of a second renaissance. *Minneapolis Star Tribune* (25 June).

McLuhan, Marshall, 1964. *Understanding media.* New York: McGraw-Hill.

Morris, David. 1995. Wireless computing could be wave of the future. *St. Paul Pioneer Press* (15 August):7A.

Mosvick, Roger K. 1982. Communication practices of managers and technical professionals in four large scale high technology industries. Paper presented at national convention, Speech Communication Association, Louisville, Kentucky.

Mosvick, Roger K. 1986. Communication practices of managers and technical professionals in high technology industries: An update. Macalester College, St. Paul, Minnesota. Manuscript.

Oslund, John J. 1995. Users of Notes know why IBM's willing to pay plenty for Lotus. *Minneapolis Star Tribune* (11 June).

Parker, Walter. 1995. Video trips take off. *St. Paul Pioneer Press* (19 June):E2.

Poole, Marshall Scott, et al. 1993. Group decision support systems and group communication: A comparison of decision making computer supported and nonsupported groups. *Communication Research* 20, 2 (April).

Rogers, Everett M., and Marcel M. Albritton. 1995. Interactive communication technologies in business organizations. *The Journal of Business Communication* 32 (April):2.

Salamone, Salvatore. 1995. Video conferencing's Achilles heels. *Byte* (August):24–25.

Schrage, Michael. 1985. New computer package helps get to the meat of meetings. *Washington Post* (18 November).

Spears, Russell, and Martin Lea. 1994. Computer mediated communication. *Communication Research* (August):427–459.

Watson, Richard T., et al. 1991. The use and adoption of Optionfinder: Keypad based group decision support system. Report to the 3M Meeting Management Institute (15 February) 2:3–5.

Williams, Margaret D. 1995. IBM will plug Lotus Notes software into global network. *St. Paul Pioneer Press* (9 August).

Appendix A

Dalkey, N. D. 1967. *Delphi*. Chicago: Rand Corp.

Delbecq, A. L., A. H. Van de Ven, and D. H. Gustafson. 1975. *Group techniques for program planning: A guide to nominal group and Delphi processes*. Glenview, Illinois: Scott, Foresman and Company.

Larson, Carl. 1969. Forms of analysis and small group problem solving. *Speech Monographs* 36:453.

Maier, Norman R. F. 1963. *Problem-solving discussion and conferences*. New York: McGraw-Hill.

Osborn, A. F. 1957. Applied imagination. New York: Scribners

Phillips, Donald. 1948. Report on discussion. *Adult Education Journal* 7 (October).

Phillips, G. M. 1966. *Communication and the small group*. Indianapolis: Bobbs-Merrill

Prince, George M. 1972. *The practice of creativity*. New York: Collier Books.

I·N·D·E·X

Decision modeling, 193
Decision support systems
(DSS), 192-194
Decision-making formats,
223, 232-244
Decisions
Authoritarian, 52-53
Consensus, 54-55,
66-67, 72, 108, 125,
131, 161-163
Criteria for, 58-60
Lack of, 126
Majority, 53-54
Minority, 54
Nonprogrammed, 50
Programmed, 50, 192
Delegation meetings,
109-110, 133
Delphi method, 223,
235-236
Deming, Edward, 66
Desktop video, 214-215,
216
Destasia, Ken, 214
Devil's advocate, 70, 72,
140, 254, 261-264
Dewey, John, 55, 232
Diachronic communication,
168-169
Disorganized meetings,
126-130
Dissent, 138-140, 158-160,
165
Drucker, Peter, v, 49, 62,
67, 68, 139, 140

E

Eakins, B. & R., 98, 99,
100
Ehlen, David, vi
Electronic conference
systems, 190, 203-216
Electronic mail (e-mail),
203, 208-211
Evaluation, 164-165, 255-
256
Computer-aided, 193
Extroverted personality,
85-86, 100
Eye contact, 99

F

Facial expression, 99
Feedback, 164-165
Fisher, B., 122
Forsythe, D., 141
Foster, W., 52
Frederick, Howard, 77
Friedman, Meyer, 87
Futurecomm, 215-216

G

Galanes, Gloria, 76, 95
Geis, F.L., 93
Gender
Assertiveness, 92
In decision making,
90-100
And nonverbal
communication,
97-100
Stereotypes, 75, 93-94
And talk time, 91-96
Gilder, George, 191
Glass, Lillian, 96
Goldhamer, E., 177
Goss, Blaine, 38
Gouran, Dennis, 69
Green, Walter, 13
Group decision support
systems (GDSS), 190,
192-194, 203
Groupthink, 67-70, 72, 262
Solutions to, 69
Groupware, 208, 211-212

H

Hackman, J., 113
Hall, Edward, 77, 78
Hall, Mildred, 77
Harms, L.S., 40, 41
Henley, Nancy, 99
Hierarchical leadership,
143-145, 165
"High machs," 89-90
High/low context
communication, 78-79
Hirokawa, Randy, 57, 65,
162-163

Hofstede, Geerte, 77, 78
Hofstra University, 8
Hoover's Handbook, 20
Hosansky, M., 112
Howell, William, 155
Hsu, Spencer, 7, 13
Humor, use of, 138
Hybrid meeting formats,
110, 223, 248-252

I

Ideal solution format, 61,
223, 238-239
Implementing solutions,
244-248
Inconclusive meetings,
124-126
Inconclusive progression,
124-125
Individualism, 79, 140-142
Influencing groups,
175-180
Information processing,
33-34
Monitoring, 46-48
Information queuing, 37,
128
Information retrieval, 198,
202
Information search
systems, 190, 191-192
Instructional groups,
231-232
Internet, 191, 212
Interrupting, 38, 85-86,
94, 126-128, 185
Introverted personality,
85-86, 100
Irrelevant discussion, 123

J

James, S.P., 86
Janis, Irving, 67, 68
Japanese decision making,
54-55, 66-67, 72
Jaroff, Leon, 213, 215
Johnson, D & F., 142
Josephs, Earl, 15

More Great Books from JIST Works, Inc.

The Customer Is Usually Wrong!
Contrary to What You've Been Told ... What You Know to Be True!
By Fred Jandt
Yes, contrary to what you've always heard, the customer is usually wrong! Beginning with this simple truth, Jandt teaches you how to maintain your business and keep your customers using his method of "win-win negotiating." A must-have for anyone who deals with the public.

ISBN: 1-57112-067-X
$12.95
Order Code: CUW

Face-to-Face Selling
Easy & Effective Sales Techniques for New & Experienced Salespeople
By Bart Breighner
The perfect primer for the sales novice, and an inspirational review for the seasoned professional, this book explains "the art of creative confrontation" and includes tips and tried and true examples of successful sales techniques. *Face-to-Face Selling* details the steps you'll need to get started and succeed in sales!

ISBN: 1-57112-065-3
$9.95
Order Code: FFS

The Perfect Memo!
Write Your Way to Career Success!
By Patricia H. Westheimer
Good, clear writing can be your ticket to career success! This book introduces SPEAKWRITE™, a powerful five-step writing technique that helps you organize and express your ideas and create better memos, letters, reports, and proposals.

ISBN: 1-57112-064-5
$12.95
Order Code: PM

Look for these and other fine books from JIST Works at your full-service bookstore, or contact us for more information.

More Great Books from JIST Works, Inc.

The Very Quick Job Search, 2nd Edition

Bet a Better Job in Half the Time!

By J. Michael Farr

The most thorough, results-oriented career planning and job search book on the market. Hailed by many as the best job search book ever, this completely revised edition includes a complete career planning section, sample resumes, information on interviewing skills, and techniques that will cut your job search time in half!

ISBN: 1-56370-181-2

$14.95

Order Code: J1812

The Quick Interview & Salary Negotiation Book

Dramatically Improve Your Interviewing Skills in Just a Few Hours!

By J. Michael Farr

Employer surveys indicate that 80% of job applicants do not present themselves well in interviews. This book explains how you can improve your interviewing skills by: creating a great first impression; telling employers what they really want to know; emphasizing your skills and accomplishments; plus much more.

ISBN: 1-56370-162-6

$12.95

Order Code: J1626

Franchise Opportunities Handbook

A Complete Guide for People Who Want to Start Their Own Franchise

By LaVerne Ludden, Ed.D.

Everything you need to know to make an informed decision about franchising. The most comprehensive, up-to-date resource of its kind, filled with practical advice and answers to commonly asked questions.

ISBN: 1-57112-073-4

$16.95

Order Code: P0734

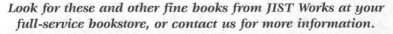

Look for these and other fine books from JIST Works at your full-service bookstore, or contact us for more information.